SocNotes

Rose Hunte

Society: The Basics

NINTH EDITION

John J. Macionis

Kenyon College

PEARSON

Prentice
Hall

Upper Saddle River, New Jersey 07458

© 2007 by PEARSON EDUCATION, INC.
Upper Saddle River, New Jersey 07458

10 9 8 7 6 5 4 3 2 1

ISBN 0-13-228502-9

Printed in the United States of America

Table of Contents

Chapter 1

Sociology: Perspective, Theory, and Method

LEARNING OBJECTIVES

- To define sociology and understand the basic components of the sociological perspective.
- To provide examples of the ways in which social forces affect our everyday lives.
- To recognize the importance of taking a global perspective in order to appreciate the interdependence of our world's nations and people.
- To recognize the benefits of using the sociological perspective.
- To be familiar with the origins of sociology.
- To identify and discuss the differences among the three major theoretical approaches used by sociologists in the analysis of society.
- To be familiar with the three ways to do sociology.
- To understand scientific and interpretive sociology.
- To review the fundamental requirements for engaging in scientific investigation using the sociological perspective.
- To appreciate the importance of research ethics.
- To be familiar with the major research methods in sociology and how to use available data.

CHAPTER OUTLINE

I. The Sociological Perspective
   A. Seeing the General in the Particular
   B. Seeing the Strange in the Familiar
   C. Seeing Personal Choice in Social Context
   D. Seeing Sociologically: Marginality and Crisis

II. The Importance of a Global Perspective

III. Applying the Sociological Perspective
   A. Sociology and Public Policy
   B. Sociology and Personal Growth
   C. Careers: The "Sociology Advantage"

IV. The Origins of Sociology
   A. Social Change and Sociology
      1. Industrial Technology
      2. The Growth of Cities

2

SOCIOLOGY: PERSPECTIVE, THEORY, AND METHOD

CHAPTER 1

_____

_____

_____

_____

_____

_____

_____

- **What** makes the sociological perspective a new and exciting way of seeing the world?

- **Why** is sociology an important tool for your future career?

- **How** do sociologists conduct research to learn about the social world?

_____

_____

_____

_____

_____

_____

The Sociological Perspective

- *Sociology*
  - *The systematic study of human society*
    - At the heart of the discipline is a distinctive point of view called—*the sociological perspective*

_____

_____

_____

_____

_____

_____

Seeing the General in the Particular

- Peter Berger (1963) described the sociological perspective
  - **Seeing the general in the particular**
    - *Sociology helps us see* general *patterns in the behavior of particular people*
    - Individuals are unique
      - Society shapes the lives of people in various categories
        - Children
        - Adults
        - Women and men
        - Rich and poor

Seeing the Strange in the Familiar

- Many people find using the sociological perspective amounts to
  - *Seeing the Strange in the Familiar*
- Looking at life sociologically requires giving up
  - the *familiar* idea we live life in terms of our own decisions
  - in favor of the *strange* notion that society shapes those decisions

Global Map 1.1 (p. 3, detail on next slide)
Women's Childbearing in Global Perspective
Is childbearing simply a matter of personal choice? A look around the world shows that it is not. In general, women living in poor countries have many more children than women in rich nations. Can you point to some of the reasons for this global disparity? In simple terms, such differences mean that if you had been born into another society (whether you are female or male), your life might be quite different from what it is now.
Sources: Data from Hamilton et al. (2005) and United Nations (2006). Map projection from Peters Atlas of the World (1990).

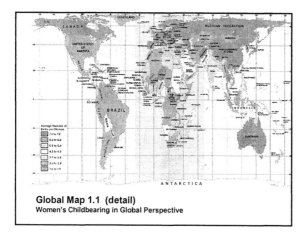

Global Map 1.1 (detail)
Women's Childbearing in Global Perspective

Seeing Personal Choice in Social Context

- Emile Durkheim (1858–1917)
    - Showed that social forces are at work
        - Provides strong evidence of how social forces affect individual behavior
- Durkheim's Logic
    - Higher suicide among Whites and men reflect greater wealth and freedom
    - Lower rate among women and people of color reflect limited social choices

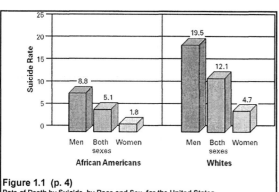

Figure 1.1 (p. 4)
Rate of Death by Suicide, by Race and Sex, for the United States
Suicide rates are higher for white people than for black people and higher for men than for women. Rates indicate the number of deaths by suicide for every 100,000 people in each category for 2003.
Source: Hoyert et al. (2006)

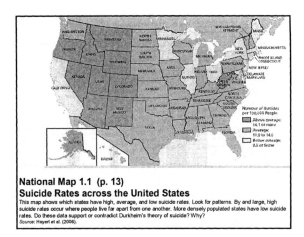

National Map 1.1 (p. 13)
Suicide Rates across the United States
This map shows which states have high, average, and low suicide rates. Look for patterns. By and large, high suicide rates occur where people live far apart from one another. More densely populated states have low suicide rates. Do these data support or contradict Durkheim's theory of suicide? Why?
Source: Hoyert et al. (2006).

Seeing Sociologically: Marginality and Crisis

- Two situations allow clear sight of how society shapes individual lives
  - Living on the margins of society
  - Living through a social crisis
- **Outsider**
  - *Not part of the dominant group and an everyday experience*
- The greater a person's marginality, the better able they are to use the sociological perspective.

- People at the margins of social life
  - Women
  - Gay people
  - People with disabilities
  - Elderly
    - These people are aware of social patterns that others rarely think about
- To become better at using the sociological perspective
  - Step back from familiar routines
  - Look at your lives with new curiosity

- Periods of change or crisis makes everyone feel off balance, encouraging the use of the sociological perspective
  - C. Wright Mills (1959)
    - Mills believed
      - Using the sociological imagination helps people understand their society and how it affects their own lives

The Importance of a Global Perspective

- **Global Perspective**
  - *The study of the larger world and our society's place in it.*
- What is the importance of a global perspective for sociology?
  - Global awareness is a logical extension of the sociological perspective.
  - Sociology shows that our place in society profoundly affects our life experiences.
  - The position of our society in the larger world system affects everyone in the U.S.

- High Income Nations
  - Nations with the highest overall standards of living
- Middle-Income Countries
  - Nations with a standard of living about average for the world as a whole
- Low-Income Countries
  - Nations with a low standard of living in which most people are poor

- Thinking globally helps us learn more about ourselves.
- In an increasingly interconnected world, we can understand ourselves to the extent that we understand others.
- Sociology is an invitation to learn a new way of looking at the world around us.
- **Now Answer:**
  - *Is this invitation worth accepting and what are the benefits of applying the sociological perspective?*

Applying the Sociological Perspective

- Three ways in which the sociological perspective can be useful
  - Sociology is at work guiding many of the laws and policies that shape our lives.
  - On an individual level, making use of the sociological perspective leads to important personal growth and expanded awareness.
  - Studying sociology is excellent preparation for the world of work.

Sociology and Public Policy

- Sociologists have helped shape public policy
  - The laws and regulations that guide how people in communities live and work
    - Racial segregation
    - School busing
    - Divorce

Sociology and Personal Growth

- Using sociology benefits us in four ways
  - The sociological perspective helps us assess the truth of "common sense."
  - The sociological perspective helps us see the opportunities in our everyday lives
  - The sociological perspective empowers us to be active participants in our society
  - The sociological perspective helps us live in a diverse world

---

Careers:
The "Sociology Advantage"

- A sociology background is excellent in preparing for the working world
- Agencies and companies want to be sure that products, programs, and policies they create get the job done at the lowest cost
- Sociologists, especially researchers, are in high demand for the above type of evaluation research

---

- Clinical Sociologists
  - Work the same as clinical psychologists
- Other fields
  - Criminal justice
  - Health care
  - Gain "sociological advantage" by learning about
    - Patterns of health and illness within a population
    - How factors such as race, gender and social class affect health

Social Change and Sociology

- Changes in Europe during the 18th and 19th centuries led to thinking about
  - Society and people's place in it
  - Spurred development of sociology
- Three significant changes transformed society
  - Rise of a factory-based economy
  - Explosive growth of cities
  - New ideas about democracy and political rights

- Industrial Technology
  - **Manufacturing**
    - *A word derived from Latin, meaning* "to make by hand"
  - By the end of the 18th century, inventors were using new sources of energy
- The Growth of Cities
  - "Enclosure Movement"
- Political Change
  - Economic development and growth of cities brought new ways of thinking

---

Science and Sociology

- Auguste Comte (1798–1857)
  - French social thinker who coined the term "sociology" in 1838
  - Saw sociology as the product of three stages of historical development:
    - Theological stage
    - Metaphysical stage
    - Scientific stage
- **Theological Stage**
  - From the beginning of human history to the end of the European Middle Ages; 1530 c.e.

- **Metaphysical Stage**
  - People saw society as a natural rather than supernatural phenomenon
  - Thomas Hobbes
    - Suggested that society reflected not the perfection of God as much as the failings of a selfish human nature
- **Scientific Stage**
  - Began with the work of early scientists
    - Nicolas Copernicus (1473–1543)
    - Isaac Newton (1642–1727)

- Comte's contribution
  - Applied the scientific approach
- **Positivism**
  - *A way of understanding based on science*
- Sociology took hold at the beginning of the 20th century in the U.S.
  - Humans are creatures of imagination and spontaneity
    - *Human behavior can never be explained by the rigid "laws of society"*

Sociological Theory

- **Theory**
  - *A statement of how and why specific facts are related*
  - Job of sociological theory
    - To explain social behavior in the real world
  - Sociologists conduct research to test and refine their theories
- Two basic questions in building theory
  - What issues should we study?
  - How should we connect the facts?

- **Theoretical Approach**
  - *A basic image of society that guides thinking and research*
  - Three theoretical approaches
    - Structural-functional approach
    - Social-conflict approach
    - Symbolic-interaction approach

The Structural-Functional Approach

- *A framework for building theory that sees society as a complex system whose parts work together to promote solidarity and stability*
- **Social Structure**
  - *Any relatively stable pattern of social behavior*
- **Social Functions**
  - *The consequences of a social pattern for the operation of society as a whole*

- This approach looks for each structure's social pattern's function to keep society going, at least in its present form
  - Structural-function owes much to Auguste Comte
- Robert K. Merton (1820–1903)
  - Expanded understanding of social function
    - Pointed out that any social structure probably has many functions
  - Distinguished between *manifest* functions and *latent* functions

- **Manifest Functions**
  - *The recognized and intended consequences of any social pattern*
- **Latent Functions**
  - *The unrecognized and unintended consequences of any social pattern*
- **Social Dysfunction**
  - *Any social pattern that may disrupt the operation of society*

- **Critical Review**
  - Main idea of the structural-functional approach is its vision of society as stable and orderly
  - Main goal of sociologists who use this approach is to figure out "what makes society tick"

The Social-Conflict Approach

- *A framework for building theory that sees society as an arena of inequality that generates conflict and change*
- Highlights how the following factors are linked to inequality
  - Class, race, ethnicity, gender, age
- Social-conflict approach is used to look at ongoing conflict between dominant and disadvantaged categories of people

Feminism and the Gender-Conflict Approach

- **Gender-Conflict Approach**
  - *A point of view that focuses on inequality and conflict between women and men*
- Gender-conflict approach is closely linked to **feminism**
  - *The advocacy of social inequality for women and men*
- Another contribution of the gender-conflict approach
  - *Awareness of the importance of women to the development of sociology*

The Race-Conflict Approach

- *A point of view that focuses on inequality and conflict between people of different racial and ethnic categories*
- Race-conflict approach points out the contributions to the development of sociology by people of color

- **Critical Review**
  - Ignores how shared values and interdependence can unify members of a society
  - Politically, social-conflict cannot claim scientific objectivity
    - Supporters note that social-conflict responds that all theoretical approaches have political consequences
  - Both functional and conflict paint society in broad strokes

The Symbolic-Interaction Approach

- Structural-functional and social-conflict approaches share a **macro-level orientation**
  - *Broad focus on social structures that shape society as a whole*
- **Micro-level orientation**
  - *A close-up focus on social interaction in specific situations*

- **Symbolic-interaction Approach**
  - *A framework for building theory that sees society as the product of the everyday interactions of individuals*
- Society is nothing more than the reality people construct for themselves as they interact with one another

---

- **Critical Review**
  - Symbolic-interaction approach reminds us that society basically amounts to people interacting
    - Micro-level sociology shows how individuals construct and experience society
  - This approach risks overlooking
    - Widespread influence of culture
  - Factors such as
    - Class
    - Gender
    - Race

Major Theoretical Approaches

	Structural-Functional Approach	Social-Conflict Approach	Symbolic-Interaction Approach
What is the level of analysis?	Macro-level	Macro-level	Micro-level
What image of society does the approach have?	Society is a system of interrelated parts that is relatively stable. Each part works to keep society operating in an orderly way. Members generally agree about what is morally right and morally wrong.	Society is a system of social inequalities based on class (Marx), gender (feminism and gender-conflict approach), and race (race-conflict approach). Society operates to benefit some categories of people and to harm others. Social inequality causes conflict that leads to social change.	Society is an ongoing process. People interact in countless settings using symbolic communications. The reality people experience is variable and changing.
What core questions does the approach ask?	How is society held together? What are the major parts of society? How are these parts linked? What does each part do to help society work?	How does society divide a population according to class, gender, race, and age? How do advantaged people protect their privileges? How do disadvantaged people challenge the system seeking change?	How do people experience society? How do people shape the reality they experience? How do behavior and meaning change from person to person and from one situation to another?

Applying Theory (p. 18)
Major Theoretical Approaches

Page 21
Race and Sport: "Stacking" in Professional Football
Does race play a part in professional sports? Looking at the various positions in professional football, we see that white players are more likely to play the central and offensive positions. What do you make of this pattern?
Source: Lapchick (2006).

Three Ways to do Sociology

- All sociologists want to learn about the social world
- Three ways to do sociological research
  - Scientific
  - Interpretive
  - Critical Sociology

Scientific Sociology

- **Science**
  - *A logical system that bases knowledge on direct, systematic observation*
- **Scientific Sociology**
  - *The study of society based on systematic observation of social behavior*
- **Empirical Evidence**
  - *Information we can verify with our senses*
- A scientific orientation often challenges what we accept as "common sense."

_____

_____

_____

_____

_____

_____

_____

Concepts, Variables, and Measurement

- **Concept**
  - *A mental construct that represents some part of the world in a simplified form*
- **Variable**
  - *A concept which changes from case to case*
- **Measurement**
  - *A procedure for determining the value of a variable in a specific case*
- **Operationalize**
  - *Stating exactly what they are measuring*

_____

_____

_____

_____

_____

_____

_____

Statistics

- **Descriptive Statistics**
  - *to "state" what is average for a large population*
  - Most commonly used descriptive statistics are:
    - **Mean**
      - Arithmetic average of all measures, obtained by adding them up and dividing by the number of cases
    - **Median**
      - The score at the halfway point in an ascending series of numbers
    - **Mode**
      - The score that occurs most often

_____

_____

_____

_____

_____

_____

_____

Reliability and Validity

- **Reliability**
  - *Consistency in measurement*
    - For measurement to be reliable, the process must yield the same results when repeated.
- **Validity**
  - *Actually measuring exactly what you intend to measure*
    - Means hitting the exact target or the bull's-eye

Correlation and Cause

- **Correlation**
  - *A relationship in which two (or more) variables change together*
    - Not just how variables change, but which variable changes the other
- **Cause and Effect**
  - *A relationship in which change in one variable causes change in another*

- Scientists refer to the *cause* as
  - *Independent Variable*
- And the *effect* as
  - *Dependent Variable*
- Understanding cause and effect is valuable because
  - Allows researchers to *predict* how one pattern of behavior will produce another

- **Spurious or False Correlation**
  - *When two variables change together but neither one causes the other*
    - Usually results from a third factor
- To be sure of a real cause and effect relationship, we must show:
  - Variables are correlated
  - The independent (causal) variable occurs before the dependant variable
  - There is no evidence that a third variable has been overlooked, causing a spurious correlation

The Ideal of Objectivity

- **Objectivity (Personal Neutrality)**
  - *To allow the facts to speak for themselves and not be influenced by the personal values and biases of the researcher*
- **Value-Relevant research**
  - *Topics the researcher cares about*
- **Value-Free research**
  - *Dedication to finding truth* as it is *rather than as we think* it should be

Interpretive Sociology

- Humans engage in *meaningful* action
- **Interpretive sociology**
  - *The study of sociology that focuses on the meanings people attach to their social world*
- Interpretive sociology differs from scientific or empirical sociology in three ways:
  - Scientific sociology focuses on *action*
    - Interpretive sociology focuses on *meaning*
  - Scientific sociology sees an *objective reality*
    - Interpretive sociology sees *reality*

- Scientific sociology favors *quantitative data*
  - Interpretive sociology favors *qualitative data*
- Scientific orientation is well-suited for research in a laboratory
- Interpretive orientation is better suited in a natural setting
  - Investigators interact with people

Weber's Concept of Verstehen

- German word for "understanding"
- Interpretive sociologist's job
  - Observe *what* people do
  - *Share* in their world of meaning
  - Appreciate *why* they act as they do
- Subjective thoughts and feelings, though difficult to measure, are the focus of interpretive sociologist's attention

---

Critical Sociology

- *The study of society that focuses on the need for social change*
  - Critical sociologists ask moral and political questions
  - Critical sociologists reject Weber's goal that
    - Sociology be value-free
    - Emphasize that sociologists should be activists in pursuit of greater social equality
  - Point of sociology is
    - "Not just to research the social world but to change it in the direction of democracy and social justice" (Feagin & Hernan, 2001:1)

- Critical sociologists
  - Seek to change society and the character of research
  - Identify personally with their research subjects and encourage them to help decide what to study and how to do their work
  - With subjects, use their findings to provide a voice for less powerful people
  - Advance the political goal of a more equal society

Sociology as Politics

- Scientific sociologists
  - Object to taking sides in this way
  - Claims critical sociology
    - Becomes political
    - Lacks objectivity
    - Cannot correct for its own biases
- Critical sociologists
  - All research is political in that it either calls for change or does not
  - Believe critical sociology is an active approach

SUMMING UP

Three Research Orientations in Sociology

	Scientific	Interpretive	Critical
What is reality?	Society is an orderly system. There is an objective reality "out there."	Society is ongoing interaction. People construct reality as they attach meanings to their behavior.	Society is patterns of inequality. Reality is that some categories of people dominate others.
How do we conduct research?	Researcher gathers empirical, ideally quantitative, data. Researcher tries to be a neutral observer	Researcher develops a qualitative account of the subjective sense people make of their world. Researcher is a participant.	Research is a strategy to bring about desired social change. Researcher is an activist.
Corresponding theoretical approach	Structural-functional approach	Symbolic-interaction approach	Social-conflict approach

Summing Up (p. 24)
Three Research Orientations in Sociology

Methods and Theory

- Each of the three ways to do sociology, scientific, interpretive, and critical stand closer to one of the theoretical approaches
  - Scientific orientation is linked to structural-functional
  - Interpretive sociology is linked to symbolic-interaction
  - Critical sociology is linked to social-conflict

Gender and Research

- **Gender**
  - *The personal traits and social positions that members of a society attach to being female or male*
- Research is affected by gender
- Gender can affect sociological research in five ways
  - Androcentricity, overgeneralizing, gender blindness, double standards, and interference

- **Androcentricity**
  - Literally means "focus on the male"
  - Approaching an issue from a male perspective
  - Researcher that tries to explain human behavior cannot ignore half of humanity
- **Overgeneralizing**
  - Occurs when sociologists gather data only from men but use that information to draw conclusions about all people

- **Gender blindness**
  - Failing to consider gender at all
  - Lives of men and women differ in many ways
- **Double standards**
  - Researchers must be careful not to judge men and women by different standards
- **Interference**
  - A study is distorted if a subject reacts to the sex of the researcher, interfering with the research operation

Research Ethics

- *Awareness that research can harm as well as help subjects and communities*
- **American Sociological Association**
  - Established formal guidelines for conducting research (1977)
    - Be skillful and fair-minded in their work
    - Disclose all research findings
    - Make results available to other sociologists
    - Make sure that subjects are not harmed
    - Stop work right away if subject is at risk of harm
    - Privacy of individuals—confidential information
    - Get informed consent

- Must include all sources of financial support
- Must have an *institutional review board* (IRB)
- Before beginning work in another country
  - Investigator must become familiar enough with that society to understand what people are
    - Likely to regard as violation of privacy
    - Likely to regard as sources of danger
  - In America's diverse society, same rule applies to studying people with a different culture

Research Methods

- *A systematic plan for doing research*
- Four methods of sociological investigation
  - Experiments
  - Surveys
  - Participant observation
  - Existing sources

Testing a Hypothesis: The Experiment

- *A research method for investigating cause and effect under highly controlled conditions*
- Test a specific **hypothesis**
  - *A statement of how two or more variables are related*
  - *An educated guess about how variables are linked – usually an if-then statement*

- Evidence needed to reject or accept the hypothesis occurs in four steps:
  - State which variable is the *independent variable* and which is the *dependent variable*
  - Measure the initial value of the dependent variable
  - Expose the dependent variable to the independent variable
  - Measure the dependent variable again to see what change, if any, took place

Asking Questions: Survey Research

- **Survey**
  - *A research method in which subjects respond to a series of statements or questions in a questionnaire or an interview*
- Survey targets some population
- Researchers usually study a **sample**
  - *A much smaller number of subjects selected to represent the entire population*

- Survey must have a specific plan for asking questions and recording answers
  - Most common is a **questionnaire**
    - *Series of written statements or questions*
  - **Interview**
    - *Researcher personally asks subjects a series of questions*
    - Gives participants freedom to respond as they wish

THE TALENTED 100: LOIS BENJAMIN'S AFRICAN AMERICAN ELITE

Sex	Age	Childhood Racial Setting	Childhood Region	Highest Educational Degree	Job Sector	Annual Income (about 1990)	Political Orientation
Male 63%	35 or younger 6%	Mostly black 71%	West 6%	Doctorate 32%	College or university 35%	More than $50,000 64%	Radical left 13%
Female 37%	36 to 54 68%	Mostly white 15%	North or Midwest 32%	Medical or law 17%	Private, for-profit 17%	$35,000 to $50,000 18%	Liberal 38%
	55 or older 26%	Racially mixed 14%	South 38%	Master's 27%	Private, nonprofit 9%	$20,000 to $34,999 12%	Moderate 28%
			Northeast 12%	Bachelor's 13%	Government 22%	Less than $20,000 6%	Conservative 5%
			Other 12%	Less 11%	Self-employed 14%		Depends on issue 14%
					Retired 3%		Unknown 2%
100%	100%	100%	100%	100%	100%	100%	100%

Source: Adapted from Lois Benjamin, *The Black Elite: Facing the Color Line in the Twilight of the Twentieth Century* (Chicago: Nelson-Hall, 1991), p. 276.

Page 29
The Talented 100: Lois Benjamin's African American Elite

In the Field: Participant Observation

- **Participant observation**
  - *A research method in which investigators systematically observe people while joining them in their routine activities*
  - **Cultural anthropologists**
    - *Use to study societies*
      - Called "Fieldwork"
  - Fieldwork makes most participant observation *exploratory* and *descriptive*
  - Participant observation has few hard and fast rules

- Critics claim:
  - Participant observation falls short of scientific standards
    - Personal impressions of a single researcher play a central role
- Strength
  - Personal approach
  - Observer can gain profound insight into people's behavior
    - Survey might disrupt a setting

Using Available Data: Existing Sources

- Sociologists make use of **existing sources**
  - *Data collected by others*
- Most widely used data are gathered by government agencies
- Using available information
- **Criticism**
  - Data may not be available in the exact form that is needed
  - Always questions about how accurate the existing data are

Four Research Methods			
	Experiment	**Survey**	**Participant Observation**	**Existing Sources**
Application	For explanatory research that specifies relationships between variables. Generates quantitative data	For gathering information about issues that cannot be directly observed, such as attitudes and values. Useful for descriptive and explanatory research. Generates quantitative or qualitative data	For exploratory and descriptive study of people in a "natural" setting. Generates qualitative data	For exploratory, descriptive, or explanatory research whenever suitable data are available
Advantages	Provides the greatest opportunity to specify cause-and-effect relationships. Replication of research is relatively easy	Sampling, using questionnaires, allows surveys of large populations. Interviews provide in-depth responses	Allows study of "natural" behavior. Usually inexpensive	Saves time and expense of data collection. Makes historical research possible
Limitations	Laboratory settings have an artificial quality. Unless the research environment is carefully controlled, results may be biased	Questionnaires must be carefully prepared and may yield a low return rate. Interviews are expensive and time-consuming	Time-consuming. Replication of research is difficult. Researcher must balance roles of participant and observer	Researcher has no control over possible biases in data. Data may only partially fit current research needs

Summing Up (p. 32)
Four Research Methods

Putting It All Together:
Ten Steps in Sociological Research

- 1. What is your topic?
- 2. What have others already learned?
- 3. What, exactly, are your questions?
- 4. What will you need to carry out research?
- 5. Might the research cause harm?
- 6. What method will you use?

- 7. How will you record the data?
- 8. What do the data tell you?
- 9. What are your conclusions?
- 10. How can you share what you have learned?

Chapter 2

Culture

LEARNING OBJECTIVES

- To begin to understand the sociological meaning of the concept of culture.
- To consider the relationship between human intelligence and culture.
- To know the components of culture and to provide examples of each.
- To identify the dominant values in our society and to recognize their interrelationships with one another and with other aspects of our culture.
- To explain how subcultures and countercultures contribute to cultural diversity.
- To begin to develop your understanding of multiculturalism.
- To differentiate between ethnocentrism and cultural relativism.
- To compare and contrast analyses of culture using structural-functional, social-conflict, and sociobiological approaches.
- To identify the consequences of culture for human freedom and constraint.

CHAPTER OUTLINE

I.   What is Culture?
  A. Culture and Human Intelligence
  B. How Many Cultures?

II.   The Elements of Culture
  A. Symbols
  B. Language
    1. Does Language Shape Reality?
  C. Values and Beliefs
    1. Key Values of U.S.
    2. Values: Often in Harmony, Sometimes in Conflict
    3. Emerging Values
    4. Values: A Global Perspective
  D. Norms
  E. Ideal and Real Culture

III. Technology and Culture
  A. Hunting and Gathering
  B. Horticulture and Pastoralism
  C. Agriculture
  D. Industry
  E. Postindustrial Information Technology

CULTURE

CHAPTER 2

- **What** is Culture?

- **Why** is it so important to understand people's cultural differences?

- **How** does culture support social inequality?

What is Culture?

- **Culture**
  - *The ways of thinking, the ways of acting, and the material objects that together form a people's way of life*
  - Non-Material Culture
    - Includes ideas created by members of a society
  - Material Culture
    - Refers to physical things

- Culture is a shared way of life or social heritage
- **Society**
  - *Refers to people who interact in a defined territory and share a culture*
- Neither society nor culture could exist without the other

- **Culture Shock**
  - *Personal disorientation when experiencing an unfamiliar way of life*
- No way of life is *"natural"* to humanity
- Animal behavior is determined by **instinct**
  - *Biological programming over which each species has no control*

Culture and Human Intelligence

- History took a crucial turn with the appearance of **primates**
  - *Have the largest brains relative to body size of all living creatures*
- 12 million years ago, primates evolved along two different lines
  - Humans
  - Great apes
  - Distant human ancestors evolved in Central Africa

- Stone Age achievements marked the points when our ancestors embarked on a distinct evolutionary course
  - Made culture their primary strategy for survival
- **Homo Sapiens**
  - *"Thinking Person"*
- Modern Homo Sapiens
  - Larger brains
  - Developed culture rapidly
  - Used wide range of tools and cave art

How Many Cultures?

- One indication of culture is language
- Globally, experts document 7,000 languages
- Coming decades may see the disappearance of hundreds of languages
- Why the decline?
  - High-technology communication
  - Increasing international migration
  - Expanding global economy
    - A ll are reducing global diversity

Global Map 2-1 (p. 47)

Language in Global Perspective

(details on next three slides)

Source: Peter's Atlas of the World (1990); updated by the author.

Society: The Basics, 9th Edition by John Macionis

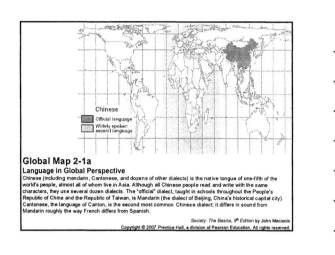

Global Map 2-1a
Language in Global Perspective
Chinese (including mandarin, Cantonese, and dozens of other dialects) is the native tongue of one-fifth of the world's people, almost all of whom live in Asia. Although all Chinese people read and write with the same characters, they use several dozen dialects. The "official" dialect, taught in schools throughout the People's Republic of China and the Republic of Taiwan, is Mandarin (the dialect of Beijing, China's historical capital city). Cantonese, the language of Canton, is the second most common Chinese dialect; it differs in sound from Mandarin roughly the way French differs from Spanish.

Society: The Basics, 9th Edition by John Macionis

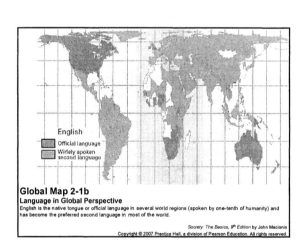

Global Map 2-1b
Language in Global Perspective
English is the native tongue or official language in several world regions (spoken by one-tenth of humanity) and has become the preferred second language in most of the world.

Society: The Basics, 9th Edition by John Macionis

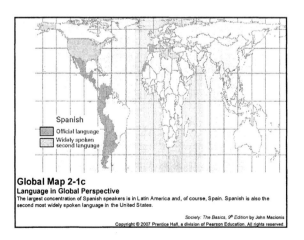

Global Map 2-1c
Language in Global Perspective
The largest concentration of Spanish speakers is in Latin America and, of course, Spain. Spanish is also the second most widely spoken language in the United States.

Society: The Basics, 9th Edition by John Macionis

National Map 2-1 (p. 56)
Language Diversity across the United States
Of more than 268 million people age five or older in the United States, the Census Bureau reports that 52 million (19 percent) speak a language other than English at home. Of these, 62 percent speak Spanish and 15 percent use an Asian language (the Census Bureau lists 29 languages, each of which is favored by more than 100,000 people). The map shows that non-English speakers are concentrated in certain regions of the country. Which ones? What do you think accounts for this pattern?
Source: U.S. Census Bureau (2003, 2006).

Society: The Basics, 9th Edition by John Macionis

THE ELEMENTS OF CULTURE

- Though cultures vary greatly, they have common elements
  - **Symbols**
  - **Language**
  - **Values**
  - **Norms**

Symbols

- Humans sense the surrounding world and give it meaning
- **Symbols**
  - *Anything that carries a particular meaning recognized by people who share a culture*
- Human capacity to create and manipulate symbols is almost limitless

34

- Entering an unfamiliar culture reminds us of the power of symbols
  - Culture shock is really the inability to "read" meaning in unfamiliar surroundings
- Culture shock is a two way process
  - Traveler *experiences* culture shock when meeting people whose way of life is different
  - Traveler can *inflict* culture shock on others by acting in ways that offend them
- Symbolic meanings also vary within a single society

Language

- **Language**
  - *A system of symbols that allows people to communicate with one another*
  - Heart of the symbolic system
    - Rules for writing differ
  - Key to **Cultural Transmission**
    - *The process by which one generation passes culture to the next*
  - Language is the key that unlocks centuries of accumulated wisdom

---

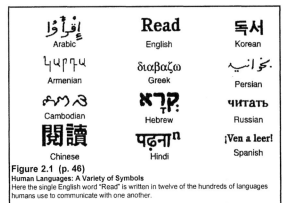

Figure 2.1 (p. 46)
Human Languages: A Variety of Symbols
Here the single English word "Read" is written in twelve of the hundreds of languages humans use to communicate with one another.

Does language shape reality?

- Edward Sapir and Benjamin Whorf
  - Claimed the answer is yes!
  - Each language has its own distinct symbols
    - Serve as the building blocks of reality
- All languages connect symbols with distinctive emotions
- Sapir-Whorf thesis
  - People see and understand the world through the cultural lens of language
  - Evidence does not support the notion that language *determines* reality the way Sapir and Whorf claimed

---

Values and Beliefs

- **Values**
  - *Culturally defined standards that people use to decide what is desirable, good, and beautiful and that serve as broad guidelines for social living*
- **Beliefs**
  - *Specific statements that people hold to be true*

Key Values of U.S. Culture

- Robin Williams Jr. (1970)
  - Ten values central to our way of life
- **1. Equal Opportunity**
  - People in the U.S. believe not in equality of condition but equality of opportunity
- **2. Individual Achievement and Personal Success**
- **3. Material Comfort**

- 4. **Activity and Work**
  - Our heroes are "doers" who get the job done
- 5. **Practicality and Efficiency**
  - Value the practical over the theoretical
- 6. **Progress**
- 7. **Science**
  - Expect scientists to solve problems and improve our lives
  - Believe that we are rational people

- 8. **Democracy and Free Enterprise**
  - Our society recognizes numerous individual rights that governments should not take away
- 9. **Freedom**
  - Favor individual initiative over collective conformity
- 10. **Racism and Group Superiority**
  - Most people in the U.S. still judge others according to gender, race, ethnicity, and social class

---

- Can you see how cultural values can shape the way people see the world?

- For example, how does our cultural emphasis on individual achievement blind us to the power of society to give some people great advantages over others?

Values: Often in Harmony, Sometimes in Conflict

- Cultural values go together
- One core cultural value contradicts another
  - Equal opportunity vs. racism and group superiority
- Value conflicts
  - Causes strain
  - Often leads to awkward balancing acts in our beliefs
  - One value is more important than another

Emerging Values

- Like all elements of culture, values change over time
- U.S. has always valued hard work
- Recently, placed increasing importance on leisure
  - Time off from work to
    - Travel
    - Read
    - Community service
  - Importance of material comfort remains strong
  - More people are seeking personal growth

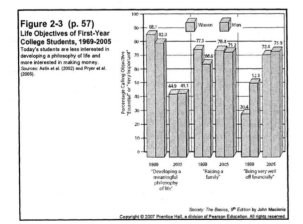

Figure 2-3 (p. 57)
Life Objectives of First-Year College Students, 1969-2005
Today's students are less interested in developing a philosophy of life and more interested in making money.
Sources: Astin et al. (2002) and Pryor et al. (2005).

Society: The Basics, 9th Edition by John Macionis

Values: A Global Perspective

- Values vary from culture to culture
- Values that are important to high-income countries differ from those in lower-income countries
- Lower-income nations develop cultures that value survival and tend to be traditional
- Higher-income nations develop cultures that value individualism and self-expression

Figure 2-2 (p. 49)
Cultural Values of Selected Countries
Higher-income countries are secular-rational and favor self-expression. The cultures of lower-income countries are more traditional and concerned with economic survival.
Source: Modernization, Cultural Change and Democracy by Ronald Inglehart and Christian Weizel, New York: Cambridge University Press, 2005.

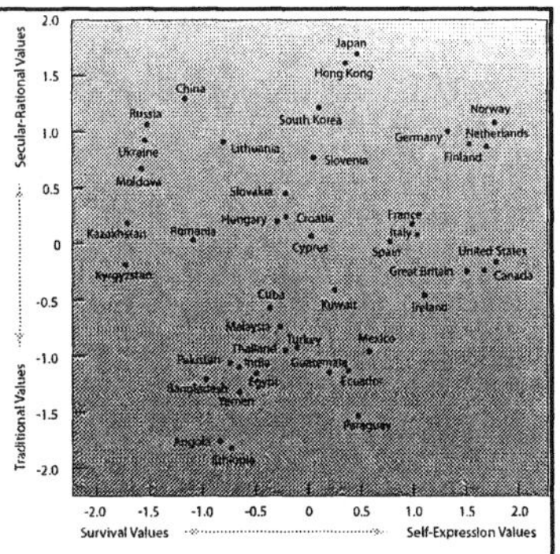

Society: The Basics, 9th Edition by John Macionis

Norms

- **Norms**
  - *Rules and expectations by which a society guides the behavior of its members*
- People respond to each other with **Sanctions**
  - *Rewards or punishments that encourage conformity to cultural norms*
- **Mores ("more rays") or Taboos**
  - *Norms that are widely observed and have great moral significance*

- **Folkways**
  - *Norms for routine or casual interaction*
  - People pay less attention to folkways
- As we learn cultural norms, we gain the capacity to evaluate our own behavior
- **Shame**
  - *The painful sense that others disapprove of our actions*
- **Guilt**
  - *A negative judgment we make of ourselves*
  - Only cultural creatures can experience shame and guilt

Ideal and Real Culture

- Values and norms do not describe actual behavior so much as they suggest how we *should* behave
- *Ideal culture* differs from *real culture*
- A culture's moral standards are important
  - "Do as I say, not as I do"

TECHNOLOGY AND CULTURE

- Every culture includes a wide range of physical human creations called *artifacts*
- Material culture can seem as strange to outsiders as their language, values, and norms
- Society's artifacts partly reflect underlying cultural values

- Material culture reflects a society's level of **technology**
  - *Knowledge that people use to make a way of life in their surroundings*
- The more complex a society's technology, the easier it is for members of that society to shape the world for themselves
- Lenski
  - A society's level of technology is crucial in determining what cultural ideas and artifacts emerge or are even possible

---

- Lenski (cont.)
  - **Sociocultural Evolution**
    - *The historical changes in culture brought about by new technology*
    - In terms of four major levels of development
      - H unting and gathering
      - H orticulture and pastoralism
      - A griculture
      - I ndustry

Hunting and Gathering

- **Hunting and gathering**
  - *The use of simple tools to hunt animals and gather vegetation for food*
  - Oldest and most basic way of living
  - Today, supports only a few societies
  - Societies are small
  - Simple and egalitarian way of life
  - Limited technology
  - As technology closes in on them, these societies are vanishing
  - Studying their way of life produced valuable information about our socio-cultural history and our fundamental ties to the natural environment

Horticulture and Pastoralism

- **Horticulture**
  - *The use of hand tools to raise crops*
- **Pastoralism**
  - *The domestication of animals*
- Many societies combine agriculture and pastoralism
- Pastoral and horticultural societies are more unequal

_____

Agriculture

- **Agriculture**
  - *Large-scale cultivation using plows harnessed to animals or machines*
  - "Dawn of Civilization" because of inventions
  - Large food surpluses
  - Agrarian society members became more specialized in their work
  - Agriculture brought about a dramatic increase in social inequity
  - Men gained pronounced power over women at all levels

_____

Industry

- **Industry**
  - *The production of goods using advanced sources of energy to drive large machinery*
  - Occurred as societies replaced muscles of animals and humans
  - Industrialization pushed aside traditional cultural values
  - Schooling is important because industrial jobs demand more skills
  - Industrial societies reduce economic inequality and weakens human community

_____

Post-Industrial Information Technology

- Many industrial societies have entered a post-industrial era
  - *New information technology*
  - Industrial societies center on factories that *make things*
  - Post-industrial production centers on computers and other electronic devices
  - Information economy changes skills that define a way of life
  - People must learn to work with symbols and society now has the capacity to create symbolic culture on an unprecedented scale

---

CULTURAL DIVERSITY

- In the U.S., we are aware of our cultural diversity
- Japan
  - Historical isolation
  - Most *monocultural* of all high-income countries
- U.S.
  - Centuries of heavy immigration
  - Most *multicultural* of all high income countries

High Culture and Popular Culture

- Cultural diversity can involve social class
  - Differences arise because cultural patterns are accessible to only some members of a society
- **High Culture**
  - *Refers to cultural patterns that distinguish a society's elite*
- **Popular Culture**
  - *Describes cultural patterns that are widespread among a society's population*

Subculture

- *Subculture*
  - *Cultural patterns that set apart some segment of a society's population*
- Easy but inaccurate to put people in sub-cultural categories
  - Almost everyone participates in many subcultures without much commitment to any one of them
  - Ethnicity and religion set people apart with tragic results

---

- Many view the U.S. as a melting pot
  - Nationalities blend into a single "American" culture
  - How accurate is the melting pot image?
    - Subcultures involve not just difference but hierarchy
    - What we view as dominant or "mainstream" culture
      - View the lives of disadvantaged people as "subculture"
- Sociologists prefer to level the playing field of society by emphasizing
  - Multiculturalism

Multiculturalism

- **Multiculturalism**
  - *A perspective recognizing the cultural diversity of the United States and promoting respect and equal standing for all cultural traditions*
  - U.S. society downplayed cultural diversity
    - Defines itself in terms of its European and especially English immigrants
- **E pluribus unum**
  - "out of many, one"
    - *Motto symbolizes not only our national political union but also the idea that the varied experiences of immigrants from around the world come together to form new ways of life*

- English way of life
  - Historians reported events from the English and European point of view
  - **Eurocentric**
    - *T he dominance of European (especially English) cultural patterns*
- Language
  - Controversial issue
  - Some believe English should be U.S. official language
  - **Afrocentrism**
    - *E mphasizing and promoting African cultural patterns*
    - *A strategy for correcting centuries of ignoring the cultural achievements of African societies and African Americans*

- Criticisms
  - Encourages divisiveness rather than unity
  - Multiculturalism actually harms minorities
  - Multicultural policies support the same racial inequality that our nation has struggled long to overcome
  - Afrocentric curriculum may deny children important knowledge and skills
  - Global war on terror spotlighted multiculturalism
    - Defense of values and a way of life

Counterculture

- Cultural diversity includes outright rejection of conventional ideas or behavior
- **Counterculture**
  - *Cultural patterns that strongly oppose those widely accepted within a society*
  - Counterculturalists favored a collective and cooperative lifestyle
    - "Being" more important than "doing"
  - Led some people to "drop out" of the larger society
  - Countercultures are still flourishing

Cultural Change

- Most basic human truth, "all things shall pass"
    - Change in one dimension of a cultural system usually sparks changes in others
- **Cultural Integration**
    - *The close relationships among various elements of a cultural system*
- Some parts of a cultural system change faster than others
- William Ogburn (1964)
    - Technology moves quickly, generating new elements of material culture faster than non-material culture can keep up

---

- **Cultural Lag**
    - *The fact that some cultural elements change more quickly than others, disrupting a cultural system*
- Cultural changes are set in motion in three ways:
    - Invention
        - The process of creating new cultural elements, which changed our way of life
    - Discovery
        - Recognizing and better understanding something already in existence
            - M any discoveries result from painstaking scientific research, and others happen by a stroke of luck

---

- **Diffusion**
    - *The spread of objects or ideas from one society to another*
    - Diffusion works the other way, too
        - M uch of what we assume is "American" actually comes from elsewhere

Ethnocentrism and Cultural Relativism

- Confucius
  - "All people are the same; it's only their habits that are different"
- **Ethnocentrism**
  - *The practice of judging another culture by the standards of one's own culture*
  - Exhibited by people everywhere
  - Also generates misunderstanding and sometimes conflict

Figure 2-4 (p. 59)
The View from "Down Under"
North American should be "up" and South America "down," or so we think. But because we live on a globe, "up" and "down" have no meaning at all. The reason this map of the Western Hemisphere looks wrong to us is not that it is geographically inaccurate; it simply violates our ethnocentric assumption that the United States should be "above" the rest of the Americas.

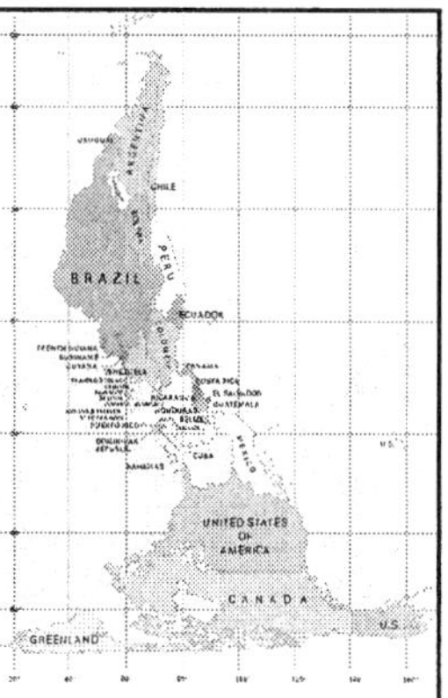

Society: The Basics, 9th Edition by John Macionis

- **Cultural Relativism**
  - *The practice of judging a culture by its own standards*
  - Alternative to ethnocentrism
  - Requires openness to unfamiliar values and norms
  - Requires the ability to put aside cultural standards known all our lives
- Businesses now know that success in the global economy depends on awareness of cultural patterns around the world
- Many companies used marketing strategies that lacked sensitivity to cultural diversity

- Cultural relativism problems
  - If almost any behavior is the norm *somewhere* in the world, does that mean everything is equally right?
  - We are all members of a single human species, what are the universal standards of proper conduct?
  - In trying to develop universal standards, how do we avoid imposing our own standards on others?

_____

_____

_____

_____

_____

_____

A Global Culture?

- English is firmly established as the preferred second language in most parts of the world
  - Are we witnessing the birth of a global culture?
- Societies around the world have more contact than ever before
  - Flow of goods
  - Flow of information
  - Flow of people

_____

_____

_____

_____

_____

_____

- **Global Economy: The Flow of Goods**
  - Global economy has spread many consumer goods throughout the world
- **Global Communication: The Flow of Information**
  - Internet and satellite-assisted communication enables people to experience events taking place thousands of miles away, often as they happen
- **Global Migration: The Flow of People**
  - Knowledge motivates people to move where they imagine life will be better

_____

_____

_____

_____

_____

_____

- **Three important limitations to the global culture thesis:**
  - Flow of goods, information, and people is uneven
  - The global culture thesis assumes that people everywhere are able to afford the new goods and services
  - Although many cultural elements have spread throughout the world, people everywhere do not attach the same meanings to them

---

THEORETICAL ANALYSIS OF CULTURE

- Sociologists investigate how culture helps us make sense of ourselves and the surrounding world
  - Examine several macro-level theoretical approaches to understanding culture
  - A micro-level approach to the personal experience of culture
    - Emphasizes how individuals conform to cultural patterns
    - How people create new patterns in their everyday lives

The Functions of Culture: Structural-Functional Analysis

- Explains culture as a complex strategy for meeting human needs
- Draws from the philosophical doctrine of *idealism*
- Structural-functional analysis helps us understand unfamiliar ways of life
- **Cultural Universals**
  - *Traits that are part of every known culture*

- Strength of structural-functional analysis lies in showing how culture operates to meet human needs
- This approach ignores cultural diversity
- Emphasizes cultural stability, downplays the importance of change

---

Inequality and Culture: Social-Conflict Analysis

- Draws attention to the link between culture and inequality
- Any cultural trait benefits some members of society at the expense of others
- Culture is shaped by a society's system of economic production

---

- Social-conflict theory is rooted in the philosophy of *materialism*
- Social conflict analysis ties our cultural values of competitiveness and material success to our country's capitalist economy
- Views capitalism as "natural"
- Strains of inequality erupt into movements for social change

- Social-conflict approach suggests that systems do not address human needs equally
- Inequality, in turn, generates pressure toward change
- Stressing the divisiveness of culture understates ways in which cultural patterns integrate members of a society

---

Evolution and Culture: Sociobiology

- **Sociobiology**
  - A theoretical approach that explores ways in which human biology affects how we create culture
  - Rests on the theory of evolution proposed by Charles Darwin's "Origin of Species"
  - Natural Selection
    - Organisms change over a long period of time

Four Principles of Natural Selection

- All living things live to reproduce themselves
- Some random variation in genes allows each species to *"try out"* new life patterns in a particular environment
- Over thousands of generations, the genes that promote reproduction survive and become dominant
- Large number of cultural universals reflects the fact that all humans are members of a single biological species

- Sociobiology provides insights into the biological roots of some cultural patterns
- Defenders state sociobiology rejects past pseudoscience of racial and gender superiority
- Research suggests that biological forces do not *determine* human behavior
- Humans *learn* behavior within a culture
- Contribution of sociobiology lies in explaining why some cultural patterns are more common and seem easier to learn than others

Culture			
	Structural-Functional Approach	Social-Conflict Approach	Sociobiology Approach
What is the level of analysis?	Macro-level	Macro-level	Macro-level
What is culture?	Culture is a system of behavior by which members of societies cooperate to meet their needs.	Culture is a system that benefits some people and disadvantages others.	Culture is a system of behavior that is partly shaped by human biology.
What is the foundation of culture?	Cultural patterns are rooted in a society's core values and beliefs.	Cultural patterns are rooted in a society's system of economic production.	Cultural patterns are rooted in humanity's biological evolution.
What core questions does the approach ask?	How does a cultural pattern help society operate? What cultural patterns are found in all societies?	How does a cultural pattern benefit some people and harm others? How does a cultural pattern support social inequality?	How does a cultural pattern help a species adapt to its environment?

Applying Theory: Culture (p. 61)

Culture and Human Freedom

- As symbolic creatures, humans cannot live without culture
- Culture is a matter of habit, which limits our choices and repetition of troubling patterns
- Culture forces us to choose as we make and remake a world for ourselves
- The better we understand the workings of culture, the better prepared we will be to use the freedom it offers

Socialization: From Infancy to Old Age

LEARNING OBJECTIVES

- To become aware of the effects of social isolation on humans and other primates.
- To become aware of the key components of Sigmund Freud's model of personality.
- To identify and describe the four stages of Jean Piaget's cognitive development theory.
- To identify and describe the stages of moral development as identified by Lawrence Kohlberg.
- To analyze Carol Gilligan's critique of Kohlberg's moral development model.
- To identify and describe Erik H. Erikson's stages of personality development.
- To consider the contributions of George Herbert Mead to the understanding of personality development.
- To compare the spheres of socialization (family, school, etc.) in terms of their effects on an individual's socialization experiences.
- To begin to understand the cross-cultural and historical patterns of death and dying.

CHAPTER OUTLINE

I. Social Experience: The Key to Our Humanity
    A.   Human Development: Nature and Nurture
        1.   The Biological Sciences: The Role of Nature
        2.   The Social Sciences: The Role of Nurture
    B.   Social Isolation
        1.   Research with Monkeys
        2.   Studies of Isolated Children

II. Understanding Socialization
    A.   Sigmund Freud's Elements of Personality
        1.   Basic Human Needs
        2.   Freud's Personality Model
        3.   Personality Development
    B.   Jean Piaget's Theory of Cognitive Development
        1.   The Sensorimotor Stage
        2.   The Preoperational Stage
        3.   The Concrete Operational Stage
        4.   The Formal Operational Stage
    C.   Lawrence Kohlberg's Theory of Moral Development
    D.   Carol Gilligan's Theory of Gender and Moral Development
    E.   George Herbert Mead's Theory of the Social Self
        1.   The Self

SOCIALIZATION: FROM INFANCY TO OLD AGE

CHAPTER 3

- **Why** is social experience the key to human personality?

- **What** familiar social settings have special importance to how we live and grow?

- **How** do our experiences change over the life course?

SOCIAL EXPERIENCE: THE KEY TO OUR HUMANITY

- *SOCIALIZATION*
  - *The lifelong social experience by which people develop their human potential and learn culture*
- Socialization is basic to human development

PERSONALITY

- *A person's fairly consistent patterns of acting, thinking, and feeling*
- Built by internalizing our surroundings
- Humans need social experience to learn their culture and to survive

---

Human Development: Nature And Nurture

- Humans depend on others to provide care needed
  - Physical growth
  - Personality development

The Biological Sciences: The Role of Nature

- *Charles Darwin*
  - Human behavior was instinctive – our "nature"
    - U.S. Economic System reflects "instinctive human competitiveness"
    - People are "born criminals"
    - Women are "naturally" emotional and men are "naturally" more rational

- People trying to understand cultural diversity also misunderstood Darwin
  - European explorers linked cultural differences to biology
  - Viewed members of less technological societies as less evolved – "less human"
  - Ethnocentric view helped colonization

The Social Sciences: The Role of Nurture

- *John B. Watson (1878-1958)*
- *Behaviorism*
  - Held that behavior is not instinctive but learned
  - People are equally human, just culturally different
  - Human behavior is rooted in nurture not nature

- Social scientists are cautious about describing *any* human behavior as instinctive
- Human life depends on the functioning of the body
- Whether you develop your inherited potential depends on how you are raised
- Nurture matters more in shaping human behavior
  - *Nurture is our nature*

Social Isolation

- Ethically, researchers cannot place human in total isolation to study what happens
- *Harry & Margaret Harlow (1962)*
  - Studied rhesus monkeys
  - Found that complete isolation for even six months seriously disturbed development
  - Unable to interact with others in a group
  - Confirmed the importance of adults in cradling infants
  - Isolation caused irreversible emotional and behavioral damage

---

- What new understanding of the familiar ad campaign "Have you hugged your child today?" do you gain from the Harlow research?

- What do studies of isolated children teach us about the importance of social experience?

Studies of Isolated Children

- *Anna*
  - Social isolation caused permanent damage
  - At age eight, mental development was less than a two year old
  - Began to use words at age ten
  - Because mother was mentally retarded, perhaps Anna was similarly challenged

- *California Case*
  - Childhood isolation resulting from parental abuse
  - At age 13, mental development of a one year old
  - Became physically healthy with intensive treatment
  - Language ability remained that of a young child

Critical Review

- Evidence points to the crucial role of social experience in forming personality
- Humans can sometimes recover from abuse and short-term isolation
- There is a point at which isolation in infancy causes permanent developmental damage

---

Understanding Socialization

- Socialization is a complex lifelong process
- Six researchers made lasting contributions to our understanding of human development

Sigmund Freud's *Elements of Personality*

- (1856-1939) Lived at a time most Europeans considered human behavior biologically fixed
- Studied personality and eventually developed the theory of psychoanalysis

---

- Basic Human Needs
  - Biology plays a major part in human development
  - Humans have two basic drives
    - Eros – need for bonding "life instinct"
    - Thanatos – aggressive drive "death instinct"
  - Opposing forces operating at an unconscious level, generating deep inner tension

---

- Freud's Model of Personality
- **Id**
  - Human being's basic drives
  - Unconscious and demand immediate satisfaction
  - Society opposes the id, which is why one of the first words a child usually learns is "no"
  - To avoid frustration, the child must learn to approach the world realistically

- **Ego**
  - A person's conscious efforts to balance innate pleasure seeking drives with the demands of society
  - Arises as we gain awareness of our distinct existence and face the fact that we cannot have everything we want

- **Superego**
  - The cultural values and norms internalized by an individual
  - Operates as our conscience
  - Begins to form as a child becomes aware of parental demands and matures as the child comes to understand that everyone's behavior should take account of cultural norms

- Personality Development
  - To the Id, the world is a jumble of physical sensations that bring pleasure or pain
  - As the superego develops, moral concepts of right and wrong are learned
  - Id and superego remain in conflict
    - Managed by the ego in a well-adjusted person
  - Conflicts not resolved in childhood may surface later on as personality disorders
  - Competing demands of self and society result in a compromise called sublimation
    - Changes selfish drives into socially acceptable behavior

Critical Review

- Critics charge that Freud's work presents humans in male terms and devalues women
- Theories are difficult to test scientifically
- Influenced everyone who later studied human personality
- Importance to sociology
  - We internalize social norms
  - Childhood experiences have a lasting impact on our personalities

_____

_____

_____

_____

_____

_____

_____

Jean Piaget's *Theory of Cognitive Development*

- (1896-1980)
- Studied human cognition
  - How people think and understand
  - Identified four stages of cognitive development

_____

_____

_____

_____

_____

_____

_____

- *Sensorimotor Stage*
  - The level of human development at which individuals experience the world only through their senses
  - First two years of life
  - "Knowing" to very young children amounts to what their senses tell them

_____

_____

_____

_____

_____

_____

_____

- *The Preoperational Stage*
  - The level of human development at which individuals first use language and other symbols
  - Between two and six, attach meanings only to specific experiences and objects
  - Lack abstract concepts
    - Cannot judge size, weight, or volume
  - About age 7, children are able to think more abstractly

_____

_____

_____

_____

_____

_____

_____

- **The Concrete Operational Stage**
  - The level of human development at which individuals first see causal connections in their surroundings
  - Between ages 7 and 11, focus on how and why things happen
  - Attach more than one symbol to an event or object

_____

_____

_____

_____

_____

_____

_____

- *The Formal Operational Stage*
  - The level of human development at which individuals think abstractly and critically
  - About age 12, begin to reason in the abstract rather than think only of concrete situations
  - As capacity for abstract thought is gained, young person also learns to understand metaphors

_____

_____

_____

_____

_____

_____

_____

Critical Review

- Freud saw the ability to engage the world unfolding in stages as the result of biological maturation and social experience
- Do people in all societies pass through all four of Piaget's stages?
- Living in a traditional society that changes slowly probably limits the capacity for abstract and critical thought

---

- **Using Piaget's concepts, can you explain why young children will reach for a nickel rather than a dime?**

Lawrence Kohlberg's *Theory of Moral Development*

- 1981
- Studied moral reasoning
  - How people come to judge situations as right or wrong
  - Development occurs in stages
- *Preconventional Level*
  - Young children experience the world in terms of pain and pleasure
  - "Rightness" amounts to "what feels good to me"

- *Conventional Level*
  - Appears in the teens
  - Young people lose some of their selfishness
  - Learn to define right and wrong in terms of what pleases parents and conforms to cultural norms
- *Postconventional Level*
  - People move beyond society's norms to consider abstract ethical principles
  - Think about ideas such as liberty, freedom, or justice
    - May argue what is lawful may not be right

Critical Review

- Kohlberg explains moral development in terms of distinct stages
- May not apply to people in all societies
- Many people in the US do not reach postconventional morality
- All research subjects were boys
  - Research cannot be generalized

Carol Gilligan's *Theory of Gender and Moral Development*

- Compare the moral development of boys and girls
- Two sexes use different standards or rightness
- Girls
  - Have *a care and responsibility perspective*
  - Judge a situation toward personal relationships and loyalties

- Impersonal rules have long governed men's lives

- Personal relationships are more relevant to women's lives

Critical Review

- Gilligan's work sharpens understanding of human development and gender issues in research
- Work does not answer whether nature or nurture is responsible in gender differences

---

George Herbert Meade's *Theory of the Social Self*

- George Herbert Mead (1863-1931)
  - Developed theory of *Social Behaviorism*
- *The Self*
  - *The part of an individual's personality composed of self-awareness and self-image*
  - Mead proposed seeing the self as the product of social experience

- *The self develops only with social experience*
  - Rejected the idea that personality is guided by biology (Freud) or biological maturation (Piaget)
  - Self develops only as individual interacts with others
  - Without interaction, body grows, but no self emerges
- *Social experience is the exchange of symbols*
  - Humans find meaning in action by imagining people's underlying intentions

- *Understanding intention requires imagining a situation from the other's point of view*
  - All symbolic interaction involves seeing ourselves as others see us
    - *Taking the role of the other*
- *The I and the Me*
  - By taking the role of the another, we become self-aware
    - Two parts of self
      - S ubject – Active and spontaneous – "I"
      - O bjective – the way we imagine others see us - "Me"

- *Development of the Self*
  - Key is learning to take the role of the other
  - Infants can only do this through *imitation* because of limited social experience
  - As children learn to use language and other symbols, the self emerges in the form of *play*
    - Assumes roles modeled on *significant others*
      - *P eople who have special importance for socialization*
  - Everyday life demands that we see ourselves in terms of cultural norms as *any* member of our society might
    - *Generalized Other*
      - *W idespread cultural norms and values we use as a reference in evaluating ourselves*

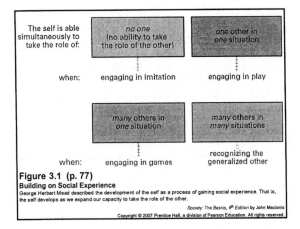

The self is able simultaneously to take the role of:

	no one (no ability to take the role of the other)	one other in one situation
when:	engaging in imitation	engaging in play
	many others in one situation	many others in many situations
when:	engaging in games	recognizing the generalized other

Figure 3.1 (p. 77)
Building on Social Experience
George Herbert Mead described the development of the self as a process of gaining social experience. That is, the self develops as we expand our capacity to take the role of the other.

Critical Review

- Mead's work explores the essence of social experience itself
- View is completely social – no biological element
- "I" and "Me" work together, unlike the "Id" and "Superego" locked in continual combat

- **Have you ever seen young children put on their parents' shoes, literally putting themselves "in the shoes" of another person?**

- **How does this help children learn to "take the role of the other"?**

Erik H. Erikson's *Eight Stages of Development*

- (1902-1994)
  - Broader view of socialization
  - Face challenges throughout the life course
- Stage 1
  - *The challenge of trust (versus mistrust)*
    - Birth to about 18 months
    - Gain a sense of trust that the world is safe

- Stage 2
  - *Toddlerhood – The challenge of autonomy (versus doubt and shame)*
    - Up to age three
    - Failure to gain self control leads to doubt in abilities
- Stage 3
  - *Preschool – The challenge of initiative (versus guilt)*
    - Four and five year olds
    - Learn to engage their surroundings or experience guilt at having failed to meet expectations

---

- Stage 4
  - *Preadolescence – The challenge of industriousness (versus inferiority)*
    - Between ages six and thirteen
    - Feel proud of accomplishments or fear they do not measure up
- Stage 5
  - *Adolescence – The challenge of gaining identity (versus confusion)*
    - Teen Years
    - Struggle to establish identity; almost all teens suffer confusion in establishing identities

- Stage 6
  - *Young Adulthood – The challenge of intimacy (versus isolation)*
    - Challenge of forming and keeping intimate relationships
    - Balancing the need to bond with the need to have a separate identity
- Stage 7
  - *Middle Adulthood – The challenge of making a difference (versus self-absorption)*
    - Challenge of middle age is to contribute to the lives of others
    - Failing leads to self-centeredness or becoming caught up in own limited concerns

- Stage 8
  - *Old Age – The challenge of integrity (versus despair)*
    - Near the end of life, people hope to look back on accomplishments with a sense of integrity
    - Those self-absorbed, old age brings a sense of despair over missed opportunities

Critical Review

- Personality formation as a lifelong process
- Success at one stage preparing to meet the next challenge
- However, not everyone faces these challenges in the exact order
- Nor is it clear that failure to meet a challenge means doom in later stages

AGENTS OF SOCIALIZATION

- **FAMILY**
- **SCHOOL**
- **PEER GROUP**
- **MASS MEDIA**

Family

- May be the most important socializing agent
- Nurture in early childhood
  - Responsibility falls on parents and other family members
  - Not all family learning results from intentional teaching
    - Also learn from the environment created by parents

- Race and Class
  - Family also gives children a social identity
    - Societies define race in various ways
  - Social class position plays a large part in shaping a child's personality
  - Research shows that class position affects amount of money parents spend on children and what they expect of them
  - All parents act in ways that encourage their children to follow in their footsteps
  - Enrichment activities represent *cultural capital*
    - Advances children's learning

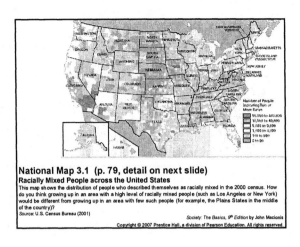

National Map 3.1 (p. 79, detail on next slide)
Racially Mixed People across the United States
This map shows the distribution of people who described themselves as racially mixed in the 2000 census. How do you think growing up in an area with a high level of racially mixed people (such as Los Angeles or New York) would be different from growing up in an area with few such people (for example, the Plains States in the middle of the country)?
Source: U.S. Census Bureau (2001)

Society: The Basics, 9th Edition by John Macionis

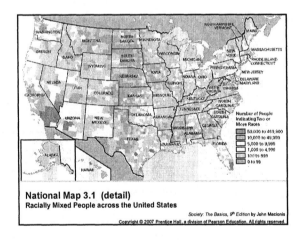

National Map 3.1 (detail)
Racially Mixed People across the United States

Society: The Basics, 9th Edition by John Macionis

The School

- Enlarges children's social world
- Encountering people who are different, children come to understand
  - Race
  - Social class position

- Gender
  - Schools socialize into gender roles
  - Continue right through to college
- What children learn
  - Schooling teaches a wide range of knowledge and skills
  - Also teach informally
    - Hidden Curriculum
  - For most, school is the first encounter with bureaucracy

The Peer Group

- *A social group whose members have interests, social position, and age in common*
- Allows children to escape the direct supervision of adults
- In a rapidly changing society, peer groups have great influence
  - Attitudinal difference may form a "generation gap"

- Peers affect short-term interests, but parental influence remains strong
- Any neighborhood or school is made up of many peer groups
- *Anticipatory Socialization*
  - *Learning that helps a person achieve a desired position*

The Mass Media

- The means for delivering impersonal communications to a vast audience
  - Powerful and influence is different than family, school, or peers
- U.S. has highest rate of TV ownership in the world
  - People with lower incomes spend the most time watching TV

Figure 3.2 (p. 80)
Television Ownership in Global Perspective
Television is popular in high- and middle-income countries, where almost every household owns at least one TV set.
Source: U.S. Census Bureau (2005) and International Telecommunication Union (2006).

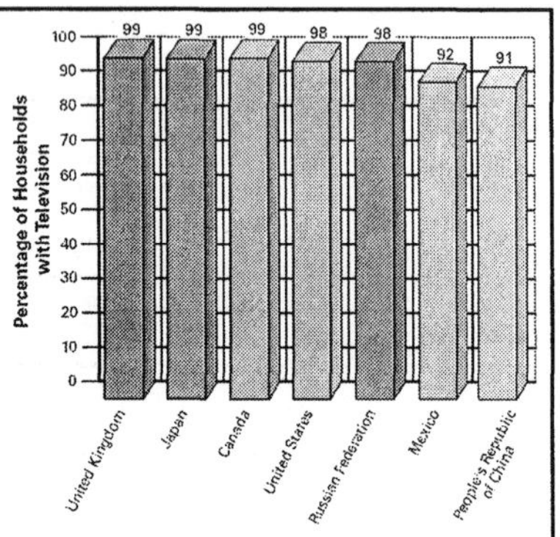

Society: The Basics, 9th Edition by John Macionis
Copyright © 2007 Prentice Hall, a division of Pearson Education. All rights reserved.

- Television and politics
  - Provokes much criticism
  - Liberal
    - Most of television history, racial and ethnic minorities have been invisible or stereotyped
    - Recently, minorities have moved to center stage
  - Conservative
    - Television and film are dominated by liberal "cultural elite"
    - "politically correct" media have advanced liberal causes
    - Not all agree –oth ers suggest TV reflects a political "spin" from both sides

74

- Television and violence
  - AMA
    - Violence in TV and film are hazardous to our health
  - Study found strong link among aggression, TV time, and video game playing of elementary school children
  - Public is concerned
  - 1997 TV rating system adopted by TV industry
  - Other spheres of social learning
    - Religion
    - Workplace
    - Military
    - Social Clubs

SOCIALIZATION AND THE LIFE COURSE

- Learning continues throughout our lives
- Society organizes human experience according to
  - Childhood
  - Adolescence
  - Adulthood
  - Old Age

Childhood

- 250 million children, half full time, work for about 50 cents an hour (see map)
- Most North Americans view childhood as a carefree time of learning and play
  - This is a new idea
- Concept of childhood is cultural not biological

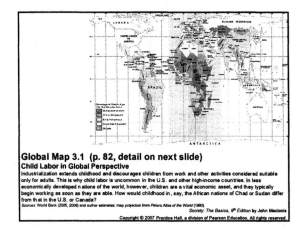

Global Map 3.1 (p. 82, detail on next slide)
Child Labor in Global Perspective
Industrialization extends childhood and discourages children from work and other activities considered suitable
only for adults. This is why child labor is uncommon in the U.S. and other high-income countries. In less
economically developed nations of the world, however, children are a vital economic asset, and they typically
begin working as soon as they are able. How would childhood in, say, the African nations of Chad or Sudan differ
from that in the U.S. or Canada?
Sources: World Bank (2005, 2006) and author estimates; map projection from Peters Atlas of the World (1990).
Society: The Basics, 9th Edition by John Macionis

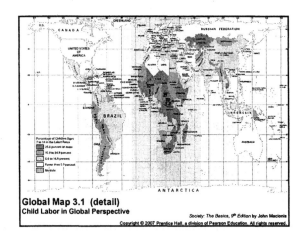

Global Map 3.1 (detail)
Child Labor in Global Perspective
Society: The Basics, 9th Edition by John Macionis

Adolescence

- Emerged as a buffer between childhood and adulthood
- Teenage turbulence comes from cultural inconsistency
  - A time of social contradictions
- Varies according to social background

Adulthood

- The time of life when most accomplishments take place
- Personalities are formed and dramatic changes cause significant change to the self
- Early adulthood – until age forty
- Middle adulthood – between forty and sixty
  - More aware of the fragility of health
  - Women face more problems than men
  - However, men realize they will never reach earlier career goals

Old Age

- The later years of adulthood and the final stage of life
- Begins around the mid-sixties
- Elderly population is growing nearly as fast as the U.S. population as a whole
- Elderly people will be more visible in everyday life – young and old will interact more
- *Gerontology*
  - *The study of aging and the elderly*

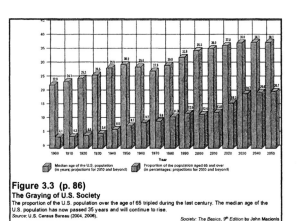

Figure 3.3 (p. 86)
The Graying of U.S. Society
The proportion of the U.S. population over the age of 65 tripled during the last century. The median age of the U.S. population has now passed 35 years and will continue to rise.
Source: U.S. Census Bureau (2004, 2006).

Society: The Basics, 9th Edition by John Macionis

- *Aging and Biology*
  - For most of our population, aging begins in middle age
  - Most older people are not disabled nor discouraged by their physical condition
- *Aging and Culture*
  - Low-income countries, elderly have influence and respect
  - *Gerontocracy*
    - *A form of social organization in which the elderly have the most wealth, power, and prestige*

- In industrial society
  - Older people live apart from their grown children
  - Rapid social change makes much of what seniors know obsolete
- *Ageism*
  - *Prejudice and discrimination against older people*
- *Aging and Income*
  - Old age means living with less income
  - Today, elderly population is doing better
    - Better income, Better health, More generous government programs

---

- **Would you favor replacing the common "senior discounts" found at many local businesses with discounts for low-income people?**

- **What about single parents with children?**

- **Explain your view?**

Death and Dying

- **Elizabeth Kubler-Ross**
  - Death as an orderly transition involving five stages
    - *Denial* – expected in a culture that doesn't talk about death
    - *Anger* –a gross injustice to the one facing death
    - *Negotiation* – bargaining with God
    - *Resignation* –acco mpanied by psychological depression
    - *Acceptance* – complete adjustment to death
- As elderly become larger part of U.S. population, expect the culture to become more comfortable with the idea of death

---

The Life Course: Patterns and Variations

- *Two major conclusions:*
  - Life course is largely a social construction
  - Life course presents certain problems and transitions that involve learning something new and unlearning familiar routines
  - Societies organize life course according to age but other forces share people's lives
  - *Cohort*
    - *A category of people with something in common, usually their age*

RESOCIALIZATION: TOTAL INSTITUTIONS

- *Total Institution*
  - *A setting in which people are isolated from the rest of society and manipulated by administrative staff*
  - Three characteristics
    - Supervision
    - Control and standardization
    - Formal rules and daily routines

- *Resocialization*
  - *Radically changing an inmate's personality by carefully controlling the environment*
    - Prisons
    - Mental hospitals
  - Two-part process
    - Break down existing identity
    - Build a new self through a system of reward and punishments
  - *Institutionalized*
    - *Living in a rigidly controlled environment without the capacity for independent living*

Chapter 4 — Social Interaction in Everyday Life

LEARNING OBJECTIVES

- To identify the characteristics of social structure.
- To discuss the relationship between social structure and individuality.
- To distinguish among the different types of statuses and roles.
- To describe and illustrate the social construction of reality.
- To see the importance of performance, nonverbal communication, idealization, and embarrassment to the "presentation of the self."
- To describe and illustrate dramaturgical analysis.
- To understand the relationship between language and gender.
- To use gender and humor to illustrate how people construct meaning in everyday life.

CHAPTER OUTLINE

I.   Social Structure: A Guide to Everyday Living

II.   Status
    A.   Ascribed Status and Achieved Status
    B.   Master Status

III. Role
    A.   Role Conflict and Role Strain
    B.   Role Exit

IV.   The Social Construction of Reality
    A.   "Street Smarts"
    B.   The Thomas Theorem
    C.   Ethnomethodology
    D.   Reality Building: Class and Culture

V.   Dramaturgical Analysis: "The Presentation of Self"
    A.   Performances
        1.   An Application: The Doctor's Office
    B.   Nonverbal Communication
        1.   Body Language and Deception
    C.   Gender and Performances
        1.   Demeanor

SOCIAL INTERACTION IN EVERYDAY LIFE

CHAPTER 4

- **How** do we create reality in our face-to-face interactions?

- **Why** do employers try to control their workers' feelings on the job as well as their behavior?

- **What** makes something funny?

SOCIAL STRUCTURE: A GUIDE TO EVERYDAY LIVING

- **SOCIAL INTERACTION**
  - *The process by which people act and react in relation to others*
- **STATUS**
  - *A social position that a person holds*
  - Generally refers to "prestige"
- **STATUS SET**
  - *All the statuses a person holds at a given time*
    - Changes over life

Ascribed and Achieved Status

- **Ascribed Status**
  - *A social position a person receives at birth or takes involuntarily later in life*
    - Matters about which we have little choice
- **Achieved Status**
  - *A social position a person takes on voluntarily that reflects a personal ability and effort*
  - People's ascribed statuses influence the statuses they achieve

---

- **Make a list of ten important statuses in your life.**

- **Indicate whether one is ascribed or achieved.**

- **Is this difficult to do?**

- **Explain your answer.**

Master Status

- *A status that has special importance for social identity, often shaping a person's entire life*
  - Can be negative as well as positive
  - Gender is a master status because all societies limit opportunities for women
  - Physical disability can serve as a master status

Role

- *Behavior expected of someone who holds a particular status*
  - A person holds a status and performs a role
  - Varies by culture
  - In every society, actual role performance varies according to a person's unique personality
  - Some societies permit more individual expression than others

- **Role Set**
  - *A number of roles attached to a single status*
    - Differs by society
    - May or may not be important to social identity

Role Conflict and Role Strain

- **Role Conflict**
  - *Conflict among the roles connected to two or more statuses*
- **Role Strain**
  - *Tension among the roles connected to a single status*

Role Exit

- **The process by which people disengage from important social roles**
  - The process of becoming an "ex"
  - Process begins as people come to doubt their ability to continue in a certain role
  - "Exes" carry with them a self-image shaped by an earlier role
  - "Exes" must also rebuild relationships with people who knew them in their earlier life

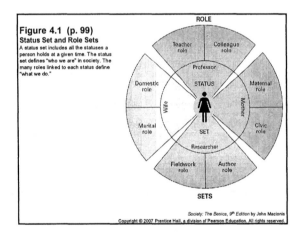

Figure 4.1 (p. 99)
Status Set and Role Sets
A status set includes all the statuses a person holds at a given time. The status set defines "who we are" in society. The many roles linked to each status define "what we do."

Global Map 4.1: Housework in Global Perspective (p. 100)
Throughout the world, housework is a major part of women's routines and identities. This is especially true in poor nations of Latin America, Africa, and Asia, where the social position of women is far below that of men. But our society also defines housework and child care as "feminine" activities, even though women and men have the same legal rights and most women work outside the home.
Source: Peters Atlas of the World (1990); updated by the author.

Global Map 4.1: Housework in Global Perspective
Detail

The Social Construction of Reality

- *"Inevitably we construct ourselves. Let me explain. I enter this house and immediately I become what I have to become, what I can become: I construct myself. That is, I present myself to you in a form suitable to the relationship I wish to achieve with you. And, of course, you do the same with me."*
  - **(Pirandello, L. (1917). The pleasure of honesty. 1962: 157-58)**

- **Social Construction of Reality**
  - *The process by which people creatively shape reality through social interaction*
    - Idea is the foundation of the symbolic-interaction approach
  - "Reality" remains unclear in everyone's minds
    - Especially in unfamiliar situations
  - Social interaction is a complex negotiation that builds reality
  - Perception of events are based on different interests and intentions

The Thomas Theorem

- **Situations that are defined as real are real in their consequences**
  - Though reality is "soft" as it is being shaped, it can become "hard" in its effects

Ethnomethodology

- ***The study of the way people make sense of their everyday surroundings***
  - Approach points out that everyday behavior rests on a number of assumptions
  - Investigate assumptions made about everyday reality by purposely breaking the rules
  - Seeing what happens gives a better idea of the "rules" of everyday social interaction
  - Rules are important to everyday reality

- **Members of every culture have rules about how close people should stand while talking.**

- **To test this assumption, during a conversation slowly move closer and closer to the other person and see what happens.**

Reality Building: Class and Culture

- How we act or what we see in our surroundings depends on our interests
- Reality construction varies even more in a global perspective
- People build reality from the surrounding culture
- Films have an effect on the reality we all experience

DRAMATURGICAL ANALYSIS: THE PRESENTATION OF SELF

- **DRAMATURGICAL ANALYSIS**
  - *The study of social interaction in terms of theatrical performance*
- **Erving Goffman (1922-1982)**
  - Analyzed social interaction
  - Explained how people live their lives like actors performing on a stage

---

- **Presentation of Self**
  - *A person's efforts to create specific impressions in the minds of others*
  - Also called "Impression Management"
  - Begins with the idea of personal performance

Performances

- *Reveal information consciously and unconsciously*
- Includes
  - Dress (costume)
  - Objects we carry (props)
  - Tone of voice and way we carry ourselves (demeanor)
  - Vary performances according to where we are (the set)

Nonverbal Communication

- **Communication using body movements, gestures, and facial expressions rather than speech**
- **Body Language**
  - Using parts of the body to convey information to others
  - Eye contact is another crucial element
  - Gestures add meaning to spoken words

- **Body Language and Deception**
  - Body language can contradict planned meaning
  - Because nonverbal communication is hard to control, it provides clues to deception
  - Recognizing dishonest performances is difficult
  - Key to detecting lies is to view the whole performance with an eye for inconsistencies

Gender and Performance

- Women are more sensitive to nonverbal communication than men
- Central element in personal performances
- **DEMEANOR**
  - *The way we act and carry ourselves*
    - Clue to social power
  - Because women generally occupy positions of less power, demeanor is also a gender issue

- **USE OF SPACE**
  - **PERSONAL SPACE**
    - *The surrounding area over which a person makes some claim to privacy*
    - Everywhere, men, because of their greater social power, often intrude into women's personal space
    - Woman moving into a man's personal space can be taken as a sign of sexual interest

- **STARING, SMILING, AND TOUCHING**
  - Women hold eye contact more than men in social conversations
  - Men stare
    - Claiming social dominance and defining women as sexual objects
  - Smiling can be a sign of trying to please or of submission
    - In a male dominated world, women smile more than men
  - Mutual touching suggests intimacy and caring
  - Touching is generally something men do to women
    - But rarely in our culture to other men

- **Watch female-male couples holding hands.**

- **Which person has the hand to the front and which has the hand to the rear?**

- **Can you see a pattern and offer an explanation?**

Idealization

- We construct performances to idealize our intentions
  - We try to convince others (and perhaps ourselves) that our actions reflect ideal cultural standards rather than selfish motives
- Rarely do people admit the more common less honorable motives
- We all use idealization to some degree

Embarrassment and Tact

- *Embarrassment*
  - *Discomfort after a spoiled performance*
  - "Losing face"
- Embarrassment is an ever-present danger because idealized performances typically contain some deception
  - One thoughtless moment can shatter the intended impression
- Curiously, an audience often overlooks flaws in performance, allowing the actor to avoid embarrassment

- **Tact**
  - *Helping someone "save face"*
  - Members of an audience actually help the performer recover from a flawed performance
  - *"Tact is the ability to describe others the way they see themselves."* **Abraham Lincoln**
  - Tact is common because embarrassment creates discomfort for the actor and everyone else
  - People who observe the awkward behavior are reminded of how fragile their own performances are
  - Although behavior is spontaneous in some respects, it is more patterned than we like to think

---

"All the world's a stage,

And all the men and women merely players:

They have their exits and their entrances;

And one man in his time plays many parts"

- **(William Shakespeare. *As You Like It.* Act 2, Scene 7)**

INTERACTIONS IN EVERYDAY LIFE: THREE APPLICATIONS

- **Three important dimensions of everyday life**
  - Emotions
  - Language
  - Humor

Emotions: The Social Construction of Feeling

- **Emotions are more commonly called feelings**
  - What we *do* matters less than how we *feel* about it
  - Emotions seem very personal because they are "inside"
  - Just as society guides our behavior, it guides our emotional life

---

- **The Biological Side of Emotions**
  - People everywhere express six basic emotions
    - Happiness
    - Sadness
    - Anger
    - Fear
    - Disgust
    - Surprise
- Emotions are powerful forces that allow us to overcome individualism and build connections with others

---

- **The Cultural Side of Emotions**
  - Culture defines *what triggers* an emotion
  - Culture provides rules for the *display* of emotions
  - Culture guides how we *value* emotions
  - Traditionally, at least, many cultures expect women to show emotions while condemning emotional expression by men as a sign of weakness
  - In some cultures this pattern is less pronounced or reversed

- **Emotions on the Job**
  - In the U.S., most people are freer to express their feelings at home than on the job
  - The typical company tries to control not only behavior but also the emotions of its employees
  - *Emotion Management*
    - *The social construction of emotions as part of everyday reality*

Language: The Social Construction of Gender

- Language conveys not only a surface message but also deeper levels of meaning
  - An important level is gender
  - Language defines men and women differently in terms of power and value

- **Language and Power**
  - Language helps men establish control over their surroundings
  - A man attaches a female pronoun to an object because doing so reflects *ownership*
  - This is also why a woman who marries traditionally takes the last name of her husband
  - Because today's women in the U.S. value independence, many now keep their own name or combine two family names

- **Language and Value**
  - Typically, the English language treats as masculine whatever has greater value, force, or significance
  - Adjective "virtuous" means "morally worthy," from the Latin "vir" meaning "man"
  - Adjective "hysterical" means "uncontrollable emotion," from the Greek "hyster" meaning "uterus"

- Language also confers a different value on the two sexes
- Use of suffixes "-ess" and "-ette" to indicate femininity usually devalue the words to which they are added
- Language both mirrors social attitudes and helps perpetuate them
- Given the importance of gender to social interaction in everyday life, it is no surprise that women and men sometimes have trouble communicating

- **How many words can you think of to describe a very sexually active female?**

- **Are they positive or negative in meaning?**

- **Repeat the same exercise for a male.**

- **What differences do you notice?**

Reality Play: The Social Construction of Humor

- Humor plays an important part in everyday life
- By using humor, we "play with reality"

_____

The Foundation of Humor

- **The Foundation of Humor**
  - Humor is produced by the social construction of reality
    - It arises as people create and contrast two different realities
  - One reality is *conventional*
    - *What people in a specific situation expect*
  - The other reality is *unconventional*
    - *An unexpected violation of cultural patterns*
  - Humor arises from the contradictions, ambiguities, and double meanings found in differing definitions of the same situation

_____

- Contrasting realities emerge from:
  - Statements that contradict themselves
  - Statements that repeat themselves
  - Statements that mix up words
  - Statements that switch around syllables
- The greater the opposition or difference between the two definitions of reality, the greater the humor

- A joke is well told if the comic times the lines to create the sharpest possible opposition between the realities
- Because the key to humor lies in the collision of realities, the climax of a joke is termed the "punch line"

- **The Dynamics of Humor: "Getting It"**
  - To "get" humor, members of an audience must understand the two realities involved well enough to appreciate the difference
  - Enjoyment of a joke is increased by the pleasure of figuring out all the pieces needed to "get it"
  - The joke makes you an *insider* compared to those who don't "get it"
  - If a joke has to be explained, it won't be very funny

- **The Topics of Humor**
  - Humor is a universal element of human culture
  - Because of different cultures, humor rarely travels well
  - The diversity of America means people will find humor in different situations
  - To everyone, topics that lend themselves to double meanings or controversy generate humor
  - Jokes can break through cultural barriers but they must touch on universal human experiences

- Controversy of humor is a fine line between what is funny and what is "sick"
- Middle Ages – *"humors"* from the Latin "humidus" meaning "moist"
  - A balance of bodily fluids that regulated a person's health
- Researchers today document the power of humor to reduce stress and improve health
  - "Laughter is the best medicine"

- At the extreme, people who always take the conventional reality lightly risk being defined as deviant or mentally ill
- Every social group considers certain topics too sensitive for humorous treatment
  - People's religious beliefs, tragic accidents, or appalling crimes are some of the subjects of "sick" jokes or no jokes at all

---

- Here is a joke about sociologists:
- *How many sociologists does it take to change a light bulb?* Answer: *None. There is nothing wrong with the light bulb; it's the system that needs to be changed!*
- What makes this joke funny?
- What sort of people are likely to get it?
- What kind of people probably won't?
- Why?

- **The Functions of Humor**
  - Humor is found everywhere because it works as a safety valve for potentially disruptive sentiments
  - Humor provides an acceptable way to discuss a sensitive topic without appearing to be serious or offensive
  - People use humor to relieve tension in uncomfortable situations

- **Humor and Conflict**
  - Humor can also be used to put down others
    - Men who tell jokes about women, for example, typically are voicing hostility towards them
    - Similarly, jokes about gay people reveal tensions about sexual orientation
  - Real conflict can be masked by humor when people choose not to bring the conflict out into the open
  - "Put-down" jokes make one category of people feel good at the expense of another

- Conflict is a driving force behind humor in most of the world
- The typical ethnic joke makes fun of some disadvantaged category of people, making the joke teller feel superior
- Humor is more important than we think
  - It is a means of mental escape from a conventional world that is not entirely to our liking
  - Many of our nation's comedians come from the ranks of the historically marginalized
  - Maintaining a sense of humor asserts our freedom, and we are never a prisoner of reality

Chapter 5 — Groups and Organizations

LEARNING OBJECTIVES

- To identify the differences between primary groups and secondary groups.
- To identify the various types of leaders associated with social groups.
- To recognize the importance of reference groups to group dynamics.
- To distinguish between in-groups and out-groups.
- To understand the relevance of group size to the dynamics of social groups.
- To identify the types of formal organizations.
- To identify and describe the basic characteristics of bureaucracy.
- To become aware of both the limitations and informal side of bureaucracy.
- To identify and discuss three important challenges of the scientific management organizational model.
- To consider the issue of the "McDonaldization" of society.
- To analyze the two opposing trends concerning the future of organizations.

CHAPTER OUTLINE

I. Social Groups
    A. Primary and Secondary Groups
    B. Group Leadership
        1. Two Leadership Roles
        2. Three Leadership Styles
    C. Group Conformity
        1. Asch's Research
        2. Milgram's Research
        3. Janis's "Groupthink"
    D. Reference Groups
        1. Stouffer's Research
    E. In-groups and Out-groups
    F. Group Size
        1. The Dyad
        2. The Triad
    G. Social Diversity: Race, Class, and Gender
    H. Networks

II. Formal Organizations
  A. Types of Formal Organizations
      1. Utilitarian Organizations
      2. Normative Organization
      3. Coercive Organizations
  B. Origins of Bureaucracy
  C. Characteristics of Bureaucracy
  D. Organizational Environment
  E. The Informal Side of Bureaucracy
  F. Problems of Bureaucracy
      1. Bureaucratic Alienation
      2. Bureaucratic Inefficiency and Ritualism
      3. Bureaucratic Inertia
      4. Oligarchy

III. The Evolution of Formal Organizations
  A. Scientific Management
  B. The First Challenge: Race and Gender
      1. Patterns of Privilege and Exclusion
      2. The "Female Advantage"
  C. The Second Challenge: The Japanese Work Organization
  D. The Third Challenge: The Changing Nature of Work
  E. The "McDonaldization" of Society
      1. McDonaldization: Basic Principles
      2. Can Rationality Be Irrational?

IV. The Future of Organizations: Opposing Trends

V. Making the Grade

GROUPS AND ORGANIZATIONS

CHAPTER 5

- **How** do groups affect how we behave?

- **Why** can "who you know" be as important as "what you know"?

- In **what** ways have large business organizations changed in recent decades?

- **SOCIAL GROUPS**
  - *The clusters of people with whom we interact in our daily lives*
- **FORMAL ORGANIZATIONS**
  - *Huge corporations and other bureaucracies*

SOCIAL GROUPS

- *Two or more people who identify with one another*
- Groups contain people with shared experiences, loyalties, and interests
- Not every collection of individuals forms a group
- The right circumstances can turn a crowd into a group

Primary and Secondary Groups

- Two types of social groups
  - *PRIMARY GROUP*
    - A small social group whose members share personal and lasting relationships
  - *SECONDARY GROUP*
    - A large and impersonal social group whose members pursue a specific goal or activity

---

- **Primary group** relationships spend a great deal of time together
- These personal and tightly integrated groups are among the first experienced in life
- Members of primary groups think of their group as an end in itself rather than as a means to other ends
- Members view each other as unique and irreplaceable

- **Secondary** relationships involve weak emotional ties and little personal knowledge of one another
- Include many more people than primary groups
- Passage of time can transform a group from secondary to primary
- Members do not think of themselves as "we"

- Primary groups display a **personal orientation**
- Secondary groups have a **goal orientation**
- Primary group members define each other according to **who** they are in terms of family ties or personal qualities
- Secondary groups look to one another for **what** they are
  - What they can do for each other

- Traits define the two groups in ideal terms
- Most real groups contain elements of both

Primary Groups and Secondary Groups		
	Primary Group ◄———————►	Secondary Group
Quality of relationships	Personal orientation	Goal orientation
Duration of relationships	Usually long-term	Variable; often short-term
Breadth of relationships	Broad, usually involving many activities	Narrow, usually involving few activities
Perception of relationships	As ends in themselves	As means to an end
Examples	Families, circles of friends	Co-workers, political organization

Summing Up (p. 122)

Group Leadership

- Important element of group dynamics is leadership
- *TWO LEADERSHIP ROLES*
  - Instrumental Leadership
  - Expressive Leadership

- **Instrumental Leadership**
  - *Group leadership that focuses on the completion of tasks*
    - Make plans
    - Give orders
    - Get things done

- **Expressive Leadership**
  - *Group leadership that focuses on the group's well-being*
    - Less of an interest in achieving goals
    - Focus on promoting the well-being of members
    - Minimize tension and conflict among members

- Instrumental leaders usually have formal, secondary relationships with other members
- Expressive leaders build more personal, primary ties
- Successful instrumental leaders enjoy more *respect* from members
- Expressive leaders receive more personal *affection*

- *THREE LEADERSHIP STYLES*
  - **Authoritarian Leadership**
    - Focuses on instrumental concerns
    - Takes personal charge of decision making
    - Demands that group members obey orders
    - Win little affection from the group
    - Is appreciated in a crisis

- **Democratic Leadership**
  - More expressive
  - Includes everyone in the decision-making process
  - Less successful in a crisis situation
  - Draw on the ideas of all members to develop creative solutions to problems

---

- **Laissez-faire Leadership**
  - Allows group to function on its own
  - "Laissez-faire" –F rench, meaning "leave it alone"
  - Least effective in promoting group goals

Group Conformity

- Groups influence the behavior of their members
  - Promoting conformity
- Solomon Asch and Stanley Milgram
  - Even strangers can encourage group conformity

- **Asch's Research**
  - Found that many of us are willing to compromise our own judgment to avoid the discomfort of being different, even from people we don't know
- **Milgram's Research**
  - People are likely to follow the directions not only of legitimate authority figures but also of groups of ordinary individuals, even when it means harming another person

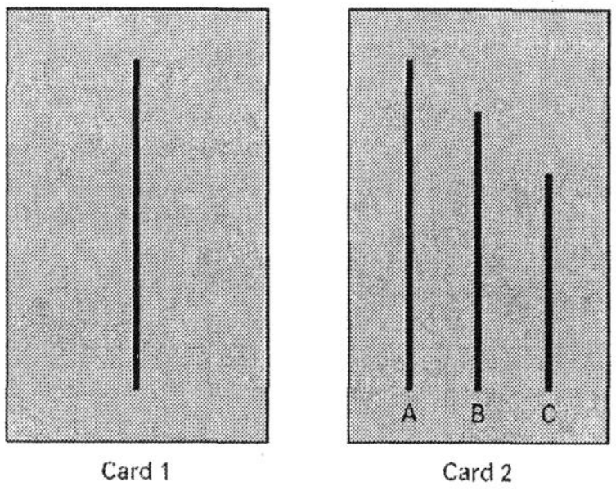

Card 1   Card 2

Figure 5.1 (p. 123)
Cards Used in Asch's Experiment in Group Conformity
In Asch's experiment, subjects were asked to match the line on Card 1 to one of the lines on Card 2. Most subjects agreed with the wrong answers given by others in their group.
Source: Asch (1952).

- Irving L. Janis's "Groupthink"
  - **GROUPTHINK**
    - *The tendency of group members to conform, resulting in a narrow view of some issue*
      - P earl Harbor, WWII
      - V ietnam War
      - Bay of Pigs, Cuba
      - I raq, 2003

Reference Groups

- *A social group that serves as a point of reference in making evaluations and decisions*
  - Used to assess our own attitudes and behavior
  - We also use groups we do not belong to for reference
  - Conforming to groups we do not belong is a strategy to win acceptance

---

- **Samuel A. Stouffer's Research**
  - We do not make judgments about ourselves in isolation
  - We do not compare ourselves with just anyone
  - In *absolute terms*, we form a subjective sense of our well-being by looking at ourselves *relative* to specific reference groups

---

In-Groups and Out-Groups

- **IN-GROUP**
  - *A social group toward which a member feels respect and loyalty*
- **OUT-GROUP**
  - *A social group toward which a person feels a sense of competition or opposition*
- Based on the idea that we have valued traits they lack

- Tensions between groups sharpen the group's boundaries and give people a clearer social identity
- Members of in-groups hold overly positive views of themselves and unfairly negative views of various out-groups
- Powerful in-group can define others as a lower-status out-group
- Many white people view people of color as an out-group

- **In terms of in-groups and out-groups, explain what happens when people who may not like each other discover they have a common enemy.**

Group Size

- Group size plays a crucial role in how group members interact
- **THE DYAD**
  - *A social group with two members*
  - Social interaction is more intense than in larger groups
  - Unstable, if either member withdraws, the group collapses

- **THE TRIAD**
  - *A social group with three members*
    - More stable than a dyad
    - As groups grow beyond three people, they become more stable and capable of withstanding the loss of one or more members
    - Reduces intense interaction
    - Based less on personal attachments and more on formal rules and regulations

Social Diversity: Race, Class, and Gender

- Race, ethnicity, class, and gender, play a part in group dynamics
- Three ways in which social diversity influences intergroup contact:
  - Large groups turn inward
  - Heterogeneous groups turn outward
  - Physical boundaries create social boundaries

- **LARGE GROUPS TURN INWARD**
  - The larger a group, the more likely its members are to concentrate relationships among themselves
  - Efforts to promote social diversity may have the unintended effect of promoting separatism

- **HETEROGENEOUS GROUPS TURN OUTWARD**
  - The more socially diverse a group is, the more likely its members are to interact with outsiders
- **PHYSICAL BOUNDARIES CREATE SOCIAL BOUNDARIES**
  - To the extent that a social group is physically segregated from others, its members are less likely to interact with other people

Figure 5.2 (p. 125)
Group Size and Relationships
As the number of people in a group increases, the number of relationships that link them increases much faster. By the time six or seven people share a conversation, the group usually divides into two. Why are relationships in smaller groups typically more intense?
Source: John J. Macionis

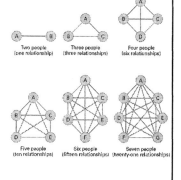

Two people (one relationship)
Three people (three relationships)
Four people (six relationships)
Five people (ten relationships)
Six people (fifteen relationships)
Seven people (twenty-one relationships)

Networks

- *A web of weak social ties*
- A "social web" expanding outward
  - Reaching great distances and including large numbers of people
- Some come close to being groups
- More commonly includes people *we know of* or who *know of us* but with whom we interact rarely

- Network ties may be weak, but they can be a powerful resource
- Based on people's colleges, clubs, neighborhoods, political parties, and personal interests
- "Privileged" networks are a valuable source of "social capital"

_____

_____

_____

_____

_____

_____

- Gender shapes networks
  - Women include more relatives (and more women)
  - Men include more co-workers (and more men)
  - Women's ties are not as powerful as typical "old boy" networks
  - As gender equality increases, male and female networks are becoming more alike

_____

_____

_____

_____

_____

_____

Global Map 5.1 (p. 128, detail on next slide)
Internet Users in Global Perspective
This map shows how the Information Revolution has affected countries around the world. In most high-income nations, at least one-third of the population uses the Internet. By contrast, only a small share of people in low-income nations does so. What effect does this have on people's access to information? What does this mean for the future in terms of global inequality?
Sources: United Nations Development Programme (2005) and International Telecommunication Union (2006).

Society: The Basics, 9th Edition by John Macionis

_____

_____

_____

_____

_____

_____

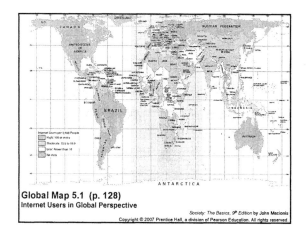

Global Map 5.1 (p. 128)
Internet Users in Global Perspective

FORMAL ORGANIZATIONS

- *Large secondary groups organized to achieve their goals efficiently*
- Differ in their impersonality and their formally planned atmosphere
- To carry out most of the tasks of organizing the 300 million members of U.S. society, reliance is on formal organizations

---

Types of Formal Organizations

- Three types of formal organizations
- Distinguished by the reasons people participate in them
  - Utilitarian Organizations
  - Normative Organizations
  - Coercive Organizations

- *UTILITARIAN ORGANIZATIONS*
  - Just about everyone who works for income belongs to this type of organization
  - Pays people for their efforts
  - Joining is usually a matter of individual choice
  - Most people must join to make a living

- *NORMATIVE ORGANIZATIONS*
  - Sometimes called *voluntary organizations*
  - People join to pursue some goal they think is morally worthwhile
  - People in the U.S. and other high income countries are most likely to join

---

- *COERCIVE ORGANIZATIONS*
  - Involuntary memberships
  - People are forced to join as a form of punishment or treatment
  - Have special physical features
  - Isolate people for a period of time to change their attitudes and behaviors

Origins of Formal Organizations

- Date back thousands of years
- Early organizations had two limitations
  - Lacked technology
  - Pre-industrial societies they were trying to rule had traditional cultures
- *TRADITION*
  - *Values and beliefs passed from generation to generation*

- Tradition makes a society conservative
  - It limits an organization's efficiency and ability to change
- *RATIONALITY*
  - *A way of thinking that emphasizes deliberate, matter-of-fact calculation of the most efficient way to accomplish a particular task*
- *RATIONALIZATION OF SOCIETY*
  - *The historical change from tradition to rationality as the main mode of human thought*

Small Groups and Formal Organizations

	Small Groups	Formal Organizations
Activities	Much the same for all members	Distinct and highly specialized
Hierarchy	Often informal or nonexistent	Clearly defined, corresponding to offices
Norms	General norms, informally applied	Clearly defined rules and regulations
Membership criteria	Variable, often based on personal affection or kinship	Technical competence to carry out assigned tasks
Relationships	Variable and typically primary	Typically secondary, with selective primary ties
Communications	Casual and face to face	Mostly formal and in writing
Focus	Person-oriented	Task-oriented

Summing Up (p. 130)

Characteristics of Bureaucracy

- **BUREAUCRACY**
  - *An organizational model rationally* designed to perform tasks efficiently
  - Official regularly create and revise policy to increase efficiency

---

- Six key elements of ideal bureaucratic organizations
  - Specialization
    - Assigns individuals to highly specialized jobs
  - Hierarchy of Offices
    - Arrange workers in vertical ranking
  - Rules and Regulations
    - Rationally enacted rules and regulations guide operation

---

- Technical Competence
  - Officials have the technical competence to carry out duties
  - Typically hire new members according to set standards and monitor performance
- Impersonality
  - Puts rules ahead of personal whim
  - Both clients and workers are treated the same

- Formal, Written Communications
  - Heart of bureaucracy is not the people but paper-work
  - Depend on formal, written memos and reports, which accumulate in vast files
- Bureaucracies carefully hires workers and limits the unpredictable effects personal taste and opinion

---

Organizational Environment

- *Factors outside an organization that affect its operations*
  - FACTORS
    - Technology
    - Economic and political trends
    - Current events
    - Available workforce
    - Other organizations

- TECHNOLOGY
  - Shapes modern organizations
- ECONOMIC AND POLITICAL TRENDS
  - All organizations are helped or hurt by periodic economic growth or recession
  - Most industries also face competition from abroad as well as changes in law

- CURRENT EVENTS
  - Significant effect on organizations that are far away
- POPULATION PATTERNS
  - Average age, typical level of education, social diversity, and size of a local community
    - Determines the available workforce and market for products or services

---

- OTHER ORGANIZATIONS
  - Contributes to the organizational environment

THE INFORMAL SIDE OF BUREAUCRACY

- In real-life organizations, humans are creative enough to resist bureaucratic regulation
- Informality may cut corners but it also provides the flexibility necessary for change
- Informality comes from the varying personalities of organizational leaders

- Qualities and quirks of individuals can have an effect on organizational success or failure
- Leaders sometimes seek to benefit personally through abuse of organizational power
- Communication is another source of organizational informality
- E-mail has allowed even the lowest-ranking employee to bypass supervisors

---

PROBLEMS OF BUREAUCRACY

- Can dehumanize and manipulate
- Some say it poses a threat to political democracy

- **BUREAUCRATIC ALIENATION**
  - Potential to *dehumanize* the people it serves
  - Impersonality that fosters efficiency also keeps officials and clients from responding to each other's unique needs
  - Formal organizations create *alienation*
    - Reduces human beings to "small cogs in a ceaselessly moving mechanism"
    - Designed to benefit humanity but people might end up serving formal organizations

- **BUREAUCRATIC INEFFICIENCY AND RITUALISM**
  - *Bureaucratic Inefficiency*
    - *T he failure of a formal organization to carry out the work it exists to perform*
    - *" **Red Tape**" – important work does not get done*
  - *Bureaucratic Ritualism*
    - *A focus on rules and regulations to the point of interfering with an organization's goals*
    - *Rul es and regulations should be a means to and end, not an end in themselves*

- **BUREAUCRATIC INERTIA**
  - *The tendency of bureaucratic organizations to perpetuate themselves*
- **OLIGARCHY**
  - *The rule of the many by the few*
  - **"Iron law of oligarchy"**
    - Pyramid shape of bureaucracy places a few leaders in charge of the resources of the entire organization
- Bureaucracy helps distance officials from the public

THE EVOLUTION OF FORMAL ORGANIZATIONS

- Problems of bureaucracy stem from two organizational traits
  - Hierarchy
  - Rigidity
- Bureaucracy is a top-down system
  - Rules and regulations are made at the top
  - Guide every part of people's work down the chain of command

Scientific Management

- *The application of scientific principles to the operation of a business or other organization*
- Involves three steps:
  - Managers observe job performance, identify operations involved, and measure the time needed for each
  - Managers analyze data and discover ways to improve job efficiency
  - Management provides guidance and incentives to increase efficiency

---

- Principles of scientific management suggest that decision-making power should rest with the owners and executives
- Formal organizations now face the challenges of:
  - Race and gender
  - Rising foreign competition
  - Changing nature of work itself

The First Challenge: Race and Gender

- In the 1960's, critics claimed big businesses engaged in unfair hiring practices
  - Routinely excluded women and other minorities from positions of power

- *PATTERNS OF PRIVILEGE AND EXCLUSION*
  - Excluding women and minorities ignores the talents of more than half the population
  - Open organization encourages leaders to seek out ideas of all employees
- *THE "FEMALE" ADVANTAGE*
  - *Patterns which help companies strive to be more flexible and democratic*
    - Women have greater communication skills
    - Women are more flexible leaders
    - Women emphasize the interconnectedness of all organizational operations

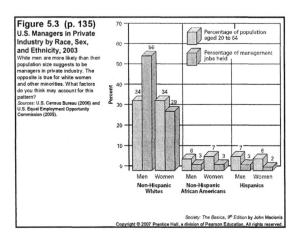

Figure 5.3 (p. 135)
U.S. Managers in Private Industry by Race, Sex, and Ethnicity, 2003
White men are more likely than their population size suggests to be managers in private industry. The opposite is true for white women and other minorities. What factors do you think may account for this pattern?
Sources: U.S. Census Bureau (2006) and U.S. Equal Employment Opportunity Commission (2005).

The Second Challenge: The Japanese Work Organization

- Japanese organizations reflect that nation's strong collective spirit
- Value cooperation
- Hired new workers in groups
  - Everyone had same salary and responsibilities
  - Fostered a sense of loyalty
  - Trained workers in all phases of operations
  - Involved workers in "quality circles"
  - Companies played a large role in the lives of workers

The Third Challenge: The Changing Nature of Work

- U.S. economy moved from industrial to postindustrial production
  - Using electronic technology to create or process information
- Differences:
  - Creative freedom
  - Competitive work teams
  - A flatter organization
  - Greater flexibility

- Postindustrial economy created two different types of work:
  - Highly skilled creative work
  - Low-skilled service work

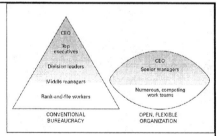

Figure 5.4 (p. 137, detail on next slide)
Two Organizational Models
The conventional model of bureaucratic organizations has a pyramid shape, with a clear chain of command. Orders flow from the top down, and reports of performance flow from the bottom up. Such organizations have extensive rules and regulations, and their workers have highly specialized jobs. More open and flexible organizations have a flatter shape, more like a football. With fewer levels in the hierarchy, responsibility for generating ideas and making decisions is shared throughout the organization. Many workers do their jobs in teams and have a broad knowledge of the entire organization's operation.
Source: John J. Macionis

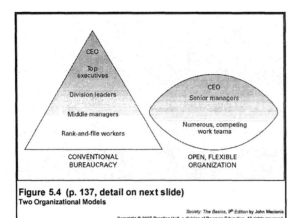

Figure 5.4 (p. 137, detail on next slide)
Two Organizational Models

The "McDonaldization" of Society

- A symbol of U.S. culture
- **"McDonaldized"**
  - *Organizational principles are coming to dominate our entire society*
  - Aspects of life are modeled on the restaurant chain

- McDonaldization: Three Principles
  - Efficiency
  - Uniformity
  - Control
- Principles limits human creativity, choice, and freedom
- *"The ultimate irrationality of McDonaldization is that people could lose control over the system and it would come to control us."*

THE FUTURE OF ORGANIZATIONS: OPPOSING TRENDS

- Postindustrial economy created more routine service jobs
- "McJobs" offer few benefits that today's highly skilled workers enjoy
- Global competition attract creative employees but costs are cut by eliminating many routine jobs
- Some people are better off than others

_____

_____

_____

_____

_____

_____

_____

Chapter 6

Sexuality and Society

LEARNING OBJECTIVES

- To gain a sociological understanding of human sexuality focusing on both biological and cultural factors.
- To become more aware of the sexual attitudes found in the United States today.
- To describe both the sexual revolution and sexual counterrevolution that occurred during the last half century in the United States.
- To discuss issues relating to the biological and social causes of sexual orientation.
- To gain a sociological perspective on several sexual controversies, including teen pregnancy, pornography, prostitution, and sexual violence and abuse.
- To discuss issues relating to human sexuality from the viewpoints offered by structural-functional, symbolic-interactionist, and social-conflict analysis.

CHAPTER OUTLINE

I. Understanding Sexuality
    A. Sex: A Biological Issue
    B. Sex and the Body
        1. Intersexual People
        2. Transsexuals
    C. Sex: A Cultural Issue
        1. Cultural Variation
    D. The Incest Taboo

II. Sexual Attitudes in the United States
    A. The Sexual Revolution
    B. The Sexual Counterrevolution
    C. Premarital Sex
    D. Sex between Adults
    E. Extramarital Sex
    F. Sex Over the Life Course

III. Sexual Orientation
    A. What Gives Us a Sexual Orientation?
        1. Sexual Orientation: A Product of Society
        2. Sexual Orientation: A Product of Biology
    B. How Many Gay People Are There?
    C. The Gay Rights Movement

IV.   Sexual Issues and Controversies
      A.   Teen Pregnancy
      B.   Pornography
      C.   Prostitution
            1.   Types of Prostitution
            2.   A Victimless Crime?
      D.   Sexual Violence: Rape and Date Rape
            1.   Rape
            2.   Date Rape

V.   Theoretical Analysis of Sexuality
      A.   Structural-Functional Analysis
            1.   The Need to Regulate Sexuality
            2.   Latent Functions: The Case of Prostitution
      B.   Symbolic-Interaction Analysis
            1.   The Social Construction of Sexuality
            2.   Global Comparisons
      C.   Social-Conflict Analysis
            1.   Sexuality: Reflecting Social Inequality
            2.   Sexuality: Creating Social Inequality
            3.   Queer Theory

VI.   Making the Grade

SEXUALITY AND SOCIETY

CHAPTER 6

- **What** was the sexual revolution, and how did it change U.S. society?

- **Why** do societies try to control people's sexual behavior?

- **How** does sexuality play a part in social inequality?

Understanding Sexuality

- Sexuality is a theme found almost everywhere
- Sex industry is a multibillion-dollar business
- U.S. culture has long treated sex as taboo

Sex: A Biological Issue

- *SEX*
  - *The biological distinction between females and males*
- From a biological viewpoint: the way humans reproduce
- Sex of an embryo guides its development

_____

_____

_____

_____

_____

_____

Sex and the Body

- *PRIMARY SEX CHARACTERISTICS*
  - *The genitals, organs used for reproduction*
- People reach sexual maturity at puberty
- *SECONDARY SEX CHARACTERISTICS*
  - *Bodily development, apart from the genitals, that distinguishes biologically mature females and males*
- Sex is not the same as gender
  - Gender is an element of culture and refers to personal traits and patterns of behavior a culture attaches to being male or female

_____

_____

_____

_____

_____

_____

- *Intersexual People*
  - *People whose bodies (including genitals) have both female and male characteristics*
  - *Hermaphrodite*
    - Has both female ovaries and male testis
  - Our culture demands that sex be clear-cut
    - Some respond to intersexuals with confusion or disgust

_____

_____

_____

_____

_____

_____

_____

- *Transexuals*
  - *People who feel they are one sex even though biologically they are the other*
  - *Transgendered*
    - *Disregarding conventional ideas about how females and males should look and behave*
  - *Gender Reassignment*
    - *Surgical alteration of the genitals, usually accompanied by hormone treatments*

Sex: A Cultural Issue

- Sexuality has a biological foundation
- Like other elements of human nature, sexuality is also a cultural issue
- Biology does not dictate specific ways of being sexual

- *CULTURAL VARIATION*
  - Every sexual practice shows variation from one society to another
  - Displaying affection varies among societies
  - Modesty is culturally variable
  - Some societies restrict sexuality and others are more permissive

The Incest Taboo

- *Incest Taboo*
  - *A norm forbidding sexual relations or marriage between certain relatives*
  - Found in every society in the world
- Reason some form of incest exists everywhere
  - *Biology* – Reproduction between close relatives of any species increases the odds of producing offspring with mental and physical problems

---

- Controlling sexuality between close relatives is a necessary element of social organization
  - Incest taboo limits sexual competition in families
  - Because family ties define people's rights and obligations toward one another, reproduction between close relatives would confuse kinship
  - By requiring people to marry outside their immediate families, the incest taboo integrates the larger society

---

National Map 6.1 (p. 149, detail on next slide)
First-Cousin Marriage Laws across the United States
There is no single view on first-cousin marriages in the United States: Twenty-four states forbid such unions, twenty allow them, and six allow them with restrictions.* In general, states that permit first-cousin marriages are found in New England, the Southeast, and the Southwest.
*Of the six states that allow first-cousin marriages with restrictions, five states permit them only when the couples are past child-bearing age.
Source: "State Laws Regarding Marriages" (2006).

Society: The Basics, 9ᵗʰ Edition by John Macionis

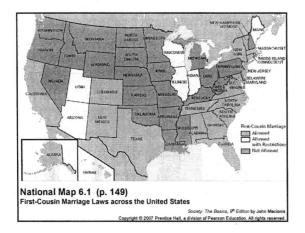

National Map 6.1 (p. 149)
First-Cousin Marriage Laws across the United States

Sexual Attitudes in the United States

- America's cultural attitudes toward sexuality has always been something of a contradiction

---

- Efforts to regulate sexuality continued into the 20th century
- U.S. culture is individualistic
  - People have the freedom to do what they wish as long as there is no direct harm to others
  - Privacy makes sex a matter of individual freedom and choice
- In the U.S. sexuality is both restrictive and permissive
  - On one hand, people view sex as a sign of personal morality
  - On the other hand, sex is a part of the mass media

- On balance, do you think the mass media encourage young people to engage in sexual activity?

- Explain

The Sexual Revolution

- Profound changes in sexual attitudes and practices over the past century
  - The "Roaring Twenties"
  - Slowed during the Great Depression and World War II
- Alfred Kinsey set the stage for the *Sexual Revolution*
  - National uproar resulted from scientists studying sex
  - People were uneasy talking about sex even in private

- Kinsey's books encouraged a new openness toward sexuality
- Sexual revolution came to age in the 60's
  - Baby boom generation was the first cohort in U.S. history to grow up with the idea that sex was part of people's lives
- Technology played a part
  - Birth control pill
- Women were historically subject to greater sexual regulation than men
  - Society's "double standard"

Figure 6-1   (p. 153)
**The Sexual Revolution: Closing
the Double Standard**
A larger share of men than women report
having had two or more sexual partners by
age twenty. But the sexual revolution
greatly reduced this gender difference.
Source: Laumann et al. (1994:198).

- Sexual revolution increased sexual activity overall
  - Changed women's behavior more than men's
- Greater openness about sexuality develops as societies become richer and the opportunities for women increase

---

The Sexual Counterrevolution

- The sexual freedom of the 1960's and 1970's were criticized as evidence of moral decline
- A conservative call for a return to "family values"
- A change from sexual freedom back to the sexual responsibility of earlier generations

- For moral reasons or concerns about STD's more people began choosing to limit their number of sexual partners or not have sex at all
- There is now greater acceptance of premarital sex as well as increasing tolerance for various sexual orientations

Premarital Sex

- **Sexual intercourse before marriage**
  - *35%* say it is "always wrong" or "almost always wrong"
  - *17%* say it is "wrong sometimes"
  - About *45%* say it is "not wrong at all"
- Society remains divided on the issue
- Premarital sex is widely accepted among young people today

- Young people can be sexually active without having intercourse
  - Increase in oral sex
    - Preferred over intercourse because does not involve risk of pregnancy
    - Can transmit diseases
- 20% of today's teens have sexual intercourse before age 15
- Half had at least one experience involving oral sex

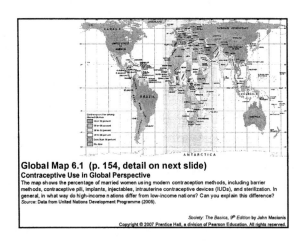

Global Map 6.1 (p. 154, detail on next slide)
Contraceptive Use in Global Perspective
The map shows the percentage of married women using modern contraception methods, including barrier methods, contraceptive pill, implants, injectables, intrauterine contraceptive devices (IUDs), and sterilization. In general, in what way do high-income nations differ from low-income nations? Can you explain this difference?
Source: Data from United Nations Development Programme (2005).

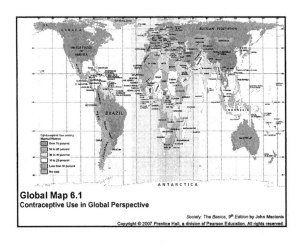

Global Map 6.1
Contraceptive Use in Global Perspective

Sex Between Adults

- Frequency of sexual activity varies widely in the U.S. population
- Married people
  - have sex with partners the most
  - Report the highest level of satisfaction with their partners
    - Physically
    - Emotionally

Extramarital Sex

- *ADULTERY*
  - *Married people having sex outside of marriage*
  - Widely condemned
  - Norm of sexual fidelity within marriage has been and remains a strong element of U.S. culture
  - Actual behavior falls short of the cultural ideal
    - 25% of married men and 10% of married women have had at least one extramarital sexual experience
    - 75% of men and 90% of women have remained sexually faithful to their partners

---

Sex Over The Life Course

- Patterns of sexual activity change with age
- Advancing age is linked to a decline in people who are sexually active
- Contrary to popular stereotypes
  - Sexual activity is a normal part of life for most older adults

---

- Does a pledge of abstinence require that someone not engage in oral sex?
  - Explain your view.

- Why do you think U.S. society has become more accepting of premarital sex but not of extramarital sex?

	Premarital Sex	Extramarital Sex
"Always wrong"	26.3%	79.9%
"Almost always wrong"	8.8	11.9
"Wrong only sometimes"	17.3	4.9
"Not wrong at all"	45.1	2.1
"Don't know"/No answer	2.5	1.2

Table 6.1 (p. 153)
How We View Premarital and Extramarital Sex
Survey Question: "There's been a lot of discussion about the way morals and attitudes about sex are changing in this country. If a man and a woman have sexual relations before marriage, do you think it is always wrong, almost always wrong, wrong only sometimes, or not wrong at all? What about a married person having sexual relations with someone other than the marriage partner?"
Source: General Social Surveys, 1972-2004: *Cumulative Codebook* (Chicago: National Opinion Research Center, 2005), p. 291.

Sexual Orientation

- **SEXUAL ORIENTATION**
  - *A person's romantic and emotional attraction to another person*
- **HETEROSEXUALITY**
  - *Sexual attraction to someone of the other sex*
- **HOMOSEXUALITY**
  - *Sexual attraction to someone of the same sex*
- **BISEXUALITY**
  - *Sexual attraction to people of both sexes*

- *ASEXUALITY*
  - *No sexual attraction to people of either sex*
- Sexual attraction is not the same as sexual behavior
- Worldwide, heterosexuality is the norm
  - Permits human reproduction
  - Most societies tolerate homosexuality

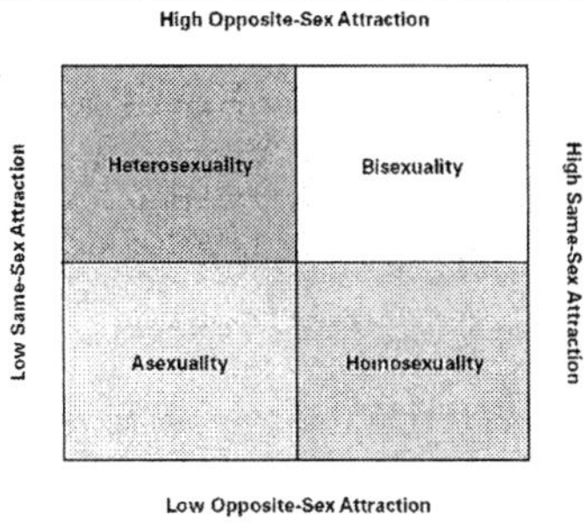

Figure 6.2 (p. 155)
Four Sexual Orientations
A person's level of same-sex attraction and opposite-sex attraction are two distinct dimensions that combine in various ways to produce four major sexual orientations.
Source: Adapted from Storms (1980).

Society: The Basics, 9th Edition by John Macionis

What Gives Us a Sexual Orientation?

- ***SEXUAL ORIENTATION: A PRODUCT OF SOCIETY***
  - *Argues that people in any society attach meanings to sexual activity*
    - Meanings differ from place to place over time
  - Patterns of homosexuality differ greatly from one society to another
  - Existence of global diverse patterns indicate that sexual expression is socially constructed

---

- ***SEXUAL ORIENTATION: A PRODUCT OF BIOLOGY***
  - *Suggests that sexual orientation is innate*
  - *LeVay*
    - Studied the brains of heterosexual and homosexual men
    - Found small but important difference in the size of the hypothalmus
      - *P art of the brain that regulates hormones*
  - Genetics may also influence sexual orientation
    - Evidence leads some researchers to think there may be a "gay gene"

How Many Gay People Are There?

- Hard question to answer
  - People are not always willing to discuss their sexuality with strangers or even family members
  - Some social scientists estimate 10%
- How homosexuality is defined makes a big difference
- Less than 1% describe themselves as bisexual
  - Many do not think of themselves as gay or straight
  - Behavior reflects elements of gay and straight living

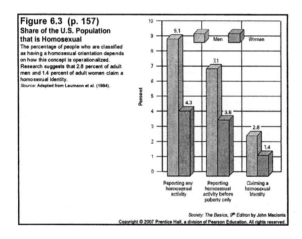

Figure 6.3 (p. 157)
Share of the U.S. Population that is Homosexual
The percentage of people who are classified as having a homosexual orientation depends on how this concept is operationalized. Research suggests that 2.8 percent of adult men and 1.4 percent of adult women claim a homosexual identity.
Source: Adapted from Laumann et al. (1994).

The Gay Rights Movement

- Change in public attitudes toward homosexuality is a result of the *Gay Rights Movement*
- 1973 – American Psychiatric Association
  - Homosexuality was not an illness but "a form of sexual behavior"
- *HOMOPHOBIA*
  - *Discomfort over close personal interaction with people thought to be gay, lesbian, or bisexual*

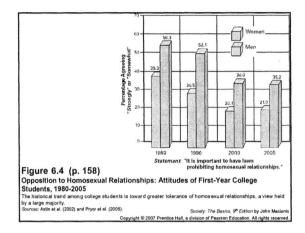

Figure 6.4 (p. 158)
Opposition to Homosexual Relationships: Attitudes of First-Year College Students, 1980-2005
The historical trend among college students is toward greater tolerance of homosexual relationships, a view held by a large majority.
Sources: Astin et al. (2002) and Pryor et al. (2005).

Society: The Basics, 9th Edition by John Macionis

- What evidence supports the position that sexual behavior is constructed by society?

- What evidence supports the position that sexual orientation is rooted in biology?

- What changes in laws regarding gay marriage do you expect in the next ten years?
  - Why?

Sexual Issues and Controversies

- Sexuality lies at the heart of a number of controversies in the United States today
  - *Teen Pregnancy*
  - *Pornography*
  - *Prostitution*
  - *Rape*

Teen Pregnancy

- Engaging in sexual intercourse demands a high level of responsibility
- Teenagers
  - May be biologically mature to conceive
  - Many are not emotionally secure
- U.S. birth rate to teens higher than all other high-income nations
- Affects young women of all racial and ethnic categories

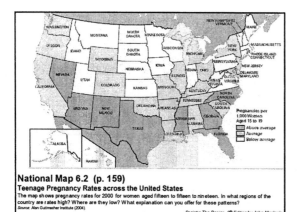

National Map 6.2 (p. 159)
Teenage Pregnancy Rates across the United States
The map shows pregnancy rates for 2000 for women aged fifteen to fifteen to nineteen. In what regions of the country are rates high? Where are they low? What explanation can you offer for these patterns?
Source: Alan Guttmacher Institute (2004).

Society: The Basics, 9th Edition by John Macionis
Copyright © 2007 Prentice Hall, a division of Pearson Education. All rights reserved.

- Weak families and low income increase the likelihood of sexual activity and unplanned children
- Raises the risk of school dropout and poverty
- Rate was higher in the 1950's than it is today
  - Abortion was illegal and led to quick marriages
  - Rate today is lower but 80% are unmarried

Pornography

- *Sexually explicit material intended to cause sexual arousal*
- U.S. Supreme Court gives local communities the power to decide what type of material
  - Violates "community standards" of decency
  - Lacks "redeeming social value"
- Very popular in U.S.
- Majority of consumers are men
- Criticized on moral grounds

- Political issue
  - Degrades women and portrays them as sexual playthings of men
- Critics claim
  - Cause of violence against women
  - Difficult to prove scientific cause and effect
  - Half of adults opine it encourages rape
- People everywhere object to sexual material
  - However, value the expression of free speech and protection of artistic expression
  - Pressure for restriction is building from conservatives and liberals

---

Prostitution

- *The selling of sexual services*
  - The "world's oldest profession"
- Most people
  - Sex should be an expression of intimacy between two people
  - Find the idea of sex for money disturbing
- Greatest in poor countries
  - Strong patriarchy
  - Traditional cultural norms limiting women's ability to earn a living

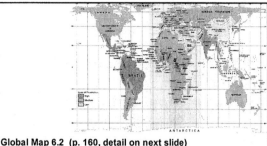

Global Map 6.2 (p. 160, detail on next slide)
Prostitution in Global Perspective

Generally speaking, prostitution is widespread in societies where women have low standing. Officially, at least, the People's Republic of China boasts of gender equality, including the elimination of "vice" such as prostitution, which oppresses women. By contrast, in much of Latin America, where patriarchy is strong, prostitution is common. In many Islamic societies, patriarchy is also strong, but religion is a counterbalance, so prostitution is limited. Western, high-income nations have a moderate amount of prostitution.
Sources: Peters Atlas of the World (1990) and Mackay (2000).

Society: The Basics, 9th Edition by John Macionis

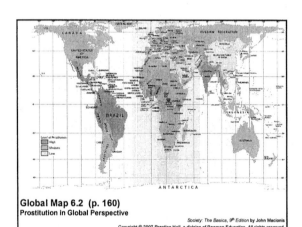

Global Map 6.2 (p. 160)
Prostitution in Global Perspective

Society: The Basics, 9th Edition by John Macionis

- *TYPES OF PROSTITUTION*
  - *Call Girls* – The top level
    - Elite prostitutes
    - Young, attractive, and well-educated
  - **"Massage Parlors"** *prostitutes* – Middle level
    - Less choice about clients
    - Receive less money
    - Keep no more than half of what they make
  - *Street-walkers* – Bottom level
    - "Work the streets" of large cities
    - Under the control of pimps who take most of their earnings
    - Some are addicted to drugs and sell sex to buy drugs

- Most offer heterosexual services
- *Gay prostitutes*
  - Sell sex after having suffered rejection by family and friends because of their orientation

---

- *A VICTIMLESS CRIME?*
  - Prostitution is against the law everywhere in the U.S.
  - Instead of enforcing laws, police stage occasional crackdowns
    - Reflects a desire to control while recognizing the impossibility of elimination
  - *Is prostitution really victimless?*
    - *Subjects many women to abuse and violence*
    - *Has a part in spreading STDs including AIDS*
    - *Many poor women become trapped in that life*
      - *E specially in low-income countries*

Sexual Violence: Rape and Date Rape

- *RAPE*
  - An expression of power
  - A violent act that uses sex
    - Hurt, humiliate, or control
  - 95,000 women report rape each year
    - Actual number is several times higher
  - *Official government definition*
    - **"The carnal knowledge of a female forcibly and against her will"**
  - Most rapists are heterosexuals

- *DATE RAPE (AQUAINTANCE RAPE)*
  - *Refers to forcible sexual violence against women by men they know*
  - Myths
    - Rape involves strangers
    - Woman must have done something to encourage the man and make him think she wanted sex
  - Rape leaves emotional and psychological scars
  - Affects the victim's ability to trust others
  - Danger of date rape is most high on college campuses
    - Promotes easy friendships and encourages trust

Theoretical Analysis of Sexuality

- Applying sociological theoretical approaches provides a better understanding of human sexuality
- *Three major approaches*
  - *Structural-functional analysis*
  - *Symbolic interaction analysis*
  - *Social-conflict analysis*

Structural-Functional Analysis

- *The Need To Regulate Sexuality*
  - Culture and social institutions regulate with *whom* and *when* people reproduce
  - Allowing sexual passion to go unchecked would threaten family life
  - No society permits a completely free choice of sexual partners
    - "Legitimate" reproduction (within marriage)
    - "Illegitimate" reproduction (outside marriage)

- *Latent Functions: The Case of Prostitution*
  - Prostitution is one way to meet the sexual needs of a large number of people who do not have ready access to sex
  - Favored because it provides sex without the "trouble" of a relationship
  - **"Men don't pay for sex; they pay so they can leave"**

- **CRITICAL REVIEW**
  - Approach helps appreciate the important role sexuality plays in the organization of society
  - Ignores gender
  - Sexual patterns change over time, just as they differ around the world

Symbolic Interaction Analysis

- Highlights how people interact and construct everyday reality
- Different people construct different realities
- Our understanding of sexuality can and does change over time

- *The Social Construction of Sexuality*
  - The changing importance of virginity
  - Young people's awareness of sex
- *Global Comparisons*
  - Different societies attach different meanings to sexuality
  - Sexual practices vary from culture to culture
    - Circumcision
    - Clitorectomy –F emale circumcision

- *CRITICAL REVIEW*
  - Strength of this approach lies in revealing the socially constructed character or familiar social patterns
  - *Limitations*
    - Not all sexual practices are so variable
    - Men everywhere have always been more likely to see women in sexual terms
    - Because this pattern is widespread –so me broader social structure must be at work

Social-Conflict Analysis

- Approach shows how sexuality reflects and perpetuates patterns of social inequality
- *Sexuality: Reflecting Social Inequality*
  - Enforcement of prostitution is uneven
  - Would so many women be involved in prostitution if they had economic opportunities equal to men
  - Categories most likely defined and treated as sexual objects
    - Those with less power – women
    - People of color compared to whites
    - Sexuality used by society to define some people as less worthy

- *Sexuality: Creating Social Inequality*
  - The root of inequality between women and men
  - Defining women in sexual terms devalues them from full human beings to objects of men's interests and attention
  - Pornography, consumed by males, is a power issue
    - Shows women focused on pleasing men
    - Supports the idea that men have power over women
  - American culture describes sexuality as sports
    - Men *"scoring"* with women
    - Violence ("slamming, banging, and hitting on")
      - Ver bs used for fighting and sex

- *Queer Theory*
  - *A body of research findings that challenges the heterosexual bias in U.S. society*
  - *Heterosexism*
    - *A view that labels anyone who is not heterosexual as* "queer"
    - Widely tolerated and sometimes within the law
    - Part of everyday culture

- *Abortion*
  - *The deliberate termination of a pregnancy*
  - Most divisive sexuality related issue of all
  - No middle ground in the debate

- **CRITICAL REVIEW**
  - Approach shows how sexuality is both cause and effect of inequality
  - Overlooks the fact that many people do not see sexuality as a power issue
  - Pays little attention to steps society has made in reducing inequality
  - Ample evidence that the Gay Rights Movement has won greater opportunities and social acceptance for gay people

---

Sexuality

	Structural-Functional Approach	Symbolic-Interaction Approach	Social-Conflict Approach
What is the level of analysis?	Macro-level	Micro-level	Macro-level
What is the importance of sexuality for society?	Society depends on sexuality for reproduction. Society uses the incest taboo and other norms to control sexuality in order to maintain social order.	Sexual practices vary among the many cultures of the world. Some societies allow individuals more freedom than others in matters of sexual behavior.	Sexuality is linked to social inequality. U.S. society regulates women's sexuality more than men's; this is part of the larger pattern of men dominating women.
Has sexuality changed over time? How?	Yes. As advances in birth control technology separate sex from reproduction, societies relax some controls on sexuality.	Yes. The meanings people attach to virginity and other sexual matters are all socially constructed and subject to change.	Yes and no. Some sexual standards have relaxed, but society still defines women in sexual terms, just as homosexual people are harmed by society's heterosexual bias.

Applying Theory (p. 164)

- Why do modern societies give people more choice about matters involving sexuality?

- What evidence can you provide showing that human sexuality is socially constructed?

- How does sexuality play a part in creating social inequality?

Chapter 7

Deviance

LEARNING OBJECTIVES

- To explain how deviance is interpreted as a product of society.
- To identify and evaluate the biological explanation of deviance.
- To identify and evaluate the sociological explanations of deviance.
- To compare and contrast different theories representative of the three major sociological approaches.
- To distinguish among the types of crime.
- To become more aware of the demographic patterns of crime in our society.
- To evaluate deviance and crime in global perspective.
- To identify and describe the elements of the American criminal justice system.

CHAPTER OUTLINE

I. What is Deviance?
    A. The Biological Context
    B. Personality Factors
    C. The Social Foundations of Deviance

II. The Functions of Deviance: Structural-Functional Analysis
    A. Durkheim's Basic Insight
        1. An Illustration: The Puritans of Massachusetts Bay
    B. Merton's Strain Theory
    C. Deviant Subcultures

III. Labeling Deviance: Symbolic-Interaction Analysis
    A. Labeling Theory
        1. Primary and Secondary Deviance
        2. Stigma
        3. Retrospective and Projective Labeling
        4. Labeling Difference as Deviance
    B. The Medicalization of Deviance
        1. The Difference Labels Make
    C. Sutherland's Differential Association Theory
    D. Hirschi's Control Theory

IV. Deviance and Inequality: Social Conflict Analysis
    A. Deviance and Power

DEVIANCE

CHAPTER 7

- **Why** does every society have deviance?

- **How** does *who* and *what* are defined as deviant reflect social inequality?

What is Deviance?

- *DEVIANCE*
  - *The recognized violation of cultural norms*
  - *CRIME*
    - *The violation of a society's formally enacted criminal law*
  - All deviant actions or attitudes have in common some element of difference that causes us to think of another person as an "outsider"
  - Not all deviance involves action or choice

Social Control

- *SOCIAL CONTROL*
  - *Attempts by society to regulate people's thoughts and behavior*
- *CRIMINAL JUSTICE SYSTEM*
  - *A formal response by police, courts, and prison officials to alleged violations of the law*
- Issues of Social organization
  - How a society defines deviance
  - Who is branded as deviant
  - What people decide to do about deviance

The Biological Context

- Early interest in criminality focused on biological causes
- *Cesare Lombroso (1835-1909)*
  - Theorized criminals stand out physically
- *Sheldon, Glueck, and Glueck (1950)*
  - Suggested body structure might predict criminality
  - A powerful build does not necessarily *cause* or *predict* criminality

- Genetic research today seeks links between biology and crime
  - Concluded that genetic factors *(especially defective genes)* together with environmental factors *(especially early abuse)* were strong predictors of adult crime and violence
  - These factors together were a better predictor of crime than either one alone

- **CRITICAL REVIEW**
  - Biological theories offer a limited explanation of crime
  - Most actions defined as deviant are carried out by people who are physically normal
  - Biological approach looks at the individual
    - Offers no insight into how some kinds of behaviors come to be defined as deviant

Personality Factors

- Psychological explanations of deviance focus on individual abnormality
- Some personality traits are inherited
- Most psychologists think personality is shaped by social experience
  - Therefore, deviance is viewed as the result of "unsuccessful" socialization
- **Reckless and Dinitz (1967)**
  - Research concluded that personality controls deviant impulses
    - *Containment theory*

- **CRITICAL REVIEW**
  - Personality patterns have some connection to deviance
  - Most serious crimes are committed by people whose psychological profiles are normal
  - Wrongdoing has more to do with the organization of society

The Functions of Deviance: Structural-Functional Analysis

- *Emile Durkheim*
  - *Deviance is a necessary element of social organization*

Durkheim's Basic Insight

- Deviance affirms cultural values and norms
- Responding to deviance clarifies moral boundaries
- Responding to deviance brings people together
- Deviance encourages social change

An Illustration: The Puritans of Massachusetts Bay

- Deviance is a necessary condition of "good" social living
- Deviance may be found in every society
  - The kind of deviance generated depends on the moral issues to be clarified
- Society creates deviants to mark its changing moral boundaries

Merton's Strain Theory

- Some deviance may be necessary for a society to function
- Too much deviance results from particular social arrangements
- The extent and kind of deviance depend on whether a society provides the *means* to achieve *cultural goals*
- Conformity lies in pursuing cultural goals through approved means

---

- *Deviance Innovation*
  - Using conventional means to achieve a culturally approved goal
- *Ritualism*
  - The inability to reach a cultural goal prompts the deviance of ritualism
- *Retreatism*
  - Rejecting both cultural goals and the means
  - Individuals "drop out"
- *Rebellion*
  - Reject cultural dimensions of success and conventional means
  - Further step is forming a counterculture alternative

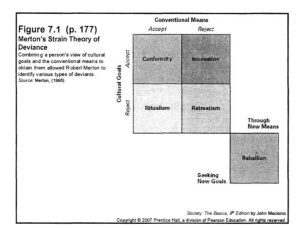

Figure 7.1 (p. 177)
Merton's Strain Theory of Deviance
Combining a person's view of cultural goals and the conventional means to obtain them allowed Robert Merton to identify various types of deviants.
Source: Merton, (1968).

Deviant Subcultures

- *Cloward and Ohlin (1966)*
  - *Deviance or conformity depends on the relative opportunity structure that frames a person's life*
- People are unable to find legal or illegal opportunities
  - *Conflict subcultures*
    - Violence is ignited by frustration and a desire for respect
  - *Retreatist subcultures*
    - Deviants drop out and abuse alcohol or drugs

- *Cohen (1977)*
  - Criminality is most common among lower-class youths-least likely to experience success
- *Miller (1970)* characterized deviant subcultures
  - *Trouble*-arising from frequent conflict
  - *Toughness*-value placed on size, strength, and agility
  - *Smartness*-ability to succeed on the streets
  - *A need for excitement*
  - *A belief in fate*-no control over their own lives
  - *A desire for freedom*-anger towards authority

- *Anderson (1994)*
  - In poor urban neighborhoods, most people manage to conform to conventional values
  - "Street Code"
    - Lifestyle of some young men
    - Neighborhood crime and violence
    - Indifference or hostility from the police
    - Parental neglect
  - Risk of jail is high

- **CRITICAL REVIEW**
  - Durkheim pointed out the functions of deviance
  - Communities do not always come together in reaction to crime
  - Merton's strain theory criticized for explaining some kinds of deviance better than others
  - Cloward and Ohlin theories assume everyone shares the same cultural standards for judging right and wrong
  - Structural-functional theories suggest that everyone who breaks the rules will be labeled deviant

- Why does biological or psychological analysis not explain deviance very well?

- Keeping in mind Durkheim's claim that society creates deviance to mark moral boundaries, why so we often define people only in terms of their deviance by calling someone an "addict" or a "thief"?

- Why do you think many of the theories discussed seem to say that crime is more common among people with lower social standing?

Labeling Deviance: Symbolic-Interaction Analysis

- Explains how people come to see deviance in everyday situations

Labeling Theory

- *The idea that deviance and conformity result not so much from what people do, as from how others respond to those actions*
- Social construction of reality is a highly variable process
  - Detection
  - Definition
  - Response

- *PRIMARY AND SECONDARY DEVIANCE*
- *Primary Deviance*
  - *Norm violations that provoke slight reaction from others and have little effect on a person's self concept*
- *Secondary Deviance*
  - *Response to primary deviance by which a person begins to take on a deviant identity and repeatedly breaks the rules*

- *STIGMA*
  - *A powerfully negative label that greatly changes a person's self-concept and social identity*
  - Operates as a master status
    - Person is discredited in the minds of others and becomes socially isolated
- *RETROSOECTIVE AND PROJECTIVE LABELING*
  - *Retrospective Labeling*
    - *A reinterpretation of the person's past in light of some present deviance*
  - *Projective Labeling*
    - *Using a deviant identity to predict future actions*

- *LABELING DIFFERENCE AS DEVIANCE*
  - *Treating behavior that is irritating or threatening not as* **"difference"** *but as deviance or mental illness*
  - Too quick to apply the label of mental illness to conditions that amount to a difference that is not liked
    - Enforces conformity to the standards of those powerful enough to impost their will on others
  - Important to think carefully about defining "difference"
    - Mentally ill are not to be blamed for their problem
    - Avoid applying such labels just to make people conform to our own standards of behavior

The Medicalization of Deviance

- The transformation of moral and legal deviance into a medical condition
  - Swaps one set of labels for another
  - Moral terms
    - "Bad" or "Good"
  - Medical terms pass no moral judgment
    - "Sick" or "Well"

- *THE DIFFERENCE LABELS MAKE*
- *Three consequences*
  - *It affects who responds to deviance*
  - *How people respond*
  - Most importantly:
    - *The two labels differ on the issue of the personal competence of the deviant person*
    - Right or wrong, we are responsible for our own behavior

Sutherland's Differential Association Theory

- Learning convention or deviant social patterns is a process that takes place in groups
- Sutherland's theory of *Differential Association*
  - *A person's tendency toward conformity or deviance depends on the amount of contact with others who encourage or reject conventional behavior*

Hirschi's Control Theory

- Control Theory
  - Social control depends on people anticipating the consequences of their behavior
- Conformity is linked to four different types of social control
  - Attachment
  - Opportunity
  - Involvement
  - Belief

- **CRITICAL REVIEW**
  - Labeling theory ignores the fact that some kinds of behavior are condemned just about everywhere
  - Research on the consequences of deviant labeling does not clearly show whether deviant labeling produces further deviance of discourages it
  - Not everyone resists being labeled as deviant; some actively seek it

Deviance and Inequality: Social-Conflict Analysis

- Links deviance to social inequality
- *Who* or *what* is labeled deviant depends on which categories of people hold power in a society

_____

_____

_____

_____

_____

_____

_____

Deviance and Power

- People labeled as deviant are typically those who share the trait of powerlessness
- Three social-conflict explanations
  - All norms and especially the laws of any society generally reflect the interests of the rich and powerful
  - Even if their behavior is called into question, the powerful have the resources to resist deviant labels
  - The widespread belief that norms and laws are natural and good masks their political character

_____

_____

_____

_____

_____

_____

_____

Deviance and Capitalism

- Deviant labels are applied to the people who interfere with the operation of capitalism
- Four reasons:
  - Capitalism is based on private control of property – threats are labeled as deviant
  - Capitalism depends on productive labor – cannot or will not work – labeled deviant
  - Capitalism depends on respect for authority figures – resist and be labeled deviant
  - Anyone who directly challenges the capitalist status quo is likely defined as deviant

_____

_____

_____

_____

_____

_____

_____

Deviance

	Structural-Functional Approach	Symbolic-Interaction Approach	Social-Conflict Approach
What is the level of analysis?	Macro-level	Micro-level	Macro-level
What is deviance? What part does it play in society?	Deviance is a basic part of social organization. By defining deviance, society sets its moral boundaries.	Deviance is part of socially constructed reality that emerges in interaction. Deviance comes into being as individuals label something as deviant.	Deviance results from social inequality. Norms, including laws, reflect the interests of powerful members of society.
What is important about deviance?	Deviance is universal: All societies contain deviance.	Deviance is variable: Any act or person may or may not be labeled as deviant.	Deviance is political: People with little power are at high risk of becoming deviant.

Applying Theory (p. 185)

- Society positively labels whatever supports the operation of capitalism
- Capitalist system tries to control those who do not fit into the system
- Social welfare and criminal justice systems blame individuals not the system for social problems

---

White-Collar Crime

- ***Crime committed by people of high social position in the course of their occupations***
  - White-collar criminals use their powerful offices to illegally enrich themselves or others
    - Cause considerable harm
  - White-collar offenses typically end up in a civil hearing rather than criminal courtroom
    - *Civil Law regulates business dealings between private parties*
    - *Criminal Law defines a person's moral responsibilities to society*

- Civil case losses pay for damage or injury but are not labeled criminal
- Rarely when white-collar criminals are charged and convicted, they escape punishment
- *CORPORATE CRIME*
  - *The illegal actions of a corporation or people on its behalf*
- *ORANIZED CRIME*
  - *A business supplying illegal goods or services*

- **CRITICAL REVIEW**
  - Approach suggests that laws and other cultural norms are created directly by the rich and powerful
    - Oversimplification because the law also protects workers, consumers, and the environment
    - Sometimes the law opposes the interests of the corporations and the rich
  - Argues that criminality springs up only to the extent that a society treats its members unequally
    - Deviance exists in all societies, whatever the economic system

---

Deviance, Race, and Gender

Hate Crimes

- A criminal act against a person or a person's property by an offender motivated by racial or other bias
- Based on
  - Race
  - Religion
  - Ancestry
  - Sexual orientation
  - Physical disability

The Feminist Perspective: Deviance and Gender

- Women have been socialized to define success in terms of relationships
- Gender influences how we define deviance because different standards judge the behavior of males and female
- Who the deviant is depends on the sex of both the audience and the actors
- Despite focus on inequality, social conflict analysis does not address the issue of gender

Crime

- *The violation of criminal laws enacted by a locality, state, or the federal government*
- All crimes have two distinct elements
  - **The *act* itself**
    - A failure to do what the law requires
  - *Criminal Intent*
    - *Mens rea* or "guilty mind"
    - Ranges from willful conduct to negligence

Types of Crime

- *Crimes against the person (Violent Crimes)*
  - *Crimes that direct violence or the threat of violence against others*
- *Crimes against property (Property Crimes)*
  - *Crimes that involve theft of property belonging to others*
- *Victimless Crimes*
  - *Violations of law in which there are no obvious victims*
  - Illegal drug use, prostitution, gambling

Criminal Statistics

- Include only crimes known to the police
- Researchers check crime statistics
  - Victimization Surveys
  - Demonstrates that the overall crime rate is three times higher than official reports indicate

---

The Street Criminal: A Profile

- Categories of people most likely to be arrested for violent and property crimes
  - *Age*
    - Rises sharply during adolescence, peeks in late teens, falls as people get older
  - *Gender*
    - Men are arrested more than twice as often as women for property crimes
    - Higher five to one ratio in violent crimes

- *Social Class*
  - Street crime is more widespread among people of lower social position
  - Most violent crimes in inner-city communities are committed by a few hard-core offenders
  - Majority of people in inner-city neighborhoods have no criminal record
  - Connection between social standing and criminality depends on what type of crime
    - Include "white-collar crime" in the definition
    - common criminal now looks more affluent and may live in a $100 million dollar home

- *Race and Ethnicity*
  - Strongly linked to crime rates
  - *Reasons for disproportionate arrests among African Americans*
    - In U.S., *race is linked to social standing*
    - *Single-parenting* has two risks
    - *Prejudice* prompts white police to arrest black people more willingly leading to over-criminalization
    - The official crime index *does not include arrests ranging from drunk driving or white-collar violations*
    - Some categories of the population have unusually low rates of arrest

Crime in a Global Perspective

- U. S. crime rate high by world standards
  - Crime arises from culture's emphasis on individual economic success
  - Extensive private ownership of guns
- Crime high in some of the largest cities of the world
  - Traditional character of low-income societies and strong family structure all local communities to control crime informally

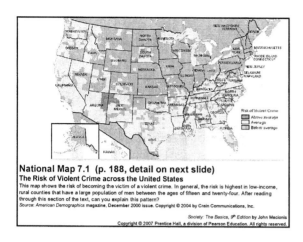

National Map 7.1 (p. 188, detail on next slide)
The Risk of Violent Crime across the United States
This map shows the risk of becoming the victim of a violent crime. In general, the risk is highest in low-income, rural counties that have a large population of men between the ages of fifteen and twenty-four. After reading through this section of the text, can you explain this pattern?
Source: American Demographics magazine, December 2000 issue. Copyright © 2004 by Crain Communications, Inc.

Society: The Basics, 9th Edition by John Macionis

National Map 7.1
The Risk of Violent Crime across the United States

Society: The Basics, 9th Edition by John Macionis

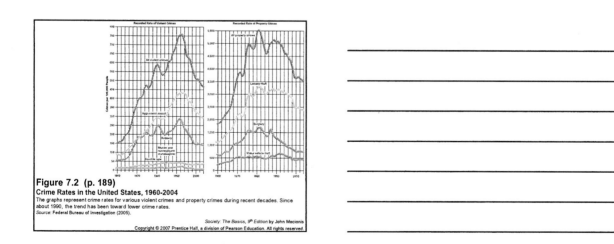

Figure 7.2 (p. 189)
Crime Rates in the United States, 1960-2004
The graphs represent crime rates for various violent crimes and property crimes during recent decades. Since about 1990, the trend has been toward lower crime rates.
Source: Federal Bureau of Investigation (2005).

Society: The Basics, 9th Edition by John Macionis

- Globalization also extends to crime
  - *Demand* issue of the drug trade in the US
  - Supply side in South America
    - 20% depend on cocaine for their livelihood
- Different countries have different strategies for dealing with crime
  - Death penalty

Global Map 7.1 (p. 192, detail on next slide)
Capital Punishment in Global Perspective
The map identifies 73 countries and territories in which the law allows the death penalty for ordinary crimes; in eleven more, the death penalty is reserved for exceptional crimes under military law or during times of war. The death penalty does not exist in 86 countries and territories; in 26 more, although the death penalty remains in law, no execution has taken place in more than ten years. Compare rich and poor nations: What general pattern do you see? In what way are the United States and Japan exceptions to this pattern?

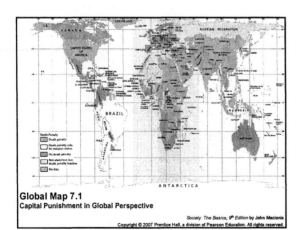

Global Map 7.1
Capital Punishment in Global Perspective

The U.S. Criminal Justice System

- *A society's formal response to crime*
  - Police
  - Courts
  - Punishment

Due Process

- **The criminal justice system must operate within the bounds of law**
- Grounded in first ten amendments to *U.S. Constitution*
  - *Offers protection to any person charged with a crime*
- Due process limits the power of government
  - Eye towards nation's cultural support of individual rights and freedoms

Police

- Serve as point of contact between a population and the criminal justice system
  - 675,734 full-time police across U.S. to monitor 300 million people
- To act quickly, size up situation in terms of six factors
  - More serious they think the situation, the more likely they make an arrest
  - Take account of the victim's wishes in an arrest
  - Odds of arrest increase the more uncooperative a suspect

- More likely to take into custody someone arrested before
- Presence of bystanders increases the chance of arrest
- All else being equal, police are more likely to arrest people of color than to arrest whites

_____

_____

_____

_____

_____

_____

_____

Courts

- Relies on an adversarial process involving attorneys
  - Defense, State, and Judge
- **PLEA BARGAINING**
  - ***A legal negotiation in which a prosecutor reduces a charge in exchange for a defendant's guilty plea***
    - Spares the system time and expense of trial
    - Sometimes pressures the innocent to plead guilty
    - Undercuts the adversarial system and the right of the defendants

_____

_____

_____

_____

_____

Punishment

- *Why does a society punish wrongdoers?*
- **RETRIBUTION**
  - *The act of moral vengeance by which society makes the offender suffer as much as the suffering caused by the crime*
- **DETERRENCE**
  - *The attempt to discourage criminality through the use of punishment*
- **REHABILITATION**
  - *A program for reforming the offender to prevent later offenses*
- **SOCIETAL PROTECTION**
  - *Rendering an offender incapable of further offenses temporarily through imprisonment or permanently by execution*

_____

_____

_____

_____

_____

_____

174

Four Justifications for Punishment	
Retribution	The oldest justification for punishment. Punishment is society's revenge for a moral wrong. In principle, punishment should be equal in severity to the crime itself.
Deterrence	An early modern approach. Crime is considered social disruption which society acts to control. People are viewed as rational and self-interested; deterrence works because the pain of punishment outweighs the pleasure of crime.
Rehabilitation	A modern strategy linked to the development of social sciences. Crime and other deviance are viewed as the result of social problems (such as poverty) or personal problems (such as mental illness). Social conditions are improved; treatment is tailored to the offender's condition.
Societal protection	A modern approach easier to carry out than rehabilitation. If society is unable or unwilling to rehabilitate offenders or reform social conditions, people are protected by the imprisonment or execution of the offender.

Summing Up (p. 195)

Society: The Basics, 9th Edition by John Macionis

- *CRITICAL REVIEW*
  - Despite extensive use of punishment
  - High *RECIDIVISM RATE*
    - *Later offenses by people previously convicted of crimes*
  - Most crimes go unpunished
  - General deterrence is difficult to investigate scientifically
  - Growing controversy over the use of the death penalty
  - Prisons provide short-term societal protection but do little to reshape attitudes or behavior

---

Community-Based Corrections

- *Correctional programs operating within society at large rather than behind prison walls*
- Three advantages:
  - Reduce costs
  - Supervision of convicts while eliminating hardships of prison life and stigma of jail
  - Not so much to punish as reform

- *Probation*
  - *A policy of permitting a convicted offender to remain in the community under conditions imposed by a court*
- *Shock Probation*
  - *A policy by which a judge orders a convicted offender to prison for a short time and then suspends the remainder of the sentence in favor of probation*
- *Parole*
  - *A policy of releasing inmates from prison to serve the remainder of their sentences in the local community under supervision of a parole officer*

- **CRITICAL REVIEW**
  - Research suggests that probation and shock probation do not significantly reduce criminal recidivism
  - Levels of crime among individuals released on parole are high
  - Criminal justice system by itself cannot eliminate crime

Chapter

8

Social Stratification

LEARNING OBJECTIVES

- To understand the four basic principles of social stratification.
- To differentiate between the caste and class systems of stratification.
- To begin to understand the relationship between ideology and stratification.
- To describe and differentiate between the structural-functional and social-conflict perspectives of stratification.
- To describe the views of Max Weber concerning the dimensions of social class.
- To have a clear sense of the extent of social inequality in the United States.
- To recognize the role of economic resources, power, occupational prestige, and schooling in the class system of the United States.
- To generally describe the various social classes in our social stratification system.
- To begin to develop a sociological sense about the nature of social mobility in the United States.

CHAPTER OUTLINE

I.   What Is Social Stratification?

II. Caste and Class Systems
    A.   The Caste System
        1.   An Illustration: India
        2.   Caste and Agrarian Life
    B.   The Class System
        1.   Meritocracy
        2.   Status Consistency
    C.   Caste and Class: The United Kingdom
        1.   The Estate System
        2.   The United Kingdom Today
    D.   Classless Societies? The Former Soviet Union
        1.   The Russian Revolution
        2.   The Modern Russian Federation
    E.   China: Emerging Social Classes
    F.   Ideology: The Power Behind Stratification
        1.   Plato and Marx on Ideology
        2.   Historical Patterns of Ideology

III. The Functions of Social Stratification
    A.   The Davis-Moore Thesis

IV.   Stratification and Conflict
    A.   Karl Marx: Class Conflict
    B.   Why No Marxist Revolution?
        1.   A Counterpoint
    C.   Max Weber: Class, Status, and Power
        1.   The Socioeconomic Status Hierarchy
        2.   Inequality in History

V.   Stratification and Interaction

VI.   Stratification and Technology: A Global Perspective
    A.   Hunting and Gathering Societies
    B.   Horticultural, Pastoral, and Agrarian Societies
    C.   Industrial Societies
    D.   The Kuznets Curve

VII.   Inequality in the United States
    A.   Income, Wealth, and Power
    B.   Schooling
    C.   Occupational Prestige
    D.   Ancestry, Race, and Gender

VIII.   Social Classes in the United States
    A.   The Upper Class
        1.   Upper-Uppers
        2.   Lower-Uppers
    B.   The Middle Class
        1.   Upper-Middles
        2.   Average-Middles
    C.   The Working Class
    D.   The Lower Class

IX.   The Difference Class Makes
    A.   Health
    B.   Values and Attitudes
    C.   Politics
    D.   Family and Gender

X.   Social Mobility
    A.   Myth Versus Reality
    B.   Mobility by Income Level
    C.   Mobility: Race, Ethnicity, and Gender
    D.   Mobility and Marriage
    E.   The American Dream: Still a Reality?
    F.   The Global Economy and the U.S. Class Structure

XI.   Poverty in the United States

SOCIAL STRATIFICATION

CHAPTER 8

- **What** is social stratification?

- **Why** does social inequality exist?

- **How** do social classes in the United States differ from one another?

What is Social Stratification?

- Defined as:
- *A system by which a society ranks and categories of people in a hierarchy*

Four Basic Principles

- *Social stratification is a trait of society, not simply a reflection of individual differences*
- *Social stratification carries over from generation to generation*
  - **Social Mobility**
    - *A change in position within the social hierarchy*
- *Social stratification is universal but variable*
- *Social stratification involves not just inequality but beliefs as well*

Caste and Class Systems

- Sociologists distinguish between
  - **Closed Systems – Caste Systems**
    - *Allow little change in social position*
  - **Open Systems – Class Systems**
    - *Permit much more social mobility*

The Caste System

- **Social stratification based on ascription, or birth**
  - Little or no social mobility
- **AN ILLUSTRATION: INDIA**
  - Four major casts or **Varna**
    - *Sanskrit, Brahmin, Kshatriya, Vaishya, Sudra*
  - Caste position determines life from birth
  - Caste guides everyday life by keeping people in the company of their "own kind"
  - Typically agrarian because agriculture demands a lifelong routine of work
  - Caste system also in South Africa

The Class System

- *Social stratification based on both birth and individual achievement*
  - Schooling and skills lead to social mobility
  - Work is no longer fixed at birth but involves some personal choice
- *MERITOCRACY*
  - A concept that refers to social stratification based on personal merit
  - Includes knowledge, abilities, and effort
  - Pure meritocracy has never existed

- *STATUS CONSISTENCY*
  - The degree of consistency in a person's social standing across various dimensions of social inequality
  - Low status consistency means that *classes* are harder to define than *castes*

Caste and Class: The United Kingdom

- Mix of meritocracy and caste in a class system
- Middle Ages, caste like system of three estates
  - 1st - Clergy-speak with the authority of God
  - 2nd – Hereditary nobility – 5% of population
  - 3rd – Commoners -- worked the land
- Industrial Revolution
  - Commoners became wealthy enough to challenge the nobility

- UNITED KINGDOM TODAY
  - Mainly a class system with caste elements based on tradition
    - Inherited wealth with high prestige to small number of families
    - Monarch – Queen Elizabeth
    - Parliament's House of Lords composed of peers
  - Control of government passed to House of Commons
    - Prime Minister and other ministers reach positions by achievement
      - elec tions

Classless Societies: The Former Soviet Union

- Union of Soviet Socialist Republics (USSR)
  - Boasted of being a classless society
  - Actually stratified into four unequal categories
    - High government officials
    - Soviet Intelligentsia and lower government officials, College professors, scientists, physicians, and engineers
    - Manual workers
    - Rural peasantry –l owest level

- The Modern Russian Federation
  - *Perestroika* – "restructuring"
  - Gorbachev's economic reforms led to one of the most dramatic social movements in history
  - 1989, Eastern Europe toppled socialist government
  - 1991, Soviet Union collapsed becoming Russian federation
  - Demonstrated that social inequality involves more than economic resources

STRUCTURAL SOCIAL MOBILITY
- *A shift in the social position of large numbers of people due more to changes in society than to individual efforts*
- 1990's
  - Structural mobility in Russian Federation turned downward
  - Private ownership increased gulf between rich and poor

China: Emerging Social Classes

- 1949 Communist Revolution
  - State control of all productive property
  - Reduced economic inequality but social differences remained
- 1978 Deng Xiaoping
  - State loosened its hold on the economy
  - Emergence of new class system
  - Mix of old political hierarchy and new business hierarchy

---

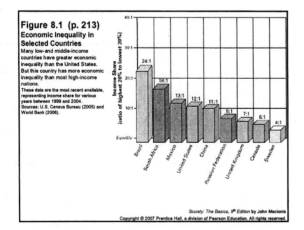

Figure 8.1 (p. 213)
Economic Inequality in Selected Countries
Many low- and middle-income countries have greater economic inequality than the United States. But this country has more economic inequality than most high-income nations.
These data are the most recent available, representing income share for various years between 1999 and 2004.
Sources: U.S. Census Bureau (2005) and World Bank (2006).

Ideology: the Power Behind Stratification

- *Ideology*
  - *Cultural beliefs that justify particular social arrangements, including patterns of inequality*
- Every culture considers some type of inequality fair
- Ideology changes with a society's economy and technology
- Historically, challenges to status quo always arise

The Functions of Social Stratification

- **STRUCTURAL FUNCTIONAL APPROACH**
  - Social stratification plays a vital part in the operation of society

The Davis-Moore Thesis

- *Social stratification has beneficial consequences for the operation of society*
  - The greater the functional importance of a position, the more rewards a society attaches to it
  - Any society can be egalitarian, but only to the extent that people are willing to let anyone perform any job
  - Positions a society considers crucial must offer enough rewards to draw talented people away from less important work

- CRITICAL REVIEW
  - How is the importance of a particular occupation assessed
  - Do rewards actually reflect the contributions someone makes to society
  - Ignores how the caste elements of social stratification can prevent the development of individual talent
  - Living in a society that places so much importance on money, overestimates the importance of high-paying work
  - Ignores how social inequality promotes conflict and revolution

Stratification and Conflict

- *Social-conflict Analysis*
  - Argues stratification provides some people with advantages over others

Karl Marx: Class Conflict

- Social stratification is rooted in people's relationship to the means of production
- *Capitalists*
  - *People who own and operate factories and other businesses in pursuits of profits*
- *Proletariats*
  - *Working people who sell their labor for wages*
- *Alienation*
  - *The experience of isolation and misery resulting from powerlessness*

- **CRITICAL REVIEW**
  - Ignores that a system of unequal rewards is needed to place people in the right jobs and to motivate people to hard work
  - The revolutionary change Marx predicted failed to happen, at least in advanced capitalist societies

Why No Marxist Revolution

- 1. Fragmentation of the capitalist class
- 2. A higher standard of living
  - Blue collar occupations
    - Lower-prestige jobs that involve mostly manual labor
  - White-collar occupations
    - Higher-prestige jobs that involve mostly mental activity
- 3. More worker organizations
- 4. Greater legal protections

Max Weber: Class, Status, and Power

- Viewed social stratification as involving three dimensions of inequality
  - *Class position* – economic inequality
  - *Status* – social prestige
  - *Power*

- *The Socioeconomic Status Hierarchy*
  - Status consistency in modern societies is low
  - *Socioeconomic Status (SES)*
    - A composite ranking based on various dimensions of social inequality
- *Inequality in History*
  - Each of Weber's three dimensions stands out at a different time in history of human societies
    - Status is main dimension in Agrarian societies
    - Class is main dimension in Industrial societies
    - Power is the main dimension with bigger government and spread of other types of organizations

- **CRITICAL REVIEW**
  - Industrial and postindustrial nations still show patterns of social inequality

Stratification and Interaction

- Micro-level analysis of social stratification
  - People's social standing affects their everyday interaction
  - People with different social standing keep their distance from one another
  - *Conspicuous consumption*
    - *Buying and using products with an eye to the "statement" they make about social position*

Social Stratification

	Structural-Functional Approach	Social-Conflict Approach	Symbolic-Interaction Approach
What is the level of analysis?	Macro-level	Macro-level	Micro-level
What is social stratification?	Stratification is a system of unequal rewards that benefits society as a whole.	Stratification is a division of a society's resources that benefits some and harms others.	Stratification is a factor that guides people's interaction in everyday life.
What is the reason for our social position?	Social position reflects personal talents and abilities in a competitive economy.	Social position reflects the way society divides resources.	The products we consume all say something about social position.
Are unequal rewards fair?	Yes. Unequal rewards boost economic production by encouraging people to work harder and try new ideas. Linking greater rewards to more important work is widely accepted.	No. Unequal rewards only serve to divide society, creating "haves" and "have-nots." There is widespread opposition to social inequality.	Maybe. People may or may not define inequality as fair. People may view their social position as a measure of self-worth, justifying inequality in terms of personal differences.

Applying Theory (p. 219)

What Stratification and Technology: A Global Perspective?

- Hunting and Gathering Societies
  - No categories of people better off than others
- Horticultural, Pastoral, and Agrarian Societies
  - Social inequality increases with rise of nobility
- Industrial Societies
  - Pushes inequality downward prompted by development of meritocracy

---

- *The Kuznets Curve*
  - *Technological advances first increase but then moderate the intensity of social stratification*
  - Greater inequality is functional for agrarian societies
  - Industrial societies benefit from less inequality
  - Social inequality around the world generally confirms the Kuznets curve
    - Income inequality reflects not just technological development but also a society's political and economic priorities
  - U.S. society now experiencing greater economic inequality suggests that long term trend may differ from Kuznets's observation half a century ago

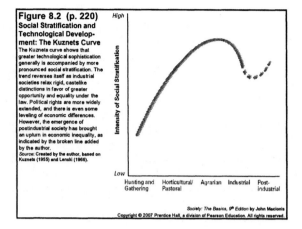

Figure 8.2 (p. 220)
Social Stratification and
Technological Develop-
ment: The Kuznets Curve
The Kuznets curve shows that
greater technological sophistication
generally is accompanied by more
pronounced social stratification. The
trend reverses itself as industrial
societies relax rigid, castelike
distinctions in favor of greater
opportunity and equality under the
law. Political rights are more widely
extended, and there is even some
leveling of economic differences.
However, the emergence of
postindustrial society has brought
an upturn in economic inequality, as
indicated by the broken line added
by the author.
Source: Created by the author, based on
Kuznets (1955) and Lenski (1966).

Society: The Basics, 9ᵗʰ Edition by John Macionis

Inequality in the United States

- U.S. differs from most European nations in never having a titled nobility
- With the exception of race, never known a caste system with rigid ranks of characterization
- U.S. society is highly stratified

Income, Wealth, and Power

- *INCOME*
  - *Earnings from work or investments*
    - The richest 20% received 48.1% of all income
    - Bottom 20% received only 4.0%
  - While a small number of people earn very high incomes, majority make do with far less
- *WEALTH*
  - *The total value of money and other assets, minus outstanding debts*
    - Wealth is distributed more unequally than income

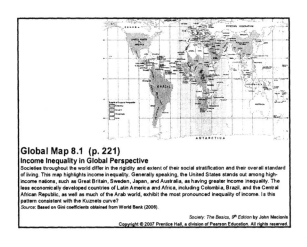

Global Map 8.1 (p. 221)
Income Inequality in Global Perspective
Societies throughout the world differ in the rigidity and extent of their social stratification and their overall standard of living. This map highlights income inequality. Generally speaking, the United States stands out among high-income nations, such as Great Britain, Sweden, Japan, and Australia, as having greater income inequality. The less economically developed countries of Latin America and Africa, including Colombia, Brazil, and the Central African Republic, as well as much of the Arab world, exhibit the most pronounced inequality of income. Is this pattern consistent with the Kuznets curve?
Source: Based on Gini coefficients obtained from World Bank (2006).

Society: The Basics, 9th Edition by John Macionis

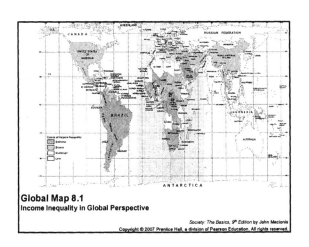

Global Map 8.1
Income Inequality in Global Perspective

Society: The Basics, 9th Edition by John Macionis

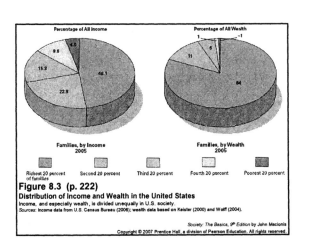

Figure 8.3 (p. 222)
Distribution of Income and Wealth in the United States
Income, and especially wealth, is divided unequally in U.S. society.
Sources: Income data from U.S. Census Bureau (2006); wealth data based on Keister (2000) and Wolff (2004).

Society: The Basics, 9th Edition by John Macionis

- *POWER*
    - In the U.S., wealth is an important source of power
    - Small proportion of families that control most of the wealth also has *the ability to shape the agenda of the entire society*
    - Sociologists argue:
        - Such concentrated wealth weakens democracy
            - The political system serves the interests of the rich
- *QUESTION:*
    - *PEOPLE OF ALL SOCIAL CLASSES HAVE THE SAME RIGHT TO VOTE. BUT CAN YOU THINK OF WAYS IN WHICH THE RICH HAVE MORE POWER TO SHAPE U.S. SOCIETY*

- *SCHOOLING*
    - Industrial societies have expanded opportunities for schooling, but some receive much more than others
    - *Affects occupation and income*
        - Most better-paying, white-collar jobs require a college degree and other advanced study
        - Blue-collar jobs
            - Require less schooling
            - Bring lower income and less prestige

TABLE 8-2

Schooling of U.S. Adults, 2004 (aged 25 and over)

	Women	Men
Not a high school graduate	**14.6%**	**15.2%**
8 years or less	6.1	6.5
9–11 years	8.5	8.7
High school graduate	**85.4**	**84.8**
High school only	32.8	31.1
1–3 years of college	26.5	24.3
College graduate or more	26.1	29.4

Source: U.S. Census Bureau (2005).

Table 8.2 (p. 223)
Schooling of U.S. Adults (aged 25 and over)

- **OCCUPATIONAL PRESTIGE**
  - Generates income and is an important source of prestige
  - High prestige given to occupations that require extensive training and generate high income
  - Less prestigious work pays less and requires less ability and schooling
  - In any society, high-prestige occupations go to privileged categories
    - Dominated by men
    - Lowest prestige jobs commonly performed by people of color

---

TABLE 8-3

The Relative Social Prestige of Selected Occupations in the United States

White-Collar Occupations	Prestige Score	Blue-Collar Occupations
Physician	86	
Lawyer	75	
College/university professor	74	
Architect	73	
Chemist	73	
Physicist/astronomer	73	
Aerospace engineer	72	
Dentist	72	

Table 8.3a (p. 224, continued on next 7 slides)
The Relative Social Prestige of Selected Occupations in the United States

TABLE 8–3

The Relative Social Prestige of Selected Occupations in the United States

White-Collar Occupations	Prestige Score	Blue-Collar Occupations
Member of the clergy	69	
Psychologist	69	
Pharmacist	68	
Optometrist	67	
Registered nurse	66	
Secondary school teacher	66	
Accountant	65	
Athlete	65	

Table 8.3b (continued)
The Relative Social Prestige of Selected Occupations in the United States

---

TABLE 8–3

The Relative Social Prestige of Selected Occupations in the United States

White-Collar Occupations	Prestige Score	Blue-Collar Occupations
Electrical engineer	64	
Elementary school teacher	64	
Economist	63	
Veterinarian	62	
Airplane pilot	61	
Computer programmer	61	
Sociologist	61	
Editor/reporter	60	

Table 8.3c (continued)
The Relative Social Prestige of Selected Occupations in the United States

---

TABLE 8–3

The Relative Social Prestige of Selected Occupations in the United States

White-Collar Occupations	Prestige Score	Blue-Collar Occupations
	60	Police officer
Actor	58	
Radio/TV announcer	55	
Librarian	54	
	53	Aircraft mechanic
	53	Firefighter
Dental hygienist	52	

Table 8.3d (continued)
The Relative Social Prestige of Selected Occupations in the United States

TABLE 8-3

The Relative Social Prestige of Selected Occupations in the United States

White-Collar Occupations	Prestige Score	Blue-Collar Occupations
Painter/sculptor	52	
Social worker	52	
	51	Electrician
Computer operator	50	
Funeral director	49	
Real estate agent	49	

Table 8.3e (continued)
The Relative Social Prestige of Selected Occupations in the United States

---

TABLE 8-3

The Relative Social Prestige of Selected Occupations in the United States

White-Collar Occupations	Prestige Score	Blue-Collar Occupations
Bookkeeper	47	
	47	Machinist
	47	Mail carrier
Musician/composer	47	
	46	Secretary
Photographer	45	
Bank teller	43	
	42	Tailor

Table 8.3f (continued)
The Relative Social Prestige of Selected Occupations in the United States

---

TABLE 8-3

The Relative Social Prestige of Selected Occupations in the United States

White-Collar Occupations	Prestige Score	Blue-Collar Occupations
	42	Welder
	40	Farmer
	40	Telephone operator
	39	Carpenter
	36	Bricklayer/stonemason
	36	Child care worker
File clerk	36	

Table 8.3g (continued)
The Relative Social Prestige of Selected Occupations in the United States

TABLE 8-3

The Relative Social Prestige of Selected Occupations in the United States

White-Collar Occupations	Prestige Score	Blue-Collar Occupations
	36	Hairdresser
	35	Baker
	34	Bulldozer operator
	31	Auto body repairer
Retail apparel salesperson	30	
	30	Truck driver
Cashier	29	
	28	Elevator operator

Table 8.3h (continued)
The Relative Social Prestige of Selected Occupations in the United States

Society: The Basics, 9th Edition by John Macionis

TABLE 8-3

The Relative Social Prestige of Selected Occupations in the United States

White-Collar Occupations	Prestige Score	Blue-Collar Occupations
	28	Garbage collector
	28	Taxi driver
	28	Waiter/waitress
	27	Bellhop
	25	Bartender
	23	Farm laborer
	23	Household laborer

Table 8.3i (continued)
The Relative Social Prestige of Selected Occupations in the United States

Society: The Basics, 9th Edition by John Macionis

TABLE 8-3

The Relative Social Prestige of Selected Occupations in the United States

White-Collar Occupations	Prestige Score	Blue-Collar Occupations
	22	Door-to-door salesperson
	22	Janitor
	09	Shoe shiner

Table 8.3j (continued)
The Relative Social Prestige of Selected Occupations in the United States

Society: The Basics, 9th Edition by John Macionis

- *ANCESTRY, RACE, AND GENDER*
  - *Nothing affects social standing as birth into a particular family (Ancestry)*
    - Has strong bearing on future schooling, occupation, and income
  - *(Race) is linked closely to social position in the U.S.*
    - Social ranking also involves ethnicity
  - *Both men and women are found in families at every social level (Gender)*
    - On average, women have less income, wealth, and occupational prestige than men
    - Single parent families headed by women are three times more likely to be poor than those headed by men

Social Classes in the United States

- Defining classes in the U.S. is difficult
  - Relatively low level of status inconsistency
  - The social mobility characteristic of class systems means that social position may change during a person's lifetime
  - *Four general rankings*
    - *Upper class*
    - *Middle class*
    - *Working class*
    - *Lower class*

The Upper Class

- Top 5% of the U.S. population
- *General rule:*
  - *The more a family's income comes from inherited wealth, the stronger the family's claim to being upper-class*
- Richest 374 people in the U.S.
  - **"Capitalists"**
    - *The owners of the means of production and most of the nation's wealth*
- Historically, composed of white Anglo-Saxon Protestants
  - Less true today

- ***UPPER-UPPERS***
  - "Blue Bloods" or "Society"
  - Less than 1% of U.S. population
  - Membership is by ascription (birth)
  - Possess enormous wealth primarily inherited
    - "Old Money"
  - Live in exclusive neighborhoods
  - Children typically attend private schools with similar others
    - Complete formal education at prestigious universities and colleges
  - Volunteer at charitable organizations
    - Help community and build networks that broaden their power

- ***LOWER-UPPERS***
  - Most of the people in this group
    - *Known as the* **"working rich"**
      - G et money by earning it rather than inheritance
    - 3 to 4% of U.S. population
    - Live in expensive neighborhoods
    - Vacation homes near water or in mountains
    - Children attend private schools and good colleges
    - *Most do not gain entry into the clubs and associations of* **"old money"** *fa milies*

The Middle Class

- 40 to 45% of U.S. population
- Tremendous influence on U.S. culture
- Commercial advertising directed at this group
- Contains far more ethnic and racial diversity than upper-class

- *UPPER-MIDDLES*
  - Average income of $100,000 to $185,000
  - 2/3rds of children attend college
    - Postgraduate degrees are common
  - Many have high prestige occupations
  - Lack power to influence national or international events
  - Often play an important role in local politics

The Working Class

- 1/3rd of population sometimes called lower-middle class
- Forms the core of the industrial proletariat
- Have little or no wealth
  - Vulnerable to financial problems
- Jobs provide little personal satisfaction
- Half own their own homes
- 1/3rd of children go to college

The Lower Class

- Remaining 20% of U.S. population
- Low income makes their lives insecure and difficult
- 37 million or 12.6% are classified as poor by federal government
- Hold low prestige jobs
- ½ complete high school; 1 in 4 reaches college
- Society segregates lower class, especially if minorities

The Difference Class Makes

- *Max Weber*
  - *Social stratification affects people's life chances*
  - Social standing linked to:
    - Health
    - Values
    - Politics
    - Family Life

- *HEALTH*
  - Children in poor families three times more likely to die during first year of life
  - On average, rich live seven years longer
    - S afer and less stressful environments, better medical care
- **VALUES AND ATTITUDES**
  - Some vary from class to class
  - *"Old Rich"* have strong sense of family history
  - Upper-uppers favor understated manners and tastes
  - Affluent people more tolerant of controversial behavior
  - Working-class grow up in an atmosphere of supervision and discipline
    - L ess likely to attend college and less tolerant

- *POLITICS*
  - Well-off people
    - Protection of wealth leads to
      - Cons ervative approach to *economic issues*
      - M ore *liberal* on *social issues*
    - Likely to *vote and join political organizations* because they are better served by the system
  - Lower social standing
    - *Economic liberals*
    - More conservative on *social issues*

- *FAMILY AND GENDER*
  - Lower class families
    - Families larger than middle class
      - E arlier marriage and less use of birth control
    - Encourage children to conform to conventional norms and respect authority
    - Divide responsibilities according to gender roles
    - Serve as sources of material assistance
  - Higher social standing
    - Pass on a different "culture capital" to children
      - Tea ch individuality and imagination
    - More egalitarian – sharing more activities and expressing greater intimacy
    - Friendships likely to share interests and leisure pursuits

---

Social Mobility

- *Upward Social Mobility*
- **Downward Social Mobility**
- **Intragenerational Social Mobility**
  - *A change in social position occurring during a person's lifetime*
- *Intergenerational Social Mobility*
  - *Upward or downward social mobility of children in relation to their parents*
- **Horizontal Social Mobility**
  - *Changing jobs at the same class level*

Myth Versus Reality

Four general conclusions–Social Mobility

1. *Social mobility over the course of the past century has been fairly high.*
2. *The long-term trend in social mobility has been upward.*
3. *Within a single generation, social mobility is usually small.*
4. *Social mobility since the 1970s has been uneven.*

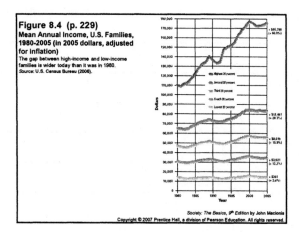

Figure 8.4 (p. 229)
Mean Annual Income, U.S. Families,
1980-2005 (in 2005 dollars, adjusted
for inflation)
The gap between high-income and low-income
families is wider today than it was in 1980.
Source: U.S. Census Bureau (2006).

Mobility: Race, Ethnicity, and Gender

- Whites always in a more privileged position
- 1980s and 1990s
  - More African Americans became wealthy
  - Overall income, however, has not changed in three decades
- Latinos
  - Average income in 2005, 64% that of whites
- Women have less chance because of the type of jobs they hold
  - Earnings gap between men and women is narrowing

Mobility and Marriage

- Marriage has an important effect on social standing
  - Married people accumulate about twice as much wealth compared to single and divorce
    - Double incomes
- Compared to singles, married men and women work harder and save more
- Divorce makes social standing go down
  - Divorced couples support two households
  - Men earn more than women
  - Divorced women lose income and benefits

202

The American Dream: Still a Reality?

- Expectation of upward social mobility is rooted in U.S. culture
- Disturbing trends
  - For many workers, earnings have stalled
  - More jobs offer little income
  - Young people are remaining at home
- Over the past generation
  - Rich have become richer
  - Low-paying jobs has brought downward mobility for millions

---

The Global Economy and the U.S. Class Structure

- High paying industrial jobs moved overseas
- U.S. serves a vast consumer market
- High paying manufacturing jobs support only 11% of workers
- Global economy is driving upward social mobility for educated people
- Same trend has hurt average workers
  - Loss of factory jobs
  - Company downsizing

Poverty in the United States

- *Relative Poverty*
  - *The deprivation of some people in relation to those who have more*
- *Absolute Poverty*
  - *A deprivation of resources that is life-threatening*

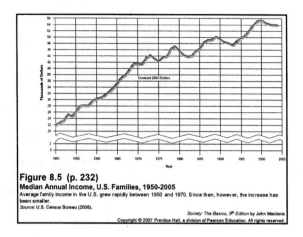

Figure 8.5 (p. 232)
Median Annual Income, U.S. Families, 1950-2005
Average family income in the U.S. grew rapidly between 1950 and 1970. Since then, however, the increase has been smaller.
Source: U.S. Census Bureau (2006).

Society: The Basics, 9th Edition by John Macionis

The Extent of Poverty

- 12.6% or 37 million of U.S. population – are classified as poor
- Relative poverty
  - Families with income below official poverty line
  - Family of four - $19,971
- Poverty line is three times what the government estimates a family will spend on food
  - Average poor family income is just 60% of the above amount
  - Typical poor family gets by on $12,000/year

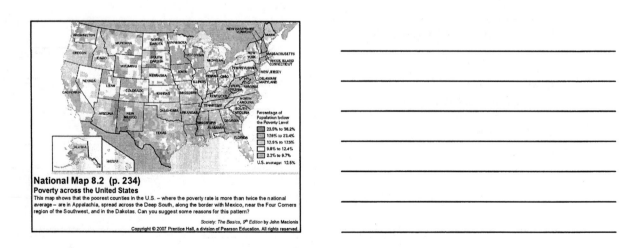

National Map 8.2 (p. 234)
Poverty across the United States
This map shows that the poorest counties in the U.S. – where the poverty rate is more than twice the national average – are in Appalachia, spread across the Deep South, along the border with Mexico, near the Four Corners region of the Southwest, and in the Dakotas. Can you suggest some reasons for this pattern?

Society: The Basics, 9th Edition by John Macionis

Who Are The Poor?

- *AGE*
  - Better retirement programs assist the elderly
  - Burden of poverty falls most heavily on children
    - 35% of the U.S. poor are children
- *RACE AND ETHNICITY*
  - 2/3rds of all poor are white
  - 25% are African American
    - Three times likely as non-Hispanic whites to be poor
  - High rates of child poverty among people of color
    - 34.5% African American children
    - 28.3% Hispanic children
    - 10.0% White children

- *GENDER AND FAMILY PATTERNS*
  - Of all poor eighteen and older
    - 61% are women; 39% are men
  - *Feminization of Poverty*
    - *The trend of women making up an increasing proportion of the poor*
    - Result of a larger trend
      - T he rapidly increasing number of households at all class levels headed by single women
    - Fifty-three percent of poor families are headed by single women
    - Households headed by women are at high risk of poverty

- *URBAN AND RURAL POVERTY*
  - Greatest concentration of poverty is found in central cities
    - 2005 poverty rate 17.0%; in suburbs – 9.3%
  - Poverty rate for urban areas as a whole-12.2%
  - Lower than the 14.5% in rural areas
  - Most of U.S. counties with the highest poverty rate are rural

Explaining Poverty

- Two opposing explanations
- *One View: Blame the Poor*
  - *The poor are primarily responsible for their own poverty*
    - *Culture of Poverty*
      - *A lower-class subculture that can destroy people's ambition to improve their lives*
- *Another View: Blame Society*
  - *Society is primarily responsible for poverty*
    - Primary cause is loss of jobs in inner cities
  - Government should fund jobs and provide affordable child care for low-income mothers and fathers

---

- **CRITICAL REVIEW**
  - Facts support "blame the poor" position
    - Major cause of poverty is not holding a job
  - *Reasons* that people do not work are more in step with the "blame society" position
    - Middle-class women can combine work and child rearing
    - Harder for poor women
      - Ca nnot afford child care
  - Effective way to reduce poverty
    - Greater supply of jobs and child care for parents who work

---

The Working Poor

- Not all poor people are jobless
- *Cause of working poverty*
  - Full-time worker earning $6.00/hr cannot lift an urban family of four above the poverty line
- Sociological evidence
  - *Society, not individual character traits, are primary source of poverty*
  - Entire categories of people face special barriers and limited opportunities

Homelessness

- Familiar stereotypes replaced by "new homelessness"
  - People out of work
    - factory closings, Rent increases, Low wages, No work at all
- Commonality of the homeless – Poverty
  - 1/3rd –substance abusers; 1/4th –mentally ill
  - Inability to cope with our complex and competitive society
- *Societal Factors*
  - Low wages and lack of low-income housing

_____

_____

_____

_____

_____

_____

_____

Class, Welfare, Politics, and Values

- Opinions about wealth and poverty also depend on politics and values
- U.S. cultural emphasis views
  - Successful people as personally worthy
  - Poor people as personally lacking
  - Explains why U.S. spends more on education than other high-income nations
  - Most are willing to accept high level of income inequality
    - Poor defined as undeserving

_____

_____

_____

_____

_____

_____

Global Stratification

LEARNING OBJECTIVES

- To define global stratification and describe the demographics of the three "economic development" categories used to classify nations of the world.
- To begin to understand both the severity and extensiveness of poverty in the low-income nations of the world.
- To recognize the extent to which women are overrepresented among the poor of the world and the factors leading to this condition.
- To identify and describe the stages of modernization.
- To recognize the problems facing women as a result of modernization in the low-income nations of the world.
- To identify the keys to combating global inequality over the next century.

CHAPTER OUTLINE

GLOBAL STRATIFICATION

CHAPTER 9

- **What** share of the world's people live in absolute poverty?

- **Why** are some of the world's countries so rich and others so poor?

- Are rich nations making global poverty better or worse? **How?**

GLOBAL STRATIFICATION: AN OVERVIEW

- Global perspective
  - Social stratification (inequality) is far greater than in the U.S.
- People in U.S. with income below the poverty line live far better than the majority of the people on the planet

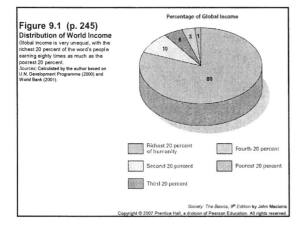

Figure 9.1 (p. 245)
Distribution of World Income
Global income is very unequal, with the richest 20 percent of the word's people earning eighty times as much as the poorest 20 percent.
Sources: Calculated by the author based on U.N. Development Programme (2000) and World Bank (2001).

Percentage of Global Income

Richest 20 percent of humanity

Second 20 percent

Third 20 percent

Fourth 20 percent

Poorest 20 percent

A Word About Terminology

- Various models of classification
- **"Three Worlds" Model**
  - "First World" – rich industrial countries
  - "Second World"-less industrialized socialist
  - "Third World"-non-industrialized poor countries
- Two reasons model does not work today
  - Grew out of cold war politics
    - Changes in Eastern Europe and Society Union collapse means there is no distinctive Second World
  - Model lumped together more than 100 countries as Third World inaccurately

---

- Revised system of classification
- *HIGH-INCOME COUNTRIES*
  - The fifty-five richest nations with the highest overall standards of living
- *MIDDLE-INCOME COUNTRIES*
  - The seventy-five nations with a standard of living about average for the world as a whole
- *LOW-INCOME COUNTRIES*
  - The remaining sixty-two nations with a low standard of living in which most people are poor
- Two advantages over "three worlds" model
  - Focuses on economic development and does not lump together all lower-income nations

High-Income Countries

- 25% of Earth's land area and lie mostly in the Northern Hemisphere

- Significant cultural differences exist

- All produce enough economic goods to enable people to lead comfortable lives

- People enjoy 79% of the world's total income

- Production is **"Capital Intensive"**
  - *Based on factories, big machinery, and advanced technology*

Global Map 9.1 (p. 247, detail on next slide)
Economic Development in Global Perspective
In high-income countries – including the U.S., Canada, Chile, Argentina, the nations of Western Europe, South Africa, Israel, Saudi Arabia, Australia, and Japan – a highly productive economy provides people, on average, with material plenty. Middle-income countries – including most of Latin America and Asia – are less economically productive, with a standard of living about average for the world as a whole but far below that of the U.S. These nations also have a significant share of poor people who are barely able to feed and house themselves. In the low-income countries of the world, poverty is severe and widespread. Although small numbers of elites live very well in the poorest nations, most people struggle to survive on a small fraction of the income common in the U.S.
Source: Based on data from UN Development Programme (2005), map projection from *Peters Atlas of the World* (1990).

Society: The Basics, 9th Edition by John Macionis

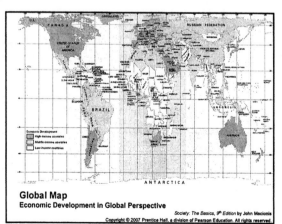

Global Map
Economic Development in Global Perspective

Society: The Basics, 9th Edition by John Macionis

Middle-Income Countries

- Industrial jobs are common
- 1/3rd of people live in rural areas
  - Poor, lack access to schools, medical care, adequate housing, and safe drinking water
- Former Soviet Union and Eastern Europe were socialist economies
- 55% of world's land area and home to 70% of humanity
  - Societies are densely populated compared to high-income countries

_____

_____

_____

_____

_____

_____

_____

Low-Income Countries

- Societies are agrarian and severe poverty
- Follow cultural traditions
- Limited industrial technology
- People's lives are shaped by hunger, disease, and unsafe housing
- People in rich nations have difficulty grasping the extent of human poverty and famine

_____

_____

_____

_____

_____

_____

_____

Global Wealthy and Poverty

- Low-income nations are home to some rich and many poor
- Most people live with incomes of a few hundred dollars a year
- Burden of poverty in low-income countries are greater than among the poor of the U.S.

_____

_____

_____

_____

_____

_____

_____

The Severity of Poverty

- Reason quality of life differs so much around the world
  - Economic productivity is lowest in regions where population growth is the highest
- High-income countries have the advantage
  - *79% of global income supporting just 18% of humanity*
- Middle-income countries
  - *20% of global income support 70% of humanity*
- *Leaves 12% of planet's population with 1% of global income*

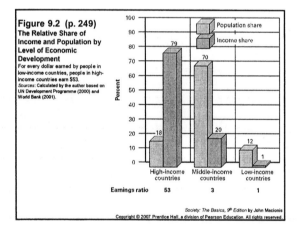

Figure 9.2 (p. 249)
The Relative Share of Income and Population by Level of Economic Development
For every dollar earned by people in low-income countries, people in high-income countries earn $53.
Sources: Calculated by the author based on UN Development Programme (2000) and World Bank (2001).

TABLE 9–1
Wealth and Well-Being in Global Perspective, 2003

Country	Gross Domestic Product (US$ billions)	GDP per Capita (PPP US$)*	Quality of Life Index
High-Income			
Norway	221	37,670	.963
Australia	522	29,632	.955
Sweden	302	26,750	.949
Canada	857	30,677	.949
United States	10,949	37,562	.944
Japan	4,301	27,967	.943
United Kingdom	1,795	27,147	.939
France	1,758	27,677	.938
South Korea	605	17,971	.901

Table 9.1a (p. 251)
Wealth and Well-Being in Global Perspective, 2003, continued on next four slides)

TABLE 9-1

Wealth and Well-Being in Global Perspective, 2003

Country	Gross Domestic Product (US$ billions)	GDP per Capita (PPP US$)*	Quality of Life Index
Middle-Income			
Eastern Europe			
Russian Federation	433	9,230	.795
Romania	57	7,277	.792
Belarus	18	6,052	.786
Ukraine	50	5,491	.766
Latin America			
Mexico	626	9,168	.814
Brazil	492	7,790	.792
Venezuela	85	4,919	.772

Table 9.1b (continued)

TABLE 9-1

Wealth and Well-Being in Global Perspective, 2003

Country	Gross Domestic Product (US$ billions)	GDP per Capita (PPP US$)*	Quality of Life Index
Asia			
Malaysia	104	9,512	.796
Thailand	143	7,595	.778
People's Republic of China	1,417	5,003	.755
Middle East			
Iran	137	6,995	.736
Syria	22	3,576	.721
Africa			
Algeria	67	6,107	.722
Botswana	8	8,714	.565

Table 9.1c (continued)

TABLE 9-1

Wealth and Well-Being in Global Perspective, 2003

Country	Gross Domestic Product (US$ billions)	GDP per Capita (PPP US$)*	Quality of Life Index
Low-Income			
Latin America			
Haiti	3	1,742	.475
Asia			
Cambodia	4	2,078	.571
Pakistan	82	2,097	.527
Bangladesh	52	1,770	.520

Table 9.1d (continued)

TABLE 9-1

Wealth and Well-Being in Global Perspective, 2003

Country	Gross Domestic Product (US$ billions)	GDP per Capita (PPP US$)*	Quality of Life Index
Africa			
Guinea	4	2,097	.466
Ethiopia	7	711	.367
Central African Republic	1	1,089	.355
Niger	3	835	.281

*These data are the United Nations' purchasing power parity (PPP) calculations, which avoid currency rate distortion by showing the local purchasing power of each domestic currency.

Source: United Nations Development Programme, *Human Development Report, 2005* (New York: United Nations Development Programme, 2005).

Table 9.1e (continued)

Relative Versus Absolute Poverty

- People in rich nations focus on *relative poverty*
  - Some people lack resources that are taken for granted by others
  - Exists in every society; rich and poor
- *Absolute poverty* is more important in the global perspective
  - Lack of resources that is life-threatening
  - Lack the nutrition necessary for health and long-term survival

---

- Global indicator of absolute poverty
  - Median age of death
  - Rich countries – most people die after 75
  - Poor countries
    - Half of all deaths occur among children under age 10

The Extent of Poverty

- Poverty is more widespread in poor countries
- Absolute poverty is greatest in Africa
  - High death rate of children
  - Half the population is malnourished
- Worldwide
- 15% or 1 billion people suffer from chronic hunger
- 400,000 people per day or 15 million die each year from hunger

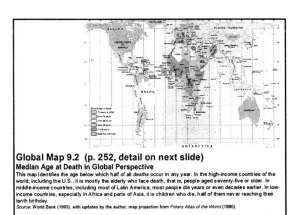

Global Map 9.2 (p. 252, detail on next slide)
Median Age at Death in Global Perspective
This map identifies the age below which half of all deaths occur in any year. In the high-income countries of the world, including the U.S., it is mostly the elderly who face death, that is, people aged seventy-five or older. In middle-income countries, including most of Latin America, most people die years or even decades earlier. In low-income countries, especially in Africa and parts of Asia, it is children who die, half of them never reaching their tenth birthday.
Source: World Bank (1993), with updates by the author; map projection from *Peters Atlas of the World* (1990).

Society: The Basics, 9th Edition by John Macionis

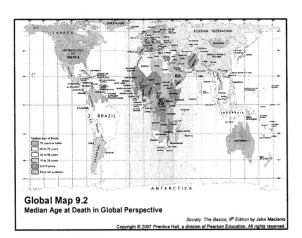

Global Map 9.2
Median Age at Death in Global Perspective

Society: The Basics, 9th Edition by John Macionis

Poverty and Children

- At least 100 million children in poor countries provide income for their families
  - Beg, steal, sell sex, or work for drug gangs
  - Means dropping out of school
  - Children are at high risk of disease and violence
- Another 100 million leave families and live on the streets
- Half of all street children found in Mexico City or Rio de Janeiro

Poverty and Women

- Rich societies
  - Women's work is undervalued, underpaid, or overlooked
- Poor societies
  - Work in sweatshops
  - Tradition keeps women out of many jobs
  - Traditional norms give women the responsibility for child rearing and household maintenance
  - Men own 90% of the land
- 70% of world's 1 billion people living in absolute poverty are women
- Women in poor countries receive little or no reproductive health care
  - limited access to birth control

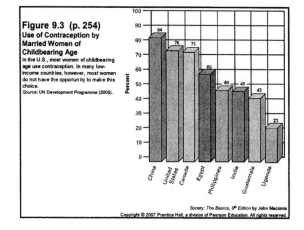

Figure 9.3 (p. 254)
Use of Contraception by Married Women of Childbearing Age
In the U.S., most women of childbearing age use contraception. In many low-income countries, however, most women do not have the opportunity to make this choice.
Source: UN Development Programme (2005).

Society: The Basics, 9th Edition by John Macionis

Slavery

- 200 million-about 3% of humanity live in conditions that amount to slavery
- Four types of slavery
  - *Chattel slavery* – one person owns another
  - *Child slavery* – desperate families let children do what they can to survive
  - *Debt bondage* – employers hold workers captive by paying them too little to meet their debts
  - *Human trafficking* – movement of men, women, and children from one place to another for forced labor

---

- *Universal Declaration of Human Rights (1948)*
  - "No one shall be held in slavery or servitude; slavery and the slave trade shall be prohibited in all their forms."
- Six decades later
  - Slavery still exists

Explanations of Global Poverty

1. *TECHNOLOGY*

   ¼ of people in low-income countries farm the land using human or animal power

2. *POPULATION GROWTH*
   - Poorest countries have the highest birth rates
   - Despite the death toll, double every five years

3. *CULTURAL PATTERNS*
   - Poor societies are usually traditional
   - Resistant to change

4. SOCIAL STRATIFICATION

Low-income nations distribute wealth unequally

5. GENDER INEQUALITY

Extreme and keep women from holding jobs

Typically means they have many children

6. GLOBAL POWER RELATIONSHIPS

COLONIALISM

- *The process by which some nations enrich themselves through political and economic control of other nations*
- Global exploitation allowed some nations to develop economically at the expense of others

---

Global Stratification: Theoretical Analysis

- Two major explanations:
  - *Modernization Theory*
  - *Dependency Theory*

Modernization Theory

- **Modernization Theory**
  - *A model of economic and social development that explains global inequality in terms of technological and cultural differences between nations*
  - Structural-functional approach
- *Historical Perspective*
  - Theory proposes that it is affluence that demands explanation
  - Industrialization's productivity improved the living standards of even the poorest people

- *The Importance of Culture*
  - Tradition as barrier to economic development
  - Technology opposed as a threat
    - Family relationships
    - Customs
    - Religious beliefs

Rostow's Stages of Modernization

1. **TRADITIONAL STAGE**
   - Socialized to honor the past
   - Cannot imagine that life can or should be different
   - Life is spiritually rich but lacking in material goods

2. **TAKE-OFF STAGE**
   - Start to use talents and imagination sparking economic growth
   - Market emerges as goods are produced
   - Greater individualism, willing to take risks, desire for material goods

---

3. **DRIVE TO TECHNOLOGICAL MATURITY**
   - Growth is a widely accepted idea that fuels pursuit of higher living standards
   - Diversified economy
   - Industrialization weakens traditional family and local community life
   - Absolute poverty reduced in nations the this stage
   - Basic schooling for all and advanced training for some
   - Social position of women steadily approaches that of men

4. HIGH MASS CONSUMPTION

- Economic development driven by industrial technology raises living standards
- Mass production stimulates mass consumption
- People learn to "need" the expanding selection of goods produced

---

The Role of Rich Nations

- High-income nations play four important roles in global economic development

1. CONTROLLING POPULATION

- Help limit population growth by exporting birth control technology

2. INCREASING FOOD PRODUCTION

- Export high-tech farming methods
- Referred to as the "Green Revolution"

---

3. INTRODUCING INDUSTRIAL TECHNOLOGY

- Introduce machinery and information technology which raises productivity
- Industrialization shifts the labor force from farming to skilled industrial and service jobs

4. PROVIDING FOREIGN AID

- Investment capital from rich nations boost prospects of poor societies
- Foreign aid help raise agricultural productivity
- Financial and technical assistance to build power plants and factories

- **CRITICAL REVIEW**
  - Most serious flaw of modernization theory
    - Has not occurred in many poor countries
  - Fails to recognize that rich nations, which benefit from the status quo, often block the path to development for poor countries
  - Treats rich and poor societies as separate worlds ignoring that the global economy affects all nations
  - Ethnocentric - Holds the world's most developed countries as the standard for judging the rest of humanity
  - Suggests that the causes of global poverty lie entirely within the poor societies themselves – blaming the victim

Dependency Theory

- *Dependency Theory*
  - *A model of economic and social development that explains global inequality in terms of the historical exploitation of poor nations by rich ones*
  - Social-conflict approach
- *Historical Perspective*
  - People living in poor countries are better off economically
  - Based on the idea that the economic positions of rich and poor nations are linked
  - Prosperity of developed countries come at the expense of less developed ones

The Importance of Colonialism
- Europeans established colonies
  - Americas, Africa, Asia
- United States
  - Alaska, Haiti, Puerto Rico, Guam, Philippines, Hawaiian Islands, Guantanamo Bay in Cuba
- European powers dominated most of the continent until early 1960s
- According to **dependency theory**
  - *Political liberation has not meant economic independence*
- **Neocolonialism**
  - *Economic relationship between rich and poor nations continue colonial pattern of domination*
  - Heart of the capitalist world economy

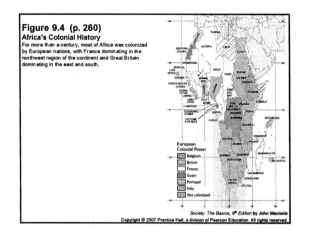

Figure 9.4 (p. 260)
Africa's Colonial History
For more than a century, most of Africa was colonized by European nations, with France dominating in the northwest region of the continent and Great Britain dominating in the east and south.

European Colonial Power
- Belgium
- Britain
- France
- Spain
- Portugal
- Italy
- Not colonized

Wallerstien's Capitalist World Economy

- *Suggests that prosperity or poverty of any country results from the operation of the global economic system*
- Rich nations are the *core* of the world economy
- Low-income nations are the *periphery* of the global economy
- *World economy*
    - Benefits rich societies by generating profits
    - Harms the rest of the world by causing poverty
    - Makes poor nations dependent on rich ones

Dependency involves three factors

1. **NARROW EXPORT-ORIENTED ECONOMIES**
    - Poor nations develop few industries of their own
2. **LACK OF INDUSTRIAL CAPACITY**
    - Poor societies depend on selling their inexpensive raw materials to rich nations and try to buy from rich nations the few expensive manufactured goods they can afford
3. **FOREIGN DEBT**
    - Unequal trade patterns plunged poor countries into debt causing high unemployment and rampant inflation

224

The Role of Rich Nations

- **Modernization theory**
  - Rich societies *produce wealth* through capital investments and new technology
- **Dependency Theory**
  - Views global inequality in terms of how countries *distribute wealth*
  - Rich nations have *overdeveloped* themselves as they *underdeveloped* the rest of the world
  - Claim that population and agricultural programs actually benefit rich nations and the ruling elites; not the poor majority

---

- **Lappe and Collins (1986)**
  - Capitalist culture encourages people to think that poverty is inevitable
  - Dependency Theory
    - Global poverty results from deliberate politics
    - World produces enough food to feed the planet
  - Contradiction of poverty amid plenty
    - Stems from rich nation policy of producing food for profit
    - Governments of poor countries support this because they need food profits to help pay off their huge foreign debt
    - Capitalist corporate structure of the global economy is at the core of this vicious cycle

---

- **CRITICAL REVIEW**
  - Dependency theory treats wealth wrongly
  - Dependency theory is wrong in blaming rich nations for global poverty
  - Dependency theory is simplistic
    - Claims capitalist market system is the cause of global inequality
    - Rich societies cannot be held responsible for corrupt and militaristic foreign leaders
    - Wrong to claim that global trade always makes rich nations richer and poor nations poorer
  - Dependency theory offers only vague solutions to global poverty

Global Poverty

	Modernization Theory	Dependency Theory
Which theoretical approach is applied?	Structural-functional approach	Social-conflict approach
How did global poverty come about?	The whole world was poor until some countries developed industrial technology, which allowed mass production and created affluence.	Colonialism moved wealth from some countries to others, making some nations poor as it made other nations rich.
What are the main causes of global poverty today?	Traditional culture and a lack of productive technology.	Neocolonialism—the operation of multi-national corporations in the global, capitalist economy.
Are rich countries part of the problem or part of the solution?	Rich countries are part of the solution, contributing new technology, advanced schooling, and foreign aid.	Rich countries are part of the problem, making poor countries economically dependent and in debt.

Applying Theory (p. 263)

Global Stratification: Looking Ahead

- Most important trend is the expansion of the global economy
- Supporters of the global economy claim
  - Expansion of trade results in benefits for all countries involved
    - Endorse NAFTA

- Greatest concern is the vast economic inequality that separates the world's nations
- Modernization and Dependency Theory offer some understanding
  - Must consider empirical evidence
  - Although all people are better off in *absolute* terms, there was almost twice as much <u>relative</u> economic inequality
- Degree of inequality has declined since 1970
- Greatest reduction in poverty took place in Asia

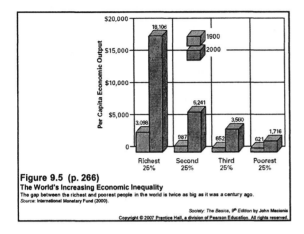

Figure 9.5 (p. 266)
The World's Increasing Economic Inequality
The gap between the richest and poorest people in the world is twice as big as it was a century ago.
Source: International Monetary Fund (2000).

Society: The Basics, 9th Edition by John Macionis

- Latin America enjoyed significant growth
  - Little overall improvement
- Half the nations of Africa are showing economic growth
  - In many countries south of the Sahara, extreme poverty has become worse
- Insight of modernization theory
  - Poverty is partly a *problem of technology*
- Insight of dependency theory
  - Global inequality is also a *political issue*

- Human community must address crucial questions
  - Distribution of resources
    - Within societies
    - Around the globe
- Though economic development raises living standards
  - Places greater strain on the natural environment

- Gulf that separates world's richest and poorest
    - Puts everyone at risk of war and terrorism
    - Poorest people challenge social arrangements that threaten their existence
- *Planetary peace can be achieved*
    - *Ensure that all people enjoy*
        - Significant measure of *dignity* and *security*

Chapter 10

Gender Stratification

GENDER STRATIFICATION

CHAPTER 10

- **How** is gender a creation of society?

- **What** differences does gender make in people's lives?

- **Why** is gender an important dimension of social stratification?

Gender and Inequality

- *GENDER*
  - *Refers to the personal traits and social positions that members of a society attach to being female or male*
  - Gender is a dimension of social organization
  - Gender involves a hierarchy
- *GENDER STRATIFICATION*
  - *The unequal distribution of wealth, power, and privilege between men and women*

Male-Female Differences

- People think gender distinctions are "natural"
  - Biology makes one sex different from the other
- 1848
  - People assumed women did not have intelligence or interests in politics
  - Reflected cultural patterns of that time and place
  - Most of the differences between men and women are socially created
- Women outperform men in the game of life
  - Men's life expectancy – 75.2 years
  - Women's life expectancy – 80.4 years

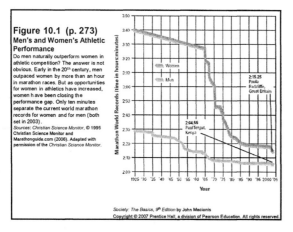

Figure 10.1 (p. 273)
Men's and Women's Athletic Performance
Do men naturally outperform women in athletic competition? The answer is not obvious. Early in the 20th century, men outpaced women by more than an hour in marathon races. But as opportunities for women in athletics have increased, women have been closing the performance gap. Only ten minutes separate the current world marathon records for women and for men (both set in 2003).
Sources: Christian Science Monitor, © 1995 Christian Science Monitor and Marathonguide.com (2006). Adapted with permission of the Christian Science Monitor.

Gender in Global Perspective

- Three important studies highlighted "masculine" and "feminine" differences
- **The Israeli Kibbutz**
  - Gender equality is one of its stated goals
  - Achieved remarkable social equality
    - Evidence that culture defines what is feminine and what is masculine

- **Margaret Mead's Research**
  - If gender is based on biological differences, people everywhere should define "feminine" and "masculine" the same
  - Studied three societies in New Guinea
    - Arapesh, Mundugumor, and Tchambuli
  - *Concluded that culture is the key to gender distinction*
    - What one society defines as masculine another may see as feminine
  - Mead's findings described as "too neat"
    - Saw the patterns she was looking for
    - "Reversal Hypothesis"

- **George Murdock's Research**
  - Broad study of 200 preindustrial societies
  - Found global agreement feminine and masculine tasks
  - Simple technology
    - Assigned roles reflecting the physical characteristics of men and women

- **CRITICAL REVIEW**
  - Global comparisons show that societies do not consistently define tasks as feminine and masculine
  - Industrialization
    - Muscle power declines
    - Reduces gender differences
  - Gender is too variable to be a simple expression of biology
  - What it means to be female and male is mostly a creation of society

Patriarchy and Sexism

- *MATRIARCHY* (**"Rule of Mothers"**)
  - *A form of social organization in which females dominate males*
    - Rarely documented in human history
- *PATRIARCHY* (**"Rule of Fathers"**)
  - *A form of social organization in which males dominate females*
    - Pattern found almost everywhere in the world
- *SEXISM*
  - *The belief that one sex is innately superior to the other*
  - Justification for patriarchy

- *The Costs of Sexism*
  - Limits the talents and ambitions of half the human population – women
  - Masculinity in U.S. culture encourages men to engage in high-risk behaviors
  - Masculinity is linked to:
    - Accidents, suicide, violence, and stress related diseases
  - *Type A Personality*
    - Cause of heart disease and almost a perfect match with behavior U.S. culture considers masculine
  - As men seek control, they lose opportunities for intimacy and trust

---

Global Map 10.1 (p. 275, detail on next slide)
Women's Power in Global Perspective
Women's social standing in relation to men's varies around the world. In general, women live better in rich countries than in poor countries. Even so, some nations stand out: In the nations of Norway, Australia, and Iceland, women come closest to social equality with men.
Source: Data from Seager (2003).

Society: The Basics, 9th Edition by John Macionis

Global Map 10.1
Women's Power in Global Perspective

- *Must Patriarchy Go On?*
  - In preindustrial societies women have little control over their lives
  - Industrialization provides choices on how to live
  - Some researchers claim
    - Biological factors "wire" the sexes with different motivations and behaviors, especially aggression
  - Most sociologists believe
    - Gender is socially constructed and can be changed
    - We do not have to stay prisoners of the past

Gender and Socialization

- Gender shapes human feelings, thoughts, and actions
- Children learn quickly how society defines male and female by age three
- *GENDER ROLES (Sex Roles)*
  - *Attitudes and activities that a society links to each sex*
  - Men expected to be leaders and women expected to be supportive

Gender and the Family

- "Is it a boy or a girl?"
  - Important because answer involves not only sex but the likely direction of a child's life
- Welcome of infants into the world
  - Pink for girls; blue for boys
- Female world revolves around cooperation and emotion
- Male world puts a premium on independence and action

Gender and the Peer Group

- Research demonstrates that young children tend to form single-sex play groups
- Peer groups teach additional lessons about gender
  - Male games reinforce masculine traits of aggression and control
  - Female peer groups encourage interpersonal skills of communication and cooperation

Gender and Schooling

- Gender shapes interests and beliefs about abilities, guiding areas of study, and career choices
- Women are now the majority (57%) of students on college campuses
  - Now represented in many fields of study that once excluded them
- Men still predominate in many fields
  - Engineering, physics, and philosophy
- Women cluster in the fine arts
  - Social sciences

Gender and the Mass Media

- Men hold center stage in television
- Historically, ads show women in the home
- Study of gender in advertising revealed that men usually appear taller than women implying male superiority
- Women are more frequently portrayed lying down appearing sexual and submissive
- Advertising perpetuates the **"beauty myth"**
  - *Society teaches women to measure their worth in terms of physical appearance*

_____

_____

_____

_____

_____

_____

_____

Gender and Social Stratification

- Gender involves more than how people think or act
- It is about social hierarchy

_____

_____

_____

_____

_____

_____

_____

Working Women and Men

- 59% of women in the work force and 71% of working women work full time
- Factors that have changed the U.S. labor force
  - Decline of farming
  - Growth of cities
  - Shrinking family size
  - Rising divorce rate
- More than half of all married couples depend on two incomes

_____

_____

_____

_____

_____

_____

_____

Gender and Occupations

- U.S. Department of Labor
  - High concentration of women in two types of jobs
    - Administrative work ("Pink Collar Jobs")
    - Service work (Food, child care, and health care)
  - Men dominate most other job categories
- Gender stratification in everyday life is easy to see
- Women are kept out of certain jobs
  - By defining some kinds of work as "masculine"
- Higher you go in the corporate world – fewer women you see

- Challenge to male domination in the workplace
  - Women who are entrepreneurs
  - Women-owned businesses employ ¼ of the entire labor force
  - Women can make opportunities for themselves apart from large, male-dominated companies

---

Figure 10.1 (p. 279)
Jobs with the Highest Concentrations of Women, 2005

TABLE 10–1
Jobs with the Highest Concentrations of Women, 2005

Occupation	Number of Women Employed	Percentage in Occupation Who Are Women
1. Preschool or kindergarten teacher	719,000	97.7%
2. Secretary or administrative assistant	3,499,000	97.3
3. Dental hygienist	132,000	97.1
4. Dental assistant	259,000	96.1
5. Dietitian or nutritionist	68,000	95.3
6. Word processor or typist	295,000	95.0
7. Child care worker	1,329,000	94.8
8. Licensed practical or licensed vocational nurse	510,000	93.4
9. Occupational therapist	85,000	92.9
10. Receptionist or information clerk	1,376,000	92.4

Source: U.S. Department of Labor (2006).

Society: The Basics, 9th Edition by John Macionis

Gender, Income and Wealth

- Women earn 77 cents for every dollar earned by men
- Differences are greater among older workers
  - Older working women have typically have less education and seniority
- Reason women earn less in the *type* of work they do
  - Still think of less important jobs as "women's work"
- Supporters of gender equality
  - Propose a policy of "comparable worth"

- Second cause of gender-based income inequality
  - Society's view of family
  - U.S. culture gives more of the responsibility of parenting to women
  - Pregnancy and raising small children keep many younger women out of the labor force
- Third factor is discrimination against women
  - Because it is illegal, it is practiced in subtle ways
  - Glass ceiling prevents many women from rising above middle management

---

- Many people think women own most of the country's wealth
  - Perhaps because they typically outlive men
- Government statistics say different
  - 55% of people with assets of 1 million or more are men
  - 12% of those identified by Forbes as the richest people in the U.S. are women

Housework: Women's "Second Shift"

- Housework presents a cultural contradiction in the U.S.
  - Essential for family life
  - Little rewards for doing it
- In U.S. and around the world
  - Care of home and children are "women's work"
- Labor force reduced the amount of housework but the share done by women remains the same

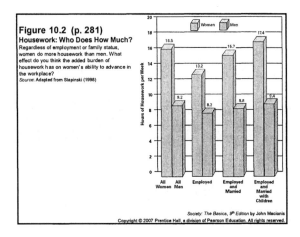

Figure 10.2 (p. 281)
Housework: Who Does How Much?
Regardless of employment or family status, women do more housework than men. What effect do you think the added burden of housework has on women's ability to advance in the workplace?
Source: Adapted from Stapinski (1998)

Gender and Education

- By 1980, women earned majority of Associate and Bachelor's degrees
- Differences in men's and women's majors are becoming smaller
- 1992 – first time – women earned a majority of postgraduate degrees
- Men still predominate some professional fields
- U.S. society still defines high-paying professions as masculine

Gender and Politics

- Nineteenth Amendment
  - Women got the right to vote
- Thousands of women hold responsible jobs in the federal government
- Change is more slow at the highest levels of power
- Women make up half of Earth's population
  - Hold just 17% of seats in the world's 185 parliaments

TABLE 10-2

Significant "Firsts" for Women in U.S. Politics

1869	Law allows women to vote in Wyoming territory.
1872	First woman to run for the presidency (Victoria Woodhull) represents the Equal Rights party.
1917	First woman elected to the House of Representatives (Jeannette Rankin of Montana).
1924	First women elected state governors (Nellie Taylor Ross of Wyoming and Miriam "Ma" Ferguson of Texas); both followed their husbands into office. First woman to have her name placed in nomination for the vice-presidency at the convention of a major political party (Lena Jones Springs, a Democrat).

Table 10.2a (p. 282, continued on next four slides)
Significant "Firsts" for Women in U.S. Politics

TABLE 10-2

Significant "Firsts" for Women in U.S. Politics

1931	First woman to serve in the Senate (Hattie Caraway of Arkansas); completed the term of her husband upon his death and won reelection in 1932.
1932	First woman appointed to the presidential cabinet (Frances Perkins, secretary of labor in the cabinet of President Franklin D. Roosevelt).
1964	First woman to have her name placed in nomination for the presidency at the convention of a major political party (Margaret Chase Smith, a Republican).

Table 10.1b (continued)

TABLE 10-2

Significant "Firsts" for Women in U.S. Politics

1972	First African American woman to have her name placed in nomination for the presidency at the convention of a major political party (Shirley Chisholm, a Democrat).
1981	First woman appointed to the U.S. Supreme Court (Sandra Day O'Connor).
1984	First woman to be successfully nominated for the vice-presidency (Geraldine Ferraro, a Democrat).
1988	First woman chief executive to be elected to a consecutive third term (Madeleine Kunin, governor of Vermont).

Table 10.1c (continued)

TABLE 10-2

Significant "Firsts" for Women in U.S. Politics

1992	Political "Year of the Woman" yields record number of women in the Senate (six) and the House (forty-eight), as well as (1) first African American woman to win election to U.S. Senate (Carol Moseley-Braun of Illinois), (2) first state (California) to be served by two women senators (Barbara Boxer and Dianne Feinstein), and (3) first woman of Puerto Rican descent elected to the House (Nydia Velazquez of New York).
1996	First woman appointed secretary of state (Madeleine Albright).

Table 10.1d (continued)

TABLE 10-2

Significant "Firsts" for Women in U.S. Politics

2000	First First Lady to win elected political office (Hillary Rodham Clinton, senator from New York).
2001	First woman to serve as national security adviser (Condoleezza Rice); first Asian American woman to serve in a presidential cabinet (Elaine Chao).
2002	Record number of women in the Senate (fourteen).
2005	First African American woman appointed secretary of state (Condoleezza Rice); record number of women in the House (sixty-seven).

Table 10.1e (continued)

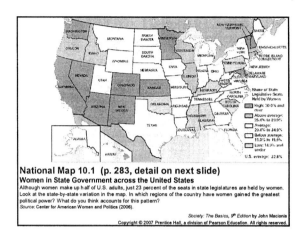

National Map 10.1 (p. 283, detail on next slide)
Women in State Government across the United States
Although women make up half of U.S. adults, just 23 percent of the seats in state legislatures are held by women. Look at the state-by-state variation in the map. In which regions of the country have women gained the greatest political power? What do you think accounts for this pattern?
Source: Center for American Women and Politics (2006).

National Map 10.1
Women in State Government across the United States

Gender and the Military

- Women have served in the armed forces since colonial times
- Women make up a growing share of the U.S. military
  - All military assignments are open to women
  - Objections include, women lack the physical strength of men
  - Military women are better educated and score higher on intelligence tests than military men

- US has a deeply held view of women as "nurturers"
  - Give life and help others
  - Clashes with the image of women trained to kill
- Women are more integrated into today's military because technology blurs the distinction between combat and non-combat personnel

---

Are Women a Minority?

- *Minority*
  - *Any category of people distinguished by physical or cultural difference that a society sets apart and subordinates*
- Economic disadvantage of being a woman
  - Women are a minority even though they outnumber men
- White women do not think of themselves in this way
  - Unlike racial minorities and ethnic minorities
  - Well represented at all levels of the class structure

- At every class level
  - Women typically have less
    - Income
    - Wealth
    - Education
    - Power
- Patriarchy makes women depend on men for social standing
  - First their fathers
  - Then their husbands

Minority Women: Intersection Theory

- ***Intersection theory***
  - *The interplay of race, class, and gender, often resulting in multiple dimensions of disadvantage*
- Disadvantages linked to race and gender combine to produce low social standing
- Differences in pay structure reflect minority women's lower positions in the occupational and educational hierarchies

---

- Gender does not operate alone
  - Class position, race and ethnicity, gender, and sexual orientation
  - Form a multilayered system that provides disadvantages for some and privileges for others

---

Violence Against Women

- In the 19th century
  - Men claimed the right to rule their households
  - Great deal of "manly" violence is still directed against women
- 387,000 aggravated assaults against women occur annually
  - 177,000 rapes/sexual assaults
  - 1.4 million simple assaults
- Gender violence is an issue on college and university campuses

- Gender-linked violence occurs where men and women interact most
  - In the home
  - Family is the most violent organization in the U.S. and women suffer most injuries
- Also occurs in casual relationships
  - Most rapes involve men known and trusted by their victims
- Extent of sexual abuse shows the tendency toward sexual violence is built into our way of life
  - All forms of violence against women express a "rape culture"

- Globally, violence against women is built into other cultures in different ways
  - *Genital mutilation*
    - *Painful and dangerous surgical procedure performed in more than 40 countries and the U.S.*

Global Map 10.2 (p. 285, detail on next slide)
Female Genital Mutilation in Global Perspective
Female genital mutilation is known to be performed in more than 40 countries around the world. Across Africa, the practice is common and affects a majority of girls in the eastern African nations of Sudan, Ethiopia, and Somalia. In several Asian nations, including India, the practice is limited to a few ethnic minorities. In the U.S., Canada, several European nations, and Australia, there are reports of the practice among some immigrants.
Source: Data from Seager (2003).

Society: The Basics, 9th Edition by John Macionis

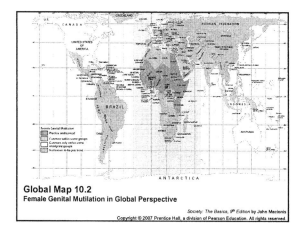

Global Map 10.2
Female Genital Mutilation in Global Perspective

Violence Against Men

- 80% of cases in which police make an arrest for a violent crime, the offender is male
- 59% of all victims of violent crime are men
- U.S. culture tends to define masculinity in terms of aggression and violence
- Men's lives involve more stress and isolation than women's lives
- Violence is built into our way of life
  - The way any culture constructs gender plays an important part in how violent or peaceful a society will be

---

Sexual Harassment

- *Refers to comments, gestures, or physical contacts of a sexual nature that are deliberate, repeated, and unwelcome*
- Most victims of sexual harassment are women
  - Our culture encourages men to be sexually assertive and see women in sexual terms
  - Most people in positions of power are men who oversee the work of women
- Sexual harassment is sometimes obvious and direct

- ***Quid pro quo*** sexual harassment
  - *One thing in return for another*
  - Violation of civil rights
- More often, problem of unwelcome sexual attention is subtle
- Based on the *effect* standard, actions add up to a *hostile environment*
  - Complex because they involve different perceptions of the same behavior

Pornography

- **Sexually explicit material that causes sexual arousal**
- Different views on what is or is not pornographic
  - Law gives communities the power to define "community standards of decency"
- Traditionally, concerns about pornography as a *moral* issue
  - Plays a part in gender stratification
  - *Power* issue because it dehumanizes women

- Concern that pornography encourages violence against women
  - Portrays them as weak and undeserving of respect
  - ½ of US adults think pornography encourages people to commit rape
- Despite material may offend about everyone
  - People defend the rights of free speech and artistic expression
- Pressure to restrict pornography has increased
  - Weakens morality and is demeaning and threatening to women

248

Theoretical Analysis of Gender

Structural-Functional Approach

- *Views society as a complex system of many separate but integrated parts*
  - Gender serves as a means to organize social life
- Over the centuries, sex-based division of labor became institutionalized and taken for granted
- Industrial technology opens up much greater range of cultural possibilities

- Ability to control reproduction gives women greater choices about how to live
- Modern societies relax traditional gender roles
  - Societies became more meritocratic
  - Rigid roles waste human talent
- Change is slow because gender is deeply rooted in culture

- **TALCOTT PARSONS: GENDER AND COMPLEMENTARITY**
  - Gender forms a complementary set of roles
    - Links women and men into family units
    - Gives each sex responsibility for carrying out important tasks
  - Gender plays an important part in socialization
    - *Instrumental qualities*
  - Society encourages gender conformity by instilling in men and women fear of rejection
  - Gender integrates society both structurally and morally

- **CRITICAL REVIEW**
  - Functionalism assumes a singular vision of society that is not shared by everyone
  - Parson's analysis ignores the personal strains and social costs of rigid gender roles
  - In the eyes of those seeking sexual equality
    - Gender *complementarity* amounts to little more than women submitting to male domination

---

Social-Conflict Analysis

- Gender involves differences not just in behavior but in power as well
- Similarity between how traditional ideas about gender benefit men and the ways oppression of racial and ethnic minorities benefits white people
- Conventional ideas about gender create division and tension

FRIEDRICH ENGELS: GENDER AND CLASS

- Capitalism intensifies male domination
  - Creates more wealth, which give greater power to men as earners and owners of property
- An expanding capitalist economy depends on turning people into consumers
- Society assigns women the task of maintaining the home to free men to work in factories
- Double exploitation of capitalism
  - Pay men low wages for labor
  - Pay women no wages at all

- CRITICAL REVIEW
  - Sees conventional families supported by traditionalists as morally good
    - A social evil
  - Social-conflict analysis minimizes the extent to which women and men live together cooperatively and often happily
  - Claim that capitalism is the root of gender stratification

---

Gender

	Structural-Functional Approach	Social-Conflict Approach
What is the level of analysis?	Macro-level	Macro-level
What does gender mean?	Parsons described gender in terms of two complementary patterns of behavior: masculine and feminine.	Engels described gender in terms of the power of one sex over the other.
Is gender helpful or harmful?	Helpful. Gender gives men and women distinctive roles and responsibilities that help society operate smoothly. Gender builds social unity as men and women come together to form families.	Harmful. Gender limits people's personal development. Gender divides society by giving power to men to control the lives of women. Capitalism makes patriarchy stronger.

Applying Theory (p. 289)

Feminism

- *The advocacy of social inequality for women and men, in opposition to patriarchy and sexism*
- "First wave" of feminist movement in U.S. began in 1840s
  - Main objective was obtaining the right to vote
- "Second wave" of feminism arose in the 1960s
  - Continues today

Basic Feminist Ideas

1. Working to increase equality
2. Expanding human choice
3. Eliminating gender stratification
4. Ending sexual violence
5. Promoting sexual freedom

Types of Feminism

- *Liberal Feminism*
  - Individuals should be free to develop their own talents and pursue their own interests
- *Socialist Feminism*
  - Capitalism increases patriarchy by concentrating wealth and power in the hands of a small number of men
- **Radical Feminism**
  - Believe that patriarchy is so firmly entrenched that even a socialist revolution would not end it

Feminism

	Liberal	Socialist	Radical
Does it accept the basic order of society?	Yes. Liberal feminism seeks change only to ensure equality of opportunity.	No. Socialist feminism supports an end to social classes and to family gender roles that encourage "domestic slavery."	No. Radical feminism supports an end to the family system.
How do women improve their social standing?	Individually, according to personal ability and effort.	Collectively, through socialist revolution.	Collectively, by working to eliminate gender itself.

Applying Theory (p. 291)

Opposition to Feminism

- Controversial because it calls for significant change
- Provokes criticism and resistance from both men and women who hold conventional ideas about gender
- Men socialized to value strength and dominance feel uneasy about feminist ideals of men as gentle and warm
- African Americans, especially women, express the greatest support of feminist goals

---

- Resistance found in academic circles
- Feminism undervalues the crucial and unique contribution women make to the development of children
- Most opposition to feminism is directed toward its socialist and radical forms
  - Support for liberal feminism is widespread

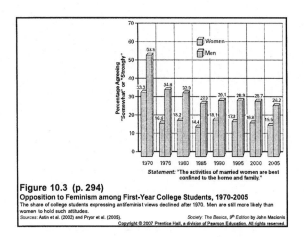

Figure 10.3 (p. 294)
Opposition to Feminism among First-Year College Students, 1970-2005
The share of college students expressing antifeminist views declined after 1970. Men are still more likely than women to hold such attitudes.
Sources: Astin et al. (2002) and Pryor et al. (2005).

Gender: Looking Ahead

- Sociologists can offer only general observations about the likely future of gender and society
- Today's economy depends a great deal on the earnings of women
- Industrialization and advances in computer technology have shifted the nature of work

---

- Birth control technology has given us greater control over reproduction
    - Women's lives are less constrained by unwanted pregnancies
- Many women and men have deliberately pursued social equality
- Greater social changes as more women assume positions of power in corporate and politics
- Despite real change, gender continues to involve controversy
    - Moving to a society where men and women will enjoy equal rights and opportunities

Chapter

11

Race and Ethnicity

LEARNING OBJECTIVES

- To develop an understanding about the biological basis for definitions of race.
- To distinguish between the biological concept of race and the cultural concept of ethnicity.
- To identify the characteristics of a minority group.
- To identify and describe the two forms of prejudice.
- To be familiar with the measurement of prejudice using the Social Distance Scale.
- To identify and describe the four theories of prejudice.
- To distinguish between prejudice and discrimination.
- To provide examples of institutional prejudice and discrimination.
- To see how prejudice and discrimination combine to create a vicious cycle.
- To describe the histories and relative statuses of each of the racial and ethnic groups identified in the text.

CHAPTER OUTLINE

I.   The Social Meaning of Race and Ethnicity
    A.   Race
        1.   Racial Types
        2.   A Trend Toward Mixture
    B.   Ethnicity
    C.   Minorities

II.   Prejudice and Stereotypes
    A.   Measuring Prejudice: The Social Distance Scale
    B.   Racism
    C.   Theories of Prejudice
        1.   Scapegoat Theory
        2.   Authoritarian Personality Theory
        3.   Culture Theory
        4.   Conflict Theory

III.   Discrimination
    A.   Institutional Prejudice and Discrimination
    B.   Prejudice and Discrimination: The Vicious Circle

IV.   Majority and Minority: Patterns of Interaction
        A.   Pluralism
        B.   Assimilation
        C.   Segregation
        D.   Genocide

V.   Race and Ethnicity in the United States
        A.   Native Americans
        B.   White Anglo-Saxon Protestants
        C.   African Americans
        D.   Asian Americans
             1.   Chinese Americans
             2.   Japanese Americans
             3.   Recent Asian Immigrants
        E.   Hispanic Americans
             1.   Mexican Americans
             2.   Puerto Ricans
             3.   Cuban Americans
        F.   Arab Americans
        G.   White Ethnic Americans

VI.   Race and Ethnicity: Looking Ahead

VII.   Making the Grade

RACE AND ETHNICITY

CHAPTER 11

- **What** are race and ethnicity, and how are they created by society?

- **Why** does the United States have so much racial and ethnic diversity?

- **How** are race and ethnicity important dimensions of social inequality today?

The Social Meaning of Race and Ethnicity

- People often confuse race and ethnicity.
- There are now millions of people in the United States who do not think of themselves in terms of a single category but as having a mix of ancestry.

Race

- *A socially constructed category of people who share biologically transmitted traits that members of a society consider important*
- Appeared among human ancestors as a result of living in different regions of the world
- Variety of racial traits found today is the product of migration
- We think of race in biological terms but it is a socially constructed concept

---

- Race is a matter of social definitions and is a highly variable concept
- The meaning and importance of race not only differ from place to place but also change over time
- Today, the Census Bureau allows people to describe themselves using more than one racial category
  - Our society officially recognizes a wide range of multiracial people

---

- *RACIAL TYPES*
  - Scientists invented the concept of race to organize the world's physical diversity
    - Caucasoid
    - Negroid
    - Mongoloid
  - Sociologists consider such terms misleading and harmful
  - There is more genetic variation *within* each category than *between* categories
  - From a biological point of view, knowing people's racial category allows us to predict nothing about them

- Categories allow societies to rank people in a hierarchy
  - Gives some more money, power, and prestige
  - Allows some people to feel they are naturally "better" than others
- Because race matters so much, societies construct racial categories in extreme ways
- *A TREND TOWARD MIXTURE*
  - Genetic traits from around the world have become mixed
  - Today, people are willing to define themselves as multiracial

_____

_____

_____

_____

_____

_____

_____

Ethnicity

- *A shared cultural heritage*
- People define themselves as members of an ethnic category that give a distinctive identity
  - Common ancestors
  - Language
  - Religion
- Like race, ethnicity is socially constructed
- Race is constructed from *biological* traits and ethnicity is constructed from *cultural* traits
- People play up or down ethnicity depending on whether they want to fit in or stand apart

_____

_____

_____

_____

_____

_____

_____

Minorities

- *Any category of people distinguished by physical or cultural difference that a society sets apart and subordinates*
  - Based on race, ethnicity, or both
- Two important characteristics
  - Share a *distinct identity*
  - Experience *subordination*
- Not all members of a minority category are disadvantaged
- Usually make up a small proportion of a society's population
  - Exceptions are South Africa and women in the U.S.

_____

_____

_____

_____

_____

_____

_____

TABLE 11–1

Racial and Ethnic Categories
in the United States, 2000

Racial or Ethnic Classification*	Approximate U.S. Population	Percentage of Total Population
Hispanic descent	**35,305,818**	**12.5%**
Mexican	20,640,711	7.3
Puerto Rican	3,406,178	1.2
Cuban	1,241,685	0.4
Other Hispanic	10,017,244	3.6

Table 11.1a (p. 303, continued on next 4 slides)
Racial and Ethnic Categories in the United States, 2000

Racial or Ethnic Classification*	Approximate U.S. Population	Percentage of Total Population
African descent	**34,658,190**	**12.3**
Nigerian	165,481	0.1
Ethiopian	86,918	<
Cape Verdean	77,103	<
Ghanaian	49,944	<
South African	45,569	<
Native American descent	**2,475,956**	**0.9**
American Indian	1,815,653	0.6
Eskimo	45,919	<
Other Native American	614,384	0.2

Table 11.1b (continued)

Racial or Ethnic Classification*	Approximate U.S. Population	Percentage of Total Population
Asian or Pacific Island descent	**10,641,833**	**3.8**
Chinese	2,432,585	0.9
Filipino	1,850,314	0.7
Asian Indian	1,678,765	0.6
Vietnamese	1,122,528	0.4
Korean	1,076,872	0.4
Japanese	796,700	0.3
Cambodian	171,937	<
Hmong	169,428	<
Laotian	168,707	<
Other Asian or Pacific Islander	1,173,997	0.4

Table 11.1c (continued)

Racial or Ethnic Classification[*]	Approximate U.S. Population	Percentage of Total Population
West Indian descent	1,869,504	0.7
Arab descent	1,202,871	0.4
Non-Hispanic European descent	194,552,774	70.9
German	42,885,162	15.2
Irish	30,528,492	10.8
English	24,515,138	8.7
Italian	15,723,555	5.6
Polish	8,977,444	3.2
French	8,309,908	3.0

Table 11.1d (continued)

Racial or Ethnic Classification[*]	Approximate U.S. Population	Percentage of Total Population
Scottish	4,890,581	1.7
Dutch	4,542,494	1.6
Norwegian	4,477,725	1.6
Two or more races	6,826,228	2.4

[*]People of Hispanic descent may be of any race. Many people also identify with more than one ethnic category. Therefore, figures total more than 100 percent.

< indicates less than 1/10 of 1 percent.

Sources: U.S. Census Bureau (2001, 2002, 2004).

Table 11.1e (continued)

National Map 11.1 (p. 304, detail on next slide)
Where the Minority Majority Already Exists
By 2000, minorities had become a majority in four states – Hawaii, California, New Mexico and Texas – and the District of Columbia. At the other extreme, Vermont and Maine have the lowest share of racial and ethnic minorities (about 2 percent). Why are states with high minority populations located in the South and Southwest? *Source:* "America 2000: A Map of the Mix," *Newsweek*, September 18, 2000, p. 48. Copyright © 2000 Newsweek, Inc. All rights reserved. Reprinted by permission.

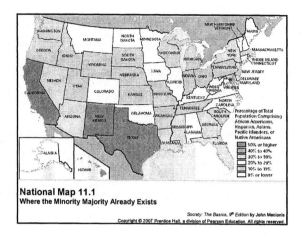

National Map 11.1
Where the Minority Majority Already Exists

Prejudice and Stereotypes

- Prejudice may target people of:
  - A particular social class
  - Sex
  - Sexual orientation
  - Age
  - Political affiliation
  - Race
  - Ethnicity

Prejudice

- A rigid and unfair generalization about an entire category of people
- Prejudices are prejudgments
  - Positive or negative
  - Rooted in culture so everyone has some measure of prejudice
- Often takes the form of *stereotypes*
  - *An exaggerated description applied to every person in some category*
  - Especially harmful to minorities in the workplace

Measuring Prejudice: The Social Distance Scale

- *SOCIAL DISTANCE*
  - *Refers to how closely people are willing to interact with members of some category*
  - *Emory Bogardus*
    - F ound that people felt more social distance from some categories than others
- Recent study found three major findings
  - Student opinion shows a trend toward greater social acceptance
  - People see less difference between various minorities
  - The terrorist attacks of September 11, 2001, may have reduced social acceptance of Arabs and Muslims

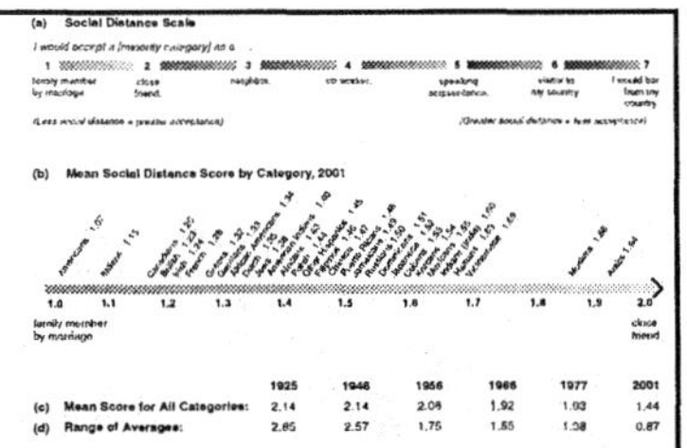

Figure 11.1 (p. 306)
Bogardus Social Distance Research (detail on next slide)

The social distance scale is a good way to measure prejudice. Part (a) illustrates the complete social distance scale, from least social distance at the far left to greatest social distance at the far right. Part (b) shows the mean (average) social distance score received by each category of people in 2001. Part (c) presents the overall mean score (the average of the scores received by all racial and ethnic categories) in specific years. These scores have fallen from 2.14 in 1925 to 1.44 in 2001, showing that students express less social distance toward minorities today than they did in the past. Part (d) shows the range of averages, the difference between the high score of 1.94 for Arabs and the low score of 1.07 for Americans). This figure has also become smaller since 1925, indicating that today's students tend to see fewer differences between various categories of people.
Source: Parrillo & Donoghue (2005).

(a) Social Distance Scale

I would accept a [minority category] as a . . .

1	2	3	4	5	6	7
family member by marriage.	close friend.	neighbor.	co-worker.	speaking acquaintance.	visitor to my country.	I would bar from my country.

(Less social distance = greater acceptance)   *(Greater social distance = less acceptance)*

(b) Mean Social Distance Score by Category, 2001

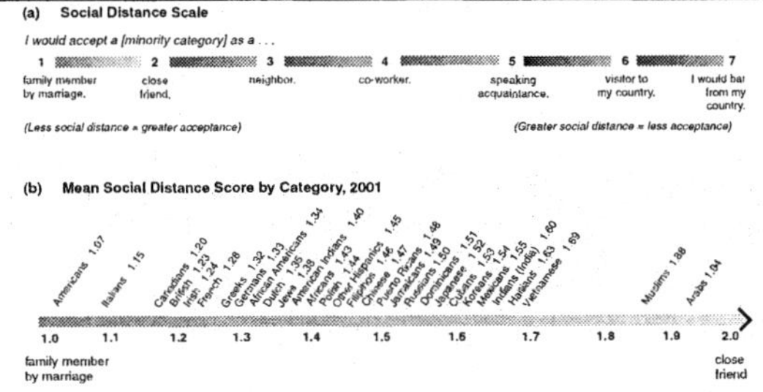

	1925	1946	1956	1966	1977	2001
(c) Mean Score for All Categories:	2.14	2.14	2.08	1.92	1.93	1.44
(d) Range of Averages:	2.85	2.57	1.75	1.55	1.38	0.87

Figure 11.1 (p. 306)
Bogardus Social Distance Research

263

Racism

- *The belief that one racial category is innately superior or inferior to another*
  - Powerful and harmful form of prejudice
  - Existed throughout world history
  - Widespread throughout the history of the U.S.
    - Today, overt racism has decreased because of Martin Luther King, Jr.'s words
      - " not by the color of their skin but by the content of their character"
  - Remains a serious problem
    - Some still argue that certain racial and ethnic categories are smarter than others

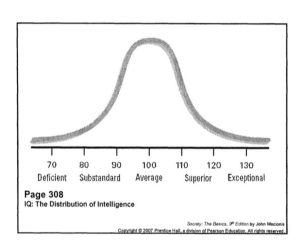

70	80	90	100	110	120	130
Deficient	Substandard		Average		Superior	Exceptional

Page 308
IQ: The Distribution of Intelligence

Theories of Prejudice

- *SCAPEGOAT THEORY*
  - *Prejudice springs from frustration among people who are themselves disadvantaged*
- *SCAPEGOAT*
  - *A person or category of people, typically with little power, whom other people unfairly blame for their own troubles*
  - Minorities often are used as scapegoats
    - T hey have little power
    - U sually are "safe targets"

AUTHORITARIAN PERSONALITY THEORY

- *AUTHORITARIAN PERSONALITY THEORY*
  - *Extreme prejudice is a personality trait of certain individuals*
  - Conclusion supported by research
    - Indicated that people who show strong prejudice toward one minority are intolerant of all minorities
  - *Authoritarian Personalities*
    - Rigidly conform to conventional cultural values
    - See moral issues as clear-cut matters of right and wrong
  - Opposite pattern also found to be true
    - People who express tolerance toward one minority are likely to be accepting of all
    - People with little education and raised by cold and demanding parents tend to develop authoritarian personalities

---

- *CULTURE THEORY*
  - *Claims that although extreme prejudice is found in certain people, some prejudice is found in everyone*
  - **"culture of prejudice"**
    - Taught to view certain categories of people as "better" or "worse" than others
- *CONFLICT THEORY*
  - *Proposes that prejudice is used a a tool by powerful people to oppress others*
  - Another conflict based argument
    - Minorities encourage "race consciousness" to win greater power and privileges

---

Discrimination

- *DISCRIMINATION*
  - *Unequal treatment of various categories of people*
- Prejudice refers to *attitudes*
- Discrimination is a matter of *action*
  - Positive or negative
  - Subtle to blatant

Institutional Prejudice and Discrimination

- ***Bias built into the operation of society's institutions***
  - Schools, hospitals, police, workplace, banks
- People are slow to condemn or recognize institutional prejudice
  - Often involves respected public officials and long-established traditions
  - ***Brown v. Board of Education of Topeka***

Prejudice and Discrimination: The Vicious Cycle

- Prejudice and discrimination reinforce each other
- ***Situations that are defined as real become real in their consequences***
- Stereotypes
  - Real to people who believe them
  - Real to those victimized by them

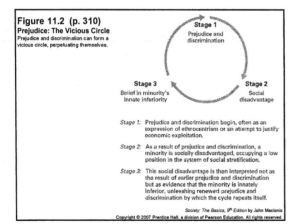

Figure 11.2 (p. 310)
Prejudice: The Vicious Circle
Prejudice and discrimination can form a vicious circle, perpetuating themselves.

Stage 1
Prejudice and discrimination

Stage 3
Belief in minority's innate inferiority

Stage 2
Social disadvantage

Stage 1: Prejudice and discrimination begin, often as an expression of ethnocentrism or an attempt to justify economic exploitation.

Stage 2: As a result of prejudice and discrimination, a minority is socially disadvantaged, occupying a low position in the system of social stratification.

Stage 3: This social disadvantage is then interpreted not as the result of earlier prejudice and discrimination but as evidence that the minority is innately inferior, unleashing renewed prejudice and discrimination by which the cycle repeats itself.

Society: The Basics, 9th Edition by John Macionis
Copyright © 2007 Prentice Hall, a division of Pearson Education. All rights reserved.

Majority and Minority: Patterns of Interaction

- Four models
  - Pluralism
  - Assimilation
  - Segregation
  - Genocide

Pluralism

- *A state in which people of all races and ethnicities are distinct but have equal social standing*
- U.S. is pluralistic to the extent that all people have equal standing under the law
- U.S. not pluralistic for three reasons
  - Although most of us value our cultural heritage, few want to live with only people exactly like ourselves
  - Our tolerance for social diversity goes only so far
  - People of various colors and cultures do not have equal social standing

Assimilation

- *The process by which minorities gradually adopt patterns of the dominant culture*
- Most minorities adopt the dominant culture
  - Avenue to upward social mobility
  - Way to escape prejudice and discrimination directed against more visible foreigners
- Amount of assimilation varies by category
- Assimilation involves changes in ethnicity but not in race

- *Miscegenation*
  - *Biological reproduction by partners of different racial categories*
  - Must occur for racial traits to diminish over generations
  - Though more common, inter-racial marriage still amounts to only 3% of all marriages

Segregation

- *The physical and social separation of categories of people*
- Segregation enforces separation that harms a minority
- **de jure segregation** (by law)
- **de facto segregation** (in fact)
- Continues in the US
- *Hypersegregation*
  - *Having little contact of any kind with people beyond the local community*

Genocide

- **The systematic killing of one category of people by another**
- Deadly form of racism and ethnocentrism
  - Violates every moral standard
- Common throughout history
- Important to recognize the degree to which U.S. society was built
  - Segregation of African Americans
  - Genocide of Native Americans

Race Ethnicity in the United States

- *Give me your tired, poor,*
- *Your huddled masses yearning to breathe free,*
- *The wretched refuse of your teeming shore,*
- *Send these, the homeless, tempest-tossed to me:*
- *I lift my lamp beside the golden door.*
  - *Emma Lazarus (Base of Statue of Liberty)*

Native Americans

- Refers to hundreds of societies who first settled the Western Hemisphere
- 15th century numbered 10 million
- By 1900, numbered 250,000
  - Centuries of conflict and genocide
- Low social standing result of cultural factors
  - Noncompetitive view of life
  - Reluctance to pursue higher education
  - Dark skin made them targets of prejudice and discrimination

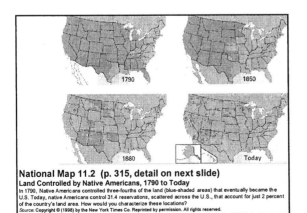

National Map 11.2 (p. 315, detail on next slide)
Land Controlled by Native Americans, 1790 to Today
In 1790, Native Americans controlled three-fourths of the land (blue-shaded areas) that eventually became the U.S. Today, native Americans control 31.4 reservations, scattered across the U.S., that account for just 2 percent of the country's land area. How would you characterize these locations?
Source: Copyright © (1998) by the New York Times Co. Reprinted by permission. All rights reserved.
Society: The Basics, 9th Edition by John Macionis

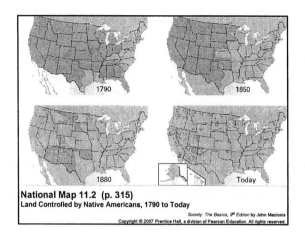

National Map 11.2 (p. 315)
Land Controlled by Native Americans, 1790 to Today

TABLE 11-2

The Social Standing of Native Americans, 2000

	Native Americans	Entire U.S. Population
Median family income	$33.144*	$50,891
Percentage in poverty	25.7%*	11.3%
Completion of four or more years of college (age 25 and over)	11.5%	24.4%

*Data are for 1999.

Sources: U.S. Census Bureau (2004, 2006).

Table 11.2 (p. 316)
The Social Standing of Native Americans, 2000

White Anglo-Saxon Protestants

- Most are of English ancestry
  - Includes Scotland and Wales
- Not subject to prejudice and discrimination
- Cultural legacy
  - English dominant language
  - Protestantism dominant religion
- Historical dominance is evident
  - Widespread use of "race" and "ethnicity" to describe everyone but them

African Americans

- Slavery was foundation of southern colonies plantation system
- 400,000 forcibly transported to U.S.
- Filth, disease, and suicide killed many
- No control over their lives
- Declaration of Independence did not apply to African Americans
- **"American Dilemma"**
  - *Democratic society's denial of basic rights and freedoms to an entire category of people*

- Resolution of the dilemma
  - African Americans defined as naturally inferior and undeserving of equality
- 13th Amendment outlawed slavery
- 14th Amendment granted citizenship to all people born in the U.S.
- 15th Amendment gave the right to vote
- *Jim Crow Laws*
  - *Institutionalized discrimination that segregated U.S. society into two racial castes*
- 20th century brought dramatic changes

- 1950s and 1960s
  - National civil rights movement
- *Black Power Movement*
  - *Gave African Americans sense of pride and purpose*
- Despite gains, continue to occupy a lower social position in U.S.
- Black unemployment twice as high as white unemployment
  - Factory jobs vital to central cities lost to other countries
- Remarkable educational progress since 1980

- Political clout has greatly increased
- People of African ancestry have struggled for social equality for 400 years
- Discrimination is illegal and research documents long-term decline in prejudice against African Americans
- Racial hierarchy persists

TABLE 11-3

The Social Standing of African Americans, 2005

	African Americans[a]	Entire U.S. Population
Median family income	$35,464	$56,194
Percentage in poverty	24.9%	12.6%
Completion of four or more years of college (age 25 and over)	17.6%	27.7%

[a] For comparison with other tables in this chapter, 2000 data are as follows: median family income, $34,204; percentage in poverty, 22.1%; completion of four or more years of college, 16.6%.

Sources: U.S. Census Bureau (2000, 2001, 2006).

Table 11.3 (p. 318)
The Social Standing of African Americans, 2005

Asian Americans

- Category marked by enormous cultural diversity
- 4% of U.S. population
- Commanded attention and respect as high achievers
- **"Model Minority"** stereotype
  - Misleading because it hides the differences in class standards and poverty found among their ranks

- *CHINESE AMERICANS*
  - Immigration began in 1849 with the gold rush
  - Economic hard times led to prejudice and discrimination
  - **"Yellow Peril"**
    - Laws passed to bar from many occupations
  - Chinese men outnumbered Chinese women twenty to one
    - High demand of Chinese women led to the loss of their natural submissiveness
  - Racial hostility
    - Moved East to urban China towns
    - Traditions and kinship networks *(Clans)*

- WWII need for labor
  - Led to end of ban on Chinese immigration
- By 1950, many experienced upward social mobility
  - Hold high prestige positions
  - Science and information technology
- Despite success, Chinese Americans still deal with subtle and sometimes blatant prejudice and discrimination
  - Poverty still high among those socially isolated in Chinatowns

---

Japanese Americans

- Immigration began slowly in the 1860s
- As number of immigrants increased to California, white hostility increased
- Differed from Chinese immigrants in three ways
  - Fewer Japanese so they escaped some of the hostility directed at the Chinese
  - Japanese knew more about the U.S. than the Chinese so assimilated better
  - Japanese preferred rural farming which made them less visible

- Japanese faced their greatest crisis after Pearl Harbor
  - Rage directed at the Japanese living in the U.S.
  - Detained in military camps by Executive Order
- Internment was criticized
  - Targeted an entire group of people
  - 2/3rds of those imprisoned were *Nisei* (U.S. citizens)
  - US also at war with Germany and Italy but no comparable action was taken against people of German and Italian ancestry

---

- Internment led to the economic devastation of Japanese Americans
- Internment ended in 1944
  - 1988 Congress awarded $20,000 to each victim for compensation
- 1999, median income of Japanese Americans was 40% above national average
- Upward social mobility encouraged cultural assimilation
  - Many abandoned their traditions
  - Some are still caught between two worlds

Recent Asian Immigrants

- Koreans, Filipinos, Indians, Vietnamese, Guamanians, and Samoans
- Overall Asian American population increased by 48% between 1990 and 2000
- Many have a strong entrepreneurial spirit
  - More likely than Latinos, three times more likely than African Americans, and eight times more likely than Native Americans to own and operate small businesses

- Japanese closest to having achieved social acceptance
- Surveys reveal greater prejudice against Asian Americans than against African Americans
- Many live in Hawaii, California, or New York
  - Incomes are high but so are costs of living
  - Many Asian Americans remain poor

TABLE 11–4
The Social Standing of Asian Americans, 2005

	All Asian Americans**	Chinese Americans*	Japanese Americans*	Korean Americans*	Filipino Americans*	Entire U.S. Population
Median family income	$68,957	$60,058	$70,849	$47,624	$65,189	$56,194
Percentage in poverty	11.1%	13.2%	9.5%	14.4%	6.2%	12.6%
Completion of four or more years of college (age 25 and over)	49.4%	48.1%	41.9%	43.8%	43.8%	27.7%

*Income data are for 1999; poverty and college completion data are for 2000.
**For comparison with other tables in this chapter, 2000 data for all Asians are as follows: median family income, $62,617; percentage in poverty, 10.6%; completion of four or more years of college, 43.9%.
Source: U.S. Census Bureau (2000, 2001, 2006).

Table 11.4 (p. 320)
The Social Standing of Asian Americans, 2005

Society: The Basics, 9th Edition by John Macionis

Hispanic Americans/ Latinos

- Number of Hispanics in U.S. topped 35 million in 2000
  - Surpassed number of African Americans at 12.3%
  - Now the largest racial or ethnic minority
- Hispanics are a cluster of distinct populations
  - Each identify with a particular ancestral nation
- Median family income is below national average

- MEXICAN AMERICANS
  - Descendants of people who lived in the part of Mexico annexed by U.S.
  - Most are recent immigrants
  - Today, more immigrants come from Mexico than from any other country
  - Almost 1/4th of Chicano families are poor
  - Still have a high dropout rate and receive less schooling than U.S. adults as a whole

- PUERTO RICANS
  - Island became U.S. possession after the Spanish-American war
  - Became citizens in 1917
  - Most live in New York City
  - Adjusting to cultural patterns is a major challenge
  - Darker skin leads to more prejudice and discrimination – most return to Puerto Rico
  - "revolving door" pattern limits assimilation
  - Most speak only Spanish which limits economic opportunity
  - Most socially disadvantaged Hispanic minority

- CUBAN AMERICANS
  - 400,000 Cubans fled to U.S. after Castro revolution in 1959
  - Most settled with others in Miami
  - Many were highly educated business and professional people
  - Median income above that of other Hispanics but still below the national average
  - 1.2 million living in U.S. today
  - Cubans are most likely to speak Spanish in their homes
  - Cultural distinctiveness and high visibility communities provoke some hostility

TABLE 11-5

The Social Standing of Hispanic Americans, 2005

	All Hispanics**	Mexican Americans*	Puerto Ricans*	Cuban Americans*	Entire U.S. Population
Median family income	$37,867	$32,263	$34,519	$44,847	$56,194
Percentage in poverty	21.8%	24.1%	23.7%	14.4%	12.6%
Completion of four or more years of college (age 25 and over)	12.1%	7.9%	14.1%	24.8%	27.7%

*Income and poverty data are for 2005; college completion data are for 2005.
**For comparison with other tables in this chapter, 2000 data for all Hispanics are as follows: median family income, $35,050; percentage in poverty, 21.2%; completion of four or more years of college, 10.6%.
Sources: U.S. Census Bureau (2000, 2001, 2005, 2006).

Table 11.5 (p. 324)
The Social Standing of Hispanic Americans, 2005

Arab Americans

- A U.S. minority that is increasing in size
- The **"Arab World"** includes twenty-two nations
- Not all are Arabs
  - Berber of Morocco; and Kurds of Iraq
- Arab cultures differ from society to society
  - Share widespread use of Arabic alphabet and language
  - Islam is dominant religion

- **"Arab"** is an ethnic category
- **"Muslim"** is a follower of Islam
- Majority of people living in Arab countries are Muslim but some Arabs are Christians or followers of other religions
- Official number given by government is 1.2 million
  - Many do not declare ethnicity so number could be twice as high
- Arab Americans choose to downplay their ethnicity to avoid prejudice and discrimination

- Terrorist attacks against U.S. and other nations has fueled a stereotype that links being Arab or Muslim with being a terrorist
  - Unfair because it blames an entire category for the actions of a few
  - Explains why social distance research show students express more negative attitudes toward Arabs that any other racial or ethnic category
  - Explains why Arabs have been the target of hate crimes
  - Explains why many feel they are subject to "ethnic profiling"
    - Threatens their privacy and civil liberties

TABLE 11–6

The Social Standing of Arab Americans, 1999

	Arab Americans	Entire U.S. Population
Median family income	$52,318	$50,046
Percentage in poverty	16.7%	12.4%
Completion of four or more years of college (age 25 and over)	41.2%*	24.4%*

*Data for for 2000.

Source: U.S. Census Bureau (2005).

Table 11.6 (p. 325)
The Social Standing of Arab Americans, 1999

Society: The Basics, 9th Edition by John Macionis

National Map 11.3 (p. 322, detail on next four slides)
The Concentration of Hispanics or Latinos, African Americans, Asian Americans, and Arab Americans, by County, 2000

In 2000, people of Hispanic or Latino descent represented 12.5 percent of the U.S. population, compared with 12.3 percent African Americans, 3.6 percent Asian Americans, and 0.4 percent Arab Americans. These maps show the geographic distribution of these categories of people in 2000. Comparing them, we see that the southern half of the U.S. is home to far more minorities than the northern half. But do they all concentrate in the same areas? What patterns do the maps reveal?

Sources: U.S. Census Bureau (2001, 2003).

Society: The Basics, 9th Edition by John Macionis

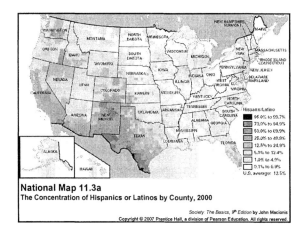

National Map 11.3a
The Concentration of Hispanics or Latinos by County, 2000

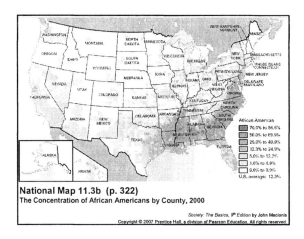

National Map 11.3b (p. 322)
The Concentration of African Americans by County, 2000

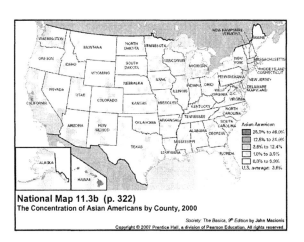

National Map 11.3b (p. 322)
The Concentration of Asian Americans by County, 2000

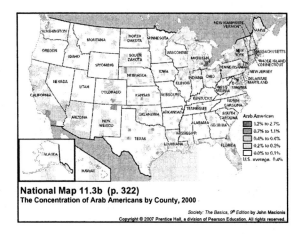

White Ethnic Americans

- Term **"White Ethnics"**
  - Recognizes ethnic heritage and social disadvantage of many white people
- Non-WASP's
  - Ireland, Poland, Germany, Italy, or other European countries
- Endured their share of prejudice and discrimination
- Congress enacted quota system limiting immigration

- Many formed supportive residential enclaves
- Some gained footholds in certain businesses and trades
- Many still live in traditional working class neighborhoods
- Those who prospered gradually assimilated
- Many descendants now make enough money to live comfortable lives
  - Ethnic heritage is now a source of pride

Race and Ethnicity: Looking Ahead

- U.S. has been, and will remain, a land of immigrants
- New arrivals face the same prejudice and discrimination experienced by those who came before them
- Recent years have witnessed *Xenophobia*
  - *Rising hostility toward foreigners*

- Today's immigrants try to blend into U.S. society without completely giving up their culture
- New arrivals still carry the traditional hope that their racial and ethnic diversity can be a source of pride rather than a badge of inferiority

Chapter 12

Economics and Politics

- To identify the elements of the economy.
- To compare the economic systems of capitalism, state capitalism, socialism, and democratic socialism.
- To explain the difference between socialism and communism.
- To describe the general characteristics and trends of work in the U.S. postindustrial society.
- To compare the four principal kinds of political systems.
- To describe the nature of the American political system of government, and discuss the principal characteristics of the political spectrum of the U.S.
- To identify the factors that increase the likelihood of war.
- To recognize the historical pattern of militarism in the United States and around the world, and to consider factors that can be used to pursue peace.

CHAPTER OUTLINE

ECONOMICS AND POLITICS

CHAPTER 12

- **What** is a social institution?

- **How** does change in the economy reshape society?

- **Why** do some critics say that the United States is not really a democracy?

THE ECONOMY: HISTORICAL OVERVIEW

- *SOCIAL INSTITUTION*
  - *A major sphere of social life, or societal subsystem, organized to meet human needs*
- *ECONOMY*
  - *The social institution that organizes a society's production, distribution, and consumption of goods and services*
  - *Goods* are commodities ranging from necessities
  - *Services* are activities that benefit people

The Agricultural Revolution

- Harnessing animals to plows 5,000 years ago led to the development of agriculture
  - 50 times more productive than hunting and gathering
- Four factors
  - Agricultural technology
  - Specialized work
  - Permanent settlements
  - Trade
    - Made the economy a distinct social institution

The Industrial Revolution

- Brought five changes to the economy
  - New sources of energy
  - Centralization of work in factories
  - Manufacturing and mass production
  - Specialization
  - Wage labor
- New laws banned child labor, set minimum wage levels, improved workplace safety, and extended schooling and political rights to a large segment of the population

The Information Revolution and Postindustrial Society

- Postindustrial Economy
  - A productive system based on service work and high technology
- Driving economic change: 3rd technological breakthrough
  - Computer
  - Three important changes
    - From tangible products to ideas
    - From mechanical skills to literacy skills
    - From factories to almost anywhere

Sectors of the Economy

- *PRIMARY SECTOR*
  - *The part of the economy that draws raw materials from the natural environment*
- *SECONDARY SECTOR*
  - *The part of the economy that transforms raw materials into manufactured goods*
- *TERTIARY SECTOR*
  - *The part of the economy that involves services rather than goods*

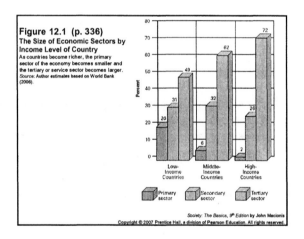

Figure 12.1 (p. 336)
The Size of Economic Sectors by Income Level of Country
As countries become richer, the primary sector of the economy becomes smaller and the tertiary or service sector becomes larger.
Source: Author estimates based on World Bank (2006).

The Global Economy

- *GLOBAL ECONOMY*
  - *Economic activity that crosses national borders*
  - 1st – global division of labor
  - 2nd – more products pass through more than one nation
  - 3rd – national governments no longer control the economic activity that takes place within their borders
  - 4th – small number of businesses, operating internationally, now control vast share of world's economic activity
  - 5th – economic globalization affects lives of U.S. workers

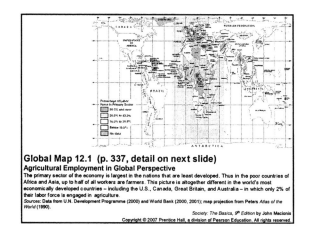

Global Map 12.1 (p. 337, detail on next slide)
Agricultural Employment in Global Perspective
The primary sector of the economy is largest in the nations that are least developed. Thus in the poor countries of Africa and Asia, up to half of all workers are farmers. This picture is altogether different in the world's most economically developed countries – including the U.S., Canada, Great Britain, and Australia – in which only 2% of their labor force is engaged in agriculture.
Sources: Data from U.N. Development Programme (2000) and World Bank (2000, 2001); map projection from Peters *Atlas of the World* (1990).

Society: The Basics, 9th Edition by John Macionis

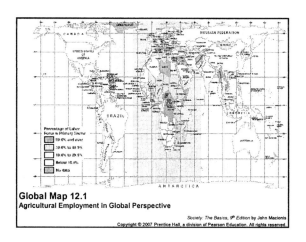

Global Map 12.1
Agricultural Employment in Global Perspective

Society: The Basics, 9th Edition by John Macionis

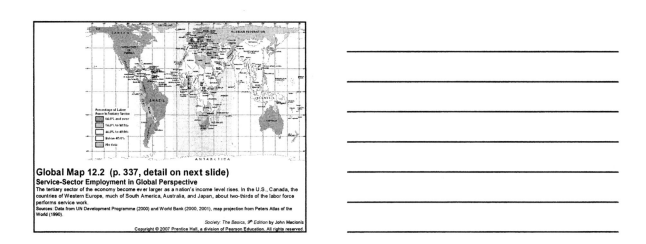

Global Map 12.2 (p. 337, detail on next slide)
Service-Sector Employment in Global Perspective
The tertiary sector of the economy become ever larger as a nation's income level rises. In the U.S., Canada, the countries of Western Europe, much of South America, Australia, and Japan, about two-thirds of the labor force performs service work.
Sources: Data from UN Development Programme (2000) and World Bank (2000, 2001), map projection from Peters Atlas of the World (1990).

Society: The Basics, 9th Edition by John Macionis

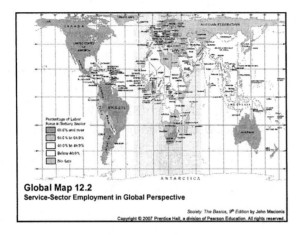

Global Map 12.2
Service-Sector Employment in Global Perspective

Economic Systems: Paths to Justice

- Two general economic models
  - Capitalism
  - Socialism
- No nation in the world is completely one or the other
  - Two ends of a continuum along which all real-world economies can be located

---

Capitalism

- *An economic system in which natural resources and means of producing goods and services are privately owned*
- Ideal capitalism has three distinctive features
  - Private ownership of property
  - Pursuit of personal profit
  - Competition and consumer choice
    - *Laissez-faire economy*
      - *P ure free-market system with no government interference*
- Capitalist system **"Justice"**
  - *Freedom of the marketplace according to self-interest*

- U.S. considered a capitalist system
  - Most businesses are privately owned
  - Not completely capitalist because government has large role in the economy
- Government owns and operates number of businesses
  - Almost all schools, roads, parks, museums, U.S. Postal Service, Amtrak railroad, entire U.S. Military
  - Played a role in the building of the Internet
  - Uses taxation and other forms of regulation to influence what companies produce

_____

- U.S. government
  - Sets minimum wage levels
  - Workplace safety standards
  - Regulates corporate mergers
  - Provides farm price supports
  - Gives income
    - Social security, public assistance, student loans, veteran's benefits
- Local, state, and federal governments are the nation's biggest employer
  - 16% non-farm labor force on payroll

_____

Socialism

- *An economic system in which natural resources and the means of producing goods and services are collectively owned*
- Three opposite features to capitalism
  - Collective ownership of property
  - Pursuit of collective goals
  - Government control of the economy
    - Centrally controlled or command economy operated by the government
- Socialist **"Justice"**
  - *Not competing to gain wealth but meeting everyone's basic needs in an equal manner*

- Paying little in wages and benefits to boost company profits in a socialist economy
  - Putting profits before people
  - Considered unjust
- World socialism declined during 1990s
  - Eastern Europe and former Soviet Union moving toward market system
- Nations in South America
  - Elected leaders moving national economies in a socialist direction

---

Welfare Capitalism and State Capitalism

- *Welfare Capitalism*
  - *An economic and political system that combines a mostly market-based economy with extensive social welfare programs*
  - Government owns some of the largest industries
    - Transportation, mass media, and health care
  - Sweden and Italy
    - Economic production is *nationalized* (State controlled)
    - High taxation aimed at the rich funds social welfare programs

---

- *State Capitalism*
  - *An economic and political system in which companies are privately owned but cooperate closely with the government*
  - Japan, Singapore, South Korea
  - Government work in partnership with large companies
    - Supply financial assistance and control foreign imports
    - Help their businesses compete in world markets

Relative Advantages of Capitalism and Socialism

- Comparing economies is difficult
  - All countries mix capitalism and socialism
  - Nations differ
    - In cultural attitudes toward work
    - Natural resources
    - Technological development
    - Patterns of trade

- **ECONOMIC PRODUCTIVITY**
- **Gross Domestic Product (GDP)**
  - *The total value of all goods and services produced annually*
- **ECONOMIC EQUALITY**
  - *Distribution of resources within the population*
  - Important measure of how well an economic system works
- **PERSONAL FREEDOM**
  - Capitalism emphasizes *freedom to pursue self-interest* and depends on freedom of producers and consumers
  - Socialism emphasizes *freedom from basic want*

Changes in Socialist and Capitalist Countries

- Capitalist economies far out-produced socialist counterparts
- Soviet socialism rigidly controlled the media and restricted individual freedoms
- Socialism did away with economic elites but increased the power of political elites
- Market economy brought increase in economic inequality

Work in the Postindustrial U.S. Economy

- Economic change occurring around the world and in the U.S.
- 2005
  - 142 million people in U.S., 2/3rds age 16 and older were working for income
  - 69.6% of men and 56.2% women had jobs

The Changing Workplace

- Family farm replaced by Corporate Agribusiness
- Industrialization swelled ranks of blue-collar workers
- 1950 white-collar revolution moved most workers from factories to service occupations
- 2005
  - 76% of labor force worked in service sector
  - 92% of new jobs created in this sector

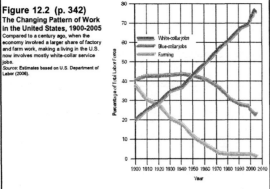

Figure 12.2 (p. 342)
The Changing Pattern of Work in the United States, 1900-2005
Compared to a century ago, when the economy involved a larger share of factory and farm work, making a living in the U.S. now involves mostly white-collar service jobs.
Source: Estimates based on U.S. Department of Labor (2006).

Labor Unions

- Decline in Labor Unions
  - Organizations that seek to improve wages and working conditions
- Widespread decline in membership
  - Shrinking industrial sector of the economy
  - Newer service jobs less likely to be unionized
- Long term future gains for unions depend on
  - Ability of unions to adapt to the new global economy
  - The need to build new international alliances

Professions

- *PROFESSION*
  - *A prestigious white-collar occupation that requires extensive formal education*
  - A *profession*, or public declaration, is made of willingness to work according to certain principles
- Four characteristics
  - Theoretical knowledge
  - Self-regulating practice
  - Authority over clients
  - Community orientation rather than self-interest

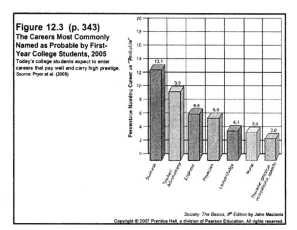

Figure 12.3 (p. 343)
The Careers Most Commonly Named as Probable by First-Year College Students, 2005
Today's college students expect to enter careers that pay well and carry high prestige.
Source: Pryor et al. (2005)

Self-Employment

- *Earning a living without being on the payroll of a large organization*
  - Was once common in the U.S.
  - Most self-employed today are small business owners
  - More likely to have blue-collar than white-collar jobs
  - Women own nearly 40% of U.S. small businesses
    - Trend is rising

_____

_____

_____

_____

_____

_____

Unemployment and Underemployment

- Every society has some level of unemployment
- Not just individual, also caused by the economy
  - Occupations become obsolete
  - Companies downsize; firms close
  - Economic recession
- African American unemployment twice the rate of Whites

_____

_____

_____

_____

_____

_____

- Economic downturn after 2000 encouraged underemployment
- Bankruptcies of large corporations
  - Left millions of workers with lower salaries
  - Jobs kept by agreeing to cuts in pay or loss of benefits

_____

_____

_____

_____

_____

_____

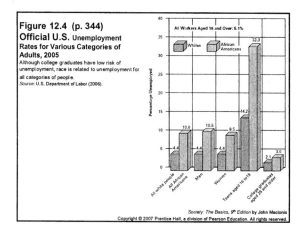

Figure 12.4 (p. 344)
Official U.S. Unemployment
Rates for Various Categories of
Adults, 2005
Although college graduates have low risk of
unemployment, race is related to unemployment for
all categories of people.
Source: U.S. Department of Labor (2006).

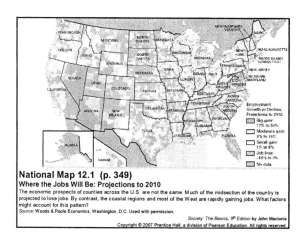

National Map 12.1 (p. 349)
Where the Jobs Will Be: Projections to 2010
The economic prospects of counties across the U.S. are not the same. Much of the midsection of the country is
projected to lose jobs. By contrast, the coastal regions and most of the West are rapidly gaining jobs. What factors
might account for this pattern?
Source: Woods & Poole Economics, Washington, D.C. Used with permission.

Workplace Diversity: Race and Gender

- Nations proportion of minorities rising rapidly
  - African American population increasing faster than White
  - Asian American population even greater
  - Increase in Hispanics greatest of all
- More workers will be women and minorities
- Employers will have to develop programs and policies
- Encourage all to work together effectively and respectfully

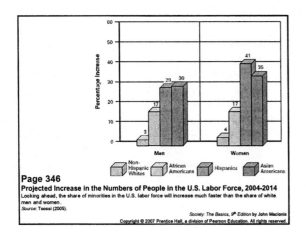

Page 346
Projected Increase in the Numbers of People in the U.S. Labor Force, 2004-2014
Looking ahead, the share of minorities in the U.S. labor force will increase much faster than the share of white men and women.
Source: Toossi (2005).

New Information Technology and Work

- Information revolution is changing what people do in a number of ways
  - Computers are deskilling labor
  - Computers are making work more abstract
  - Computers limit workplace interaction
  - Computers increase employer's control of workers
  - Computers allow companies to relocate work
- Technology is not socially neutral

Corporations

- *An organization with a legal existence, including rights and liabilities, separate from that of its members*
- Incorporating makes an organization a legal entity
  - Protects the wealth of owners from lawsuits
  - Lower tax rate on the company's profits

Economic Concentration

- Most U.S .corporations are small
  - Assets less than $500,000
- Largest corporations dominate nations economy
- ExxonMobil
  - Largest U.S. corporation
  - 208 billion in total assets

Conglomerates and Corporate Linkages

- *CONGLOMERATE*
  - *Giant corporations composed of smaller corporations*
  - Form as
    - Corporations enter new markets
    - Spin off new companies
    - Mergers
- Conglomerates are linked because they own each other's stock

- Corporations are linked through
  - *INTERLOCKING DIRECTORATES*
    - *Networks of people who serve as directors of many corporations*
- Linkages encourage illegal activity
  - Price fixing
    - Companies share information about their pricing policies

297

Corporations: Are They Competitive

- **MONOPOLY**
  - *The domination of a market by a single producer*
  - Forbidden by federal law
- **OLIGOPOLY**
  - *The domination of a market by a few producers*
  - Legal and common
- Federal government seeks regulation to protect the public interest
  - Often too little, too late resulting in harm to millions

_____

_____

_____

_____

_____

_____

Corporations and the Global Economy

- Corporations now account for most of the planet's economic output
- Biggest are based in U.S., Japan, and Western Europe
  - Their marketplace is the entire world
- Know that poor countries contain most of the world's people and resources
  - Modernization theory – raises living standards
  - Dependency theorists – increase inequality

_____

_____

_____

_____

_____

_____

The Economy: Looking Ahead

- Society must face the challenge of providing millions with language and computer skills needed in the new economy
- Second transformation is the expansion of the global economy
- World analysts are rethinking conventional economic models

_____

_____

_____

_____

_____

_____

- Two conclusions on long-term effects
  - The economic future of U.S. and other nations will be played out in the global arena
  - Imperative that we address the urgent challenges of global inequality and population increase
- Gap between rich and poor may steer our planet toward peace or war

Politics: Historical Overview

- *POLITICS*
  - *The social institution that distributes power, sets a society's goals, and makes decisions*
- *POWER*
  - *The ability to achieve desired ends despite resistance from others*
- *GOVERNMENT*
  - *A formal organization that directs the political life of a society*

- *AUTHORITY*
  - *Power that people perceive as legitimate rather than coercive*
  - *TRADITIONAL AUTHORITY*
    - *Power legitimized by respect for long established cultural patterns*
    - May seem almost sacred
    - Declines as societies industrialize
  - *RATIONAL-LEGAL AUTHORITY*
    - Sometimes called *BUREAUCRATIC AUTHORITY*
    - *Power legitimized by rationally enacted law*
      - A uthority flows from offices in governments

- *CHARISMATIC AUTHORITY*
  - *Power legitimized by the extraordinary personal qualities (charisma) of a leader*
  - These leaders aim to radically transform society
    - A lways controversial
    - F ew die of old age
  - *ROUTINIZATION OF CHARISMA*
    - *T he transformation of charismatic authority into some combination of traditional and bureaucratic authority*

Politics in Global Perspective

- Four categories
  - Monarchy
  - Democracy
  - Authoritarianism
  - Totalitarianism

Monarchy

- *A political system in which a single family rules from generation to generation*
- Commonly found in agrarian societies
- Today, 28 nations have royal families
- *Absolute Monarchs*
  - *Claim a monopoly of power based on divine right*
  - Exercise virtually absolute control over their people
- *Constitutional Monarchies*
  - *Monarchs are little more than symbolic heads of state – nobility reigns; elected officials rule*

Democracy

- A political system that gives power to the people as a whole
- Representative Democracy
  - Authority is in the hands of leaders who compete for office in elections
- Most high-income countries claim democracy
  - Industrialization and democracy go together
  - Both require a literate populace
- Democracy and rational-legal authority are linked

Global Map 12.3 (p. 353, detail on next slide)
Political Freedom in Global Perspective
In 2005, a total of 89 of the world's 192 nations, containing 46% of all people, were politically "free"; that is, they offered their citizens extensive political rights and civil liberties. Another 58 countries, which included 18 percent of the world's people, were "partly free," with more limited rights and liberties. The remaining 45 nations, home to 36% of humanity, fall into the category of "not free." In these countries, government sharply restricts individual initiative. Between 1980 and 2005, democracy made significant gains, largely in Latin America and Eastern Europe. In Asia, India (containing 1 billion people) returned to the "free" category in 1999. In 2000, Mexico joined the ranks of nations considered "free" for the first time.
Source: Freedom House (2006).

Society: The Basics, 9th Edition by John Macionis

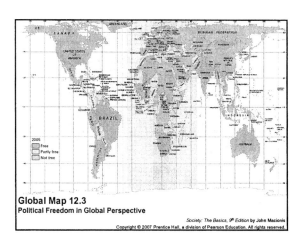

Global Map 12.3
Political Freedom in Global Perspective

Society: The Basics, 9th Edition by John Macionis

- High-income countries are not truly democratic
- Two reasons:
  - Problem of bureaucracy
  - Economic inequality
- Democratic nations do provide many rights and freedoms

Authoritarianism

- ***A political system that denies the people participation in government***
- Indifferent to people's needs
- Offers people no voice in selecting leaders
- Absolute monarchies
  - Saudi Arabia
  - Bahrain
  - Military Junta of Ethiopia

Totalitarianism

- ***A highly centralized political system that extensively regulates people's lives***
- Emerged as governments gained the ability to exert rigid control over a population
- Have a total concentration of power
  - Allow no organized opposition
- Socialization in totalitarian societies is highly political
  - Seek obedience and commitment to the system

A Global Political System?

- Though most of today's economic activity is international
- World remains divided in nation-states
- United Nations (1945) was a small step towards global government
  - Political role in world affairs is limited
- Politics has become a global process
  - Multinationals represent a new political order
- Information revolution moved national politics onto the world stage

---

- *Nongovernmental Organizations (NGO's)*
  - Amnesty International
  - Greenpeace
  - Seek to advance global issues
    - Human rights
  - Will continue to play a role in expanding the global political culture

---

Politics in the United States

- U.S. is a representative democracy
- Political development reflects cultural history as well as capitalist economy

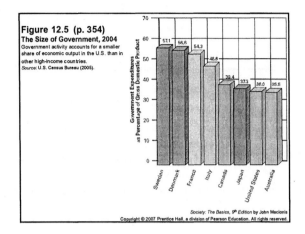

Figure 12.5 (p. 354)
The Size of Government, 2004
Government activity accounts for a smaller
share of economic output in the U.S. than in
other high-income countries.
Source: U.S. Census Bureau (2005).

U.S. Culture and the Rise of the Welfare State

- Political culture of U.S. summed in one word
  - *Individualism*
- *Welfare State*
  - *A system of government agencies and programs that provides benefits to the population*
  - Some programs especially important to the poor
  - Result of a gradual increase in the size and scope of government

---

The Political Spectrum

- Ranges
  - Extremely liberal on the left
  - Extremely conservative on the right
- Helps in understanding the ways people think about the economy
- *Economic Issues*
  - *Focus on economic inequality*
  - Liberals support extensive government regulation to reduce income inequality
  - Conservatives want limited government
    - Allow market forces more freedom

- *Social Issues*
  - *Moral questions about how people ought to live*
  - Social Liberals
    - Support equal rights and opportunities for all categories of people
    - View abortion as a matter of individual choice
    - Oppose the death penalty because it has been unfairly applied to minorities
  - Social Conservatives
    - "Family values" agenda
    - Support traditional gender roles
    - Oppose gay families, affirmative action
    - Condemn abortion as morally wrong
    - Support the death penalty

- Republican Party
  - Conservative on economic and social issues
- Democratic Party is more liberal
- Both support big government when it advances their aims
- Most people mix conservative and liberal attitudes
- High-income people hold conservative views
- Low-income are the opposite
- Women tend to be more liberal than men

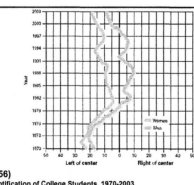

Figure 12.6 (p. 356)
Left-Right Political Identification of College Students, 1970-2003
Student attitudes moved to the right after 1970 and shifted left in the mid-1990s. College women tend to be a bit more liberal than college men.
Sources: Astin et al. (2002) and Sax et al. (2003).
Society: The Basics, 9th Edition by John Macionis

Party Identification

- Party identification in this country is weak
- Reason why each of the major two gains or loses power from election to election
  - 44% favor Democratic Party
  - 38% favor Republican Party
  - 18% are Independent
- Rural-Urban Divide
- Urban areas typically vote Democratic
- Rural areas vote Republican

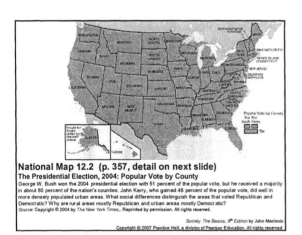

National Map 12.2 (p. 357, detail on next slide)
The Presidential Election, 2004: Popular Vote by County
George W. Bush won the 2004 presidential election with 51 percent of the popular vote, but he received a majority in about 80 percent of the nation's counties. John Kerry, who gained 48 percent of the popular vote, did well in more densely populated urban areas. What social differences distinguish the areas that voted Republican and Democratic? Why are rural areas mostly Republican and urban areas mostly Democratic?
Source: Copyright © 2004 by The New York Times,. Reprinted by permission. All rights reserved.

Society: The Basics, 9th Edition by John Macionis

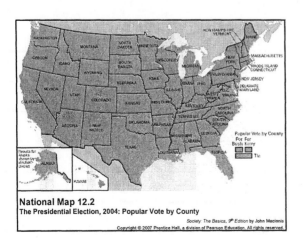

National Map 12.2
The Presidential Election, 2004: Popular Vote by County
Society: The Basics, 9th Edition by John Macionis

Special-Interest Groups

- *People organized to address some economic or social issue*
- Employ *LOBBYISTS* to support goals
- *Political Action Committees (PAC's)*
  - *Formed by special interest groups to raise and spend money in support of political aims*
- *Does having the most money matter in public elections?* *YES!*
  - 90% of the candidates with the most money end up winning

Voter Apathy

- Disturbing fact
  - Many people don't care enough about politics to vote
- Women and men are equally likely to vote
- People over 65 twice as likely to vote than college age adults
- Apathy amounts to indifference
  - Most people are content with their lives
- Apathy reflects alienation from politics
  - People deeply dissatisfied with society

Should Convicted Criminals Vote?

- All states except Vermont and Maine have laws that bar felons from voting
  - 5 million people in U.S. have lost their right to vote
- Legislatures in most of the fifty states say that government can take away political rights as a type of punishment
- May be politically motivated
  - Convicted felons show 2-1 preference for Democratic over Republican candidates

Theoretical Analysis of Power in Society

- Sociologists have long debated how power is spread throughout the U.S. population
- Decision making is complex and often takes place behind closed doors
- Three competing models
  - Pluralist Model
  - Power Elite Model
  - Marxist Model

The Pluralist Model

- *An analysis of politics that sees power as spread among many competing interest groups*
- Pluralists claim:
  - Politics is an arena of negotiation
  - Organizations operate as veto groups
    - Realizing some goals but mostly keeping opponents from achieving all of theirs
  - Political process relies heavily on creating alliances and compromises so that policies gain wide support

The Power Elite Model

- An analysis of politics that sees power as concentrated among the rich
- Based on social-conflict theory
- Upper class holds most of society's wealth, prestige, power
- Power elite in charge of three major sectors of U.S. society
  - Economy, government, and military
- Move from one sector to another building power as they go

- Power-elite theorists say U.S. is not a democracy
  - Economic and political system give a few people so much power that the average person's voice cannot be heard
  - Reject pluralist idea that various center of power serve as checks and balances on one another

The Marxist Model

- An analysis that explains politics in terms of the operation of a society's economic system
- Rejects the idea that U.S. is a political democracy
- Marxist model sees bias rooted in the nation's institutions
- Marx believed that a society's economic system shapes its political system
- Power elites are creations of a capitalist economy

- The problem is the system itself
  - "Political Economy of Capitalism"
  - As long as the U.S. has a predominantly capitalist economy, the majority of people will be shut out of politics, just as they are exploited in the workplace

Power Beyond the Rules

- Politics is always a matter of disagreement over a society's goals and means to achieve them
- Political systems try to settle controversy within a system of rules
- Political activity sometimes breaks the rules or even tries to do away with the entire system

---

Politics

	Pluralist Model	Power-Elite Model	Marxist Political-Economy Model
Which theoretical approach is applied?	Structural-functional approach	Social-conflict approach	Social-conflict approach
How is power spread throughout society?	Power is spread widely, so that all groups have some voice.	Power is concentrated in the hands of top business, political, and military leaders.	Power is directed by the operation of the capitalist economy.
Is the United States a democracy?	Yes. Power is spread widely enough to make the country a democracy.	No. Power is too concentrated for the country to be a democracy.	No. The capitalist economy sets political decision making, so the country is not a democracy.

Applying Theory (p. 359)

Revolution

- ***POLITICAL REVOLUTION***
  - *The overthrow of one political system in order to establish another*
  - Involves change in the type of system itself
- Traits of Revolutions
  - Rising expectations
  - Unresponsive government
  - Radical leadership by intellectuals
  - Establishing a new legitimacy

Terrorism

- *Acts of violence or the threat of violence used as a political strategy by an individual or a group*
  - Political act beyond the rules of established political systems
- Terrorists paint violence as a legitimate political tactic
- Terrorism is used not just by groups but also governments against their own people

---

- Democratic societies reject terrorism in principle but are especially vulnerable to terrorists because they give broad civil liberties to their people and have less extensive police networks
- Terrorism is always a matter of definition

War and Peace

- *WAR*
  - *Organized, armed conflict among the people of two or more nations, directed by their governments*
- Understanding war is crucial
- Humanity now has weapons that can destroy the entire planet

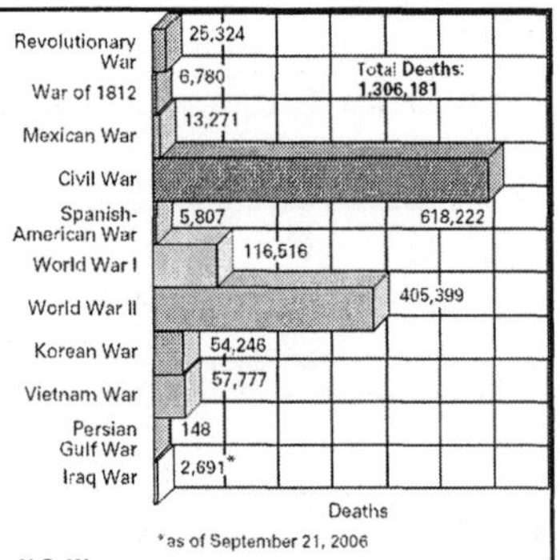

Figure 12.7 (p. 362)
Deaths of Americans in Eleven U.S. Wars
Almost half of all U.S. deaths in war occurred during the Civil War (1861-1865)
Sources: Compiled from various sources by Maris A. Vinovskis (1989) and the author.

The chart shows the following data:

- Revolutionary War: 25,324
- War of 1812: 6,780
- Mexican War: 13,271
- Civil War: 618,222
- Spanish-American War: 5,807
- World War I: 116,516
- World War II: 405,399
- Korean War: 54,246
- Vietnam War: 57,777
- Persian Gulf War: 148
- Iraq War: 2,691 *

Total Deaths: 1,306,181

Deaths

* as of September 21, 2006

The Causes of War

- Like other forms of social behavior, warfare is a product of society more common in some places than in others
- Five factors promote war:
  - Perceived threats
  - Social problems
  - Political objectives
  - Moral objectives
  - The absence of alternatives

Social Class and the Military

- Military has few young people who are rich and few who are very poor
- Working-class people
  - Look to the military for a job
  - Money to go to college
  - Get out of town
- Most volunteers are from the South

Is Terrorism a New Kind of War?

- War historically followed certain patterns
- Terrorism breaks the patterns
  - Identity and organizations are not known
  - Those involved may deny responsibility
- Terrorism is an expression of anger and hate intended to create widespread fear
- Terrorism is asymmetrical conflict

Cost and Causes of Militarism

- Defense is U.S. government's second biggest expenditure after social security
- U.S. emerged as the world's single military superpower
  - More military might than the next nine nations combined
- Military-Industrial Complex
  - The close association of the federal government, the military, and defense industries
- Regional conflict final reason for militarism

Nuclear Weapons

- "The unleashed power of the atom has changed everything *save our modes of thinking*, and we thus drift toward unparalleled catastrophe."
- By 2025, as many as 50 countries could have the ability to fight a nuclear war
- Such a trend makes any regional conflict very dangerous to the entire planet

Mass Media and War

- Iraq War was first in which television crews traveled with U.S. troops
- The power of the mass media to provide selective information to a worldwide audience means that television and other media may be almost important to the outcome of a conflict as the military doing the fighting

Pursuing Peace

- Most recent approaches to peace:
  - Deterrence
    - *Mutual Assured Destruction (MAD)*
  - High-technology defense
    - *Strategic Defense Initiative (SDI)*
  - Diplomacy and Disarmament
  - Resolving underlying Conflict

Politics: Looking Ahead

- Inconsistencies between democratic ideals and low turnout at the polls
- Global rethinking of political models
  - Discussion includes broader range of political systems
- Still face the danger of war in many parts of the world
  - New superpowers are likely to arise
  - Regional conflicts and terrorism are likely to continue

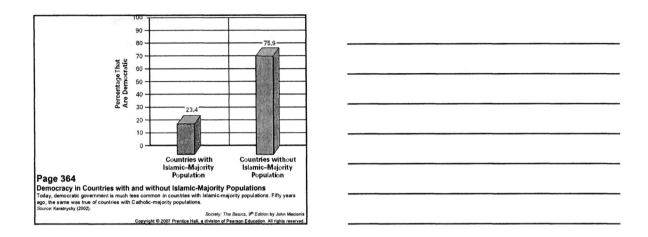

Page 364

Democracy in Countries with and without Islamic-Majority Populations

Today, democratic government is much less common in countries with Islamic-majority populations. Fifty years ago, the same was true of countries with Catholic-majority populations.
Source: Karatnycky (2002).

Family and Religion

LEARNING OBJECTIVES

- To define and illustrate basic concepts relating to the social institutions of kinship, family, and marriage.
- To gain a cross-cultural perspective of the social institutions of kinship, family, and marriage.
- To analyze the social institutions of kinship, family, and marriage using the structural-functional, social-conflict, and symbolic-interaction perspectives.
- To describe the traditional life course of the U.S. family.
- To recognize the impact of social class, race, ethnicity, and gender socialization on the family.
- To define basic concepts relating to the sociological analysis of religion.
- To describe how industrialization and science affect religious beliefs and practices.
- To discuss the basic demographic patterns concerning religious affiliation, religiosity, secularization, and religious revival in the U.S. today.

CHAPTER OUTLINE

I. Family: Basic Concepts

II. Family: Global Variations
   A. Marriage Patterns
   B. Residential Patterns
   C. Patterns of Descent
   D. Patterns of Authority

III. Theoretical Analysis of Family
   A. Functions of Family: Structural-Functional Analysis
   B. Inequality and Family: Social-Conflict Analysis
   C. Constructing Family Life: Micro-Level Analysis
      1. The Symbolic-Interaction Approach
      2. The Social-Exchange Approach

IV. Stages of Family Life
   A. Courtship and Romantic Love
   B. Settling In: Ideal and Real Marriage
   C. Child Rearing
   D. The Family in Later Life

V. U.S. Families: Class, Race, and Gender
   A. Social Class
   B. Ethnicity and Race
      1. American Indian Families

FAMILY AND RELIGION

CHAPTER 13

- **What** is family?

- **How** is religion linked to social inequality?

- **Why** are both the family and religion changing in today's world?

FAMILY: BASIC CONCEPTS

- **Family**
  - *A social institution found in all societies that unites people in cooperative groups to care for one another, including any children*
  - **Kinship**
    - *A social bond based on common ancestry, marriage, or adoption*
  - **Marriage**
    - *A legal relationship, usually involving economic cooperation as well as sexual activity and childbearing*

Family: Global Variations

- *Extended Family*
  - *A family composed of parents and children as well as other kin*
  - Also called *consanguine family*
    - Includes everyone with "shared blood"
- *Nuclear Family*
  - *A family composed of one or two parents and their children*
  - Also called *conjugal family*

Marriage Patterns

- *Endogamy*
  - *Marriage between people of the same social category*
  - Limits marriage prospects
- *Exogamy*
  - *Marriage between people of different social categories*
- *Monogamy*
  - *Marriage that unites two partners*
  - Permitted by law in higher-income nations

- *Polygamy*
  - *Marriage that unites a person with two or more spouses*
  - Permitted by many lower-income nations
  - Two forms:
    - *Polygyny* (Most common)
      - *A form of marriage that unites one man and two or more women*
    - *Polyandry*
      - *U nites one woman and two or more men*
      - *E xtremely rare and is found in Tibet*

- Historical preference for monogamy:
  - Supporting several spouses is very expensive
  - Number of men and women in most societies is roughly equal

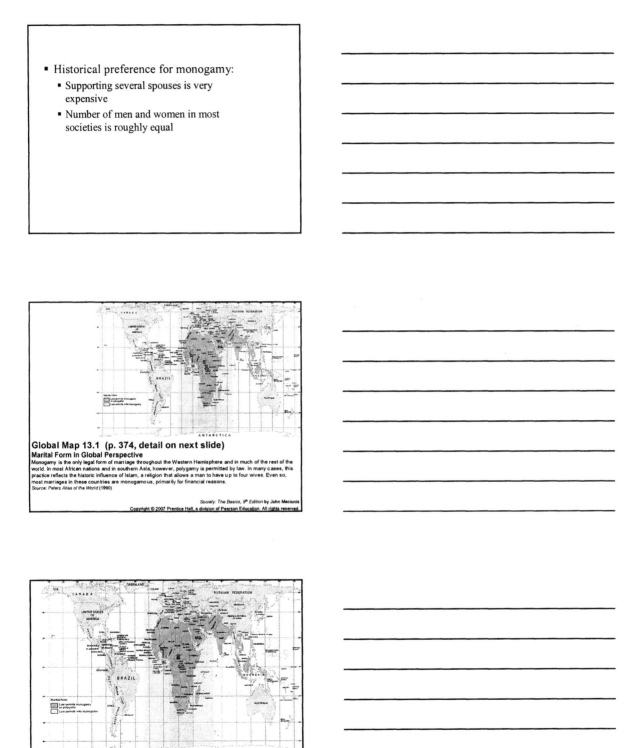

Global Map 13.1 (p. 374, detail on next slide)
Marital Form in Global Perspective
Monogamy is the only legal form of marriage throughout the Western Hemisphere and in much of the rest of the world. In most African nations and in southern Asia, however, polygamy is permitted by law. In many cases, this practice reflects the historic influence of Islam, a religion that allows a man to have up to four wives. Even so, most marriages in these countries are monogamous, primarily for financial reasons.
Source: Peters Atlas of the World (1990)

Society: The Basics, 9th Edition by John Macionis

Global Map 13.1
Marital Form in Global Perspective

Society: The Basics, 9th Edition by John Macionis

Residential Patterns

- Societies regulate mate selection and where a couple may live
- Preindustrial societies
  - Newlyweds live with one set of parents for protection, support, and assistance
- *Patrilocality*
  - *Live with or near the husband's family*
- *Matrilocality*
  - *Live with or near the wife's family*
- *Neolocality*
  - *Married couple lives far apart from both sets of parents*
  - Pattern of industrial societies

Patterns of Descent

- **Descent**
  - *Refers to the system by which members of a society trace kinship over generations*
  - **Patrilineal Descent** (most common)
    - Traces kinship through males and property flows from fathers to sons
  - **Matrilineal Descent**
    - By which people define only the mother's side as kin and property passes to daughters
    - Found in horticultural societies

- **Bilateral Decent**
  - Children recognize people on both father and mother's side
  - Property passes from parents to both sons and daughters

Patterns of Authority

- In industrial societies
  - Men are still typically head of households
  - Most U.S. parents give children their father's last name
- **Egalitarian Families**
  - Evolving more as share of women in the labor force goes up

---

THEORETICAL ANALYSIS OF FAMILY

- Structural-functional Analysis
- Social-conflict and Feminist Analysis
- Micro-level Analysis

Functions of Family: Structural-Functional Analysis

- Family sometimes called the "backbone of society"
  - Socialization
  - Regulation of sexual activity
    - *Incest Taboo*
      - *A norm forbidding sexual relations or marriage between certain relatives*
  - Social placement
  - Material and emotional security

- **Critical Review**
  - Approach glosses over the diversity of U.S. family life
  - Ignores how other social institutions could meet at least some of the same human needs
  - Overlooks the negative aspects of family life, including patriarchy and family violence

---

Inequality and Family:
Social-Conflict and Feminist Analysis

- Considers family as central to our way of life
- Points how family perpetuates inequality
  - Property and inheritance
  - Patriarchy
  - Race and ethnicity

- **Critical Review**
- **Friedrich Engels**
  - Family criticized as part and parcel of capitalism
  - Noncapitalist societies also have families and family problems
  - Family may be linked to social inequality but it carries out societal functions not easily accomplished by other means

Constructing Family Life: Micro-Level Analysis

- **The Symbolic-Interaction Approach**
  - Family offers opportunity for intimacy
  - Build emotional bonds
  - Parents are authority figures
- **The Social-Exchange Approach**
  - Describes courtship and marriage as forms of negotiation
  - Dating allows the assessment of advantages and disadvantages of a potential spouse
  - Terms of exchange are converging for men and women

- **Critical Review**
  - Misses the bigger picture
    - Experience of family life is similar for people in the same social and economic categories

Family

	Structural-Functional Approach	Social-Conflict and Feminist Approaches	Symbolic-Interaction and Social-Exchange Approaches
What is the level of analysis?	Macro-level	Macro-level	Micro-level
What is the importance of family for society?	The family performs vital tasks, including socializing the young and providing emotional and financial support for members. The family helps regulate sexual activity.	The family perpetuates social inequality by handing down wealth from one generation to the next. The family supports patriarchy as well as racial and ethnic inequality.	The symbolic-interaction approach explains that the reality of family life is constructed by members in their interaction. The social-exchange approach shows that courtship typically brings together people who offer the same level of advantages.

Applying Theory (p. 377)

STAGES OF FAMILY LIFE

- Several distinct stages of family life across the life course
  - Courtship and romantic love
  - Ideal and real marriage
  - Child rearing
  - Family in later life

Courtship and Romantic Love

- **Arranged Marriages**
  - *Alliances between two extended families of similar social standing and usually involve an exchange not just of children but also of wealth and favors*
  - Eroded and weakened by industrialization
- **Romantic Love**
  - *Affection and sexual passion toward another person*
  - Motivates young people to form families of their own
- **Homogamy**
  - *Marriage between people with the same social characteristics*

Settling In: Ideal and Real Marriage

- U.S. culture gives idealized picture of marriage
- Sexuality also a source of disappointment
  - Frequency of marital sex declines over time
- **Infidelity**
  - *Sexual activity outside marriage*
  - Another area where reality does not match the ideal

Child Rearing

- Despite demands, U.S. adults overwhelmingly identify raising children as one of life's great joys
- Big families pay off in preindustrial societies
  - Children supplied needed labor
  - High death rate
- Industrialization transformed children from asset to liability
- Parenting is expensive, lifelong commitment
- *Family and Medical Leave Act of 1993*
  - Allows up to 90 days unpaid leave from work

Family in Later Life

- Increasing life expectancy in U.S.
  - Couples who stay married do so for a longer time
- "Empty Nest"
  - Requires adjustments
  - Less sexual passion, more understanding and commitment
- Adults in midlife now provide more care for aging parents

- "Baby Boomers" in their 60's are known as the "Sandwich Generation"
  - Many, especially women, spend many years caring for aging parents as they did for their children
- Final and most difficult transition in married life
  - Death of a spouse
  - Wives typically outlive husbands because of greater life expectancy
  - Challenge greater for men
    - Fewer friends than widows
    - Lack housekeeping skills

U.S. FAMILIES: CLASS, RACE, AND GENDER

- Dimensions of inequality
  - Social class, ethnicity, race, and gender
  - Powerful forces that shape marriage and family life

Social Class

- Social class determines
  - Family's financial security and range of opportunities
- What women hope for and what they end up with is linked to their social class
- Boys and girls from affluent families
  - Enjoy better mental and physical health
  - Develop more self-confidence
  - Go on to greater achievement than children born to poor parents

Ethnicity and Race

- **American Indian Families**
  - Wide variety of family types
  - Migration create "fluid households" with changing membership
  - Those who leave tribal reservations for cities are better off than those who stay behind
    - Hard time finding work on reservations
    - Cannot easily form stable marriages
    - Alcoholism and drug abuse shatter ties between parent and child

- **Latino Families**
  - Enjoy the loyalty and support of extended families
  - Marriage considered an alliance of families
  - Prize **"Machismo"**
    - *Strength, daring, and sexual conquest among men and treating women with respect but also close supervision*
  - Assimilation changing traditional patterns
  - Many Hispanic families suffer stress
    - Unemployment
    - Other poverty related problems

- **African American Families**
  - Typical African American family earns 63% of national average
  - Three times likely as whites to be poor
  - Difficulty maintaining stable family life under these circumstances
  - African American women are more likely to be single heads of households
    - Always at high risk of poverty
  - African American families with both wife and husband are much stronger economically
    - 68% of African American children born to single women

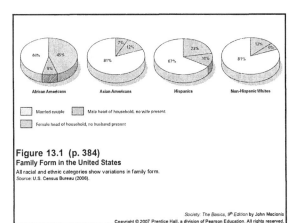

Figure 13.1 (p. 384)
Family Form in the United States
All racial and ethnic categories show variations in family form.
Source: U.S. Census Bureau (2006).

- **Ethnically and Racially Mixed Marriages**
    - Interracial marriage was illegal in 16 states
    - Actual proportion of mixed marriages is 4%
        - Shows that race still matters in social relations
    - Single most common mixed marriage
        - White husband with Asian wife – 14%
    - Most likely to live in the West
    - Hawaii, Alaska, California, Nevada, and Oklahoma
        - 10% of all married couples are interracial

- **Gender**
    - Few marriages have two equal partners
    - Many expect husband to be older and taller and have important, better-paid jobs
    - Positive stereotype of carefree bachelor contrasts sharply to the negative image of the lonely spinster
        - Suggests women are fulfilled only through being wives and mothers
    - Married women actually have poorer mental health, less happiness, and more passive attitudes than single women
    - Men more eager after divorce to find wife than widow is in finding a husband

TRANSITION AND PROBLEMS IN FAMILY LIFE

- Ann Landers
    - One marriage in twenty is wonderful
    - Five in twenty are good
    - Ten in twenty are tolerable
    - Remaining four are "pure hell"

Divorce

- Causes of Divorce
  - Individualism is on the rise
  - Romantic love fades
  - Women are less dependent on men
  - Many of today's marriages are stressful
  - Divorce is socially acceptable
  - A divorce is easier to get

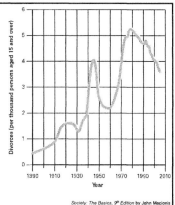

Figure 13.2 (p. 385)
Divorce Rate for the United States, 1890-2005
Over the long term, the U.S. divorce rate has gone up. Since about 1980, however, the trend has been downward.
Source: Munson & Sutton (2006).

- **Who Divorces**
  - Young couples are at greatest risk
    - Especially after brief courtship
    - Lack money and emotional maturity
  - Also rises if couple marries after an unexpected pregnancy
  - People whose parents divorce have a higher divorce rate
  - More common if both partners have successful careers
  - Men and women who divorce once are more likely to divorce again
    - High-risk factors follow from one marriage to another

- **Divorce and Children**
  - Mothers gain custody but fathers earn more income
  - Well-being of many children depend on court-ordered child support payments
  - Courts award child support in 60% of all divorces involving children
    - Half of children legally entitled receive partial or no payments at all
  - 3.5 million deadbeat dads
  - Federal legislation requires employers to withhold money from earnings of fathers and mothers who fail to pay

Remarriage and Blended Families

- Four out of five people who divorce remarry
- **Blended Families**
  - *Composed of children and some combination of biological parents and stepparents*
- Blended families must define who is part of the nuclear family
- Adjustments are necessary
- Offer both young and old the chance to relax rigid family roles

Family Violence

- *Emotional, physical, or sexual abuse of one family member by another*
- Family is the most violent group in society with the exception of the police and the military

- **Violence Against Women**
  - Often unreported to police
  - 700,000 people are victims of domestic violence each year
  - 33% of women are victims of homicide by spouses or ex-spouses
  - Women are more likely to be injured by a family member than a stranger
  - *Marital Rape Laws*
    - Found in all fifty states
  - Communities across U.S. established shelters to provide counseling and temporary housing for women and children of domestic violence

- **Violence Against Children**
  - 3 million reports of child abuse and neglect each year
    - 1,500 involve a child's death
  - Involves more than physical injury
    - Misuse of power and trust to damage child's well-being
  - Child abusers conform to no stereotype
    - More likely to be women than men
  - All abusers share one trait
    - All abused themselves as children
  - Violence in close relationships is learned
  - Violence begets violence

ALTERNATIVE FAMILY FORMS

- Recent decades, U.S. society has displayed increasing diversity in family life
  - One-parent families
  - Cohabitation
  - Gay and Lesbian couples
  - Singlehood

One-Parent Families

- 31% of U.S. families with children under 18 have one parent in the household
- Single parenthood increases a woman's risk of poverty
  - Limits her ability to work and further education
- Growing up in a one-parent family puts children at a disadvantage

Cohabitation

- *The sharing of a household by an unmarried couple*
- Appeals to more independent minded people and those who favor gender equality
- Evidence suggests cohabitating may discourage marriage
  - Partners become used to low-commitment relationships
- In separation, involvement of both parents, especially with respect to financial support, is highly uncertain

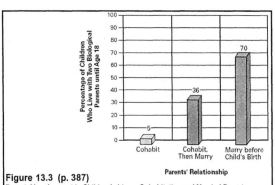

Figure 13.3 (p. 387)
Parental Involvement in Children's Lives: Cohabitating and Married Parents
Marriage increases the odds that parents will share the same household with their child.
Source: Phillips (2001).

Gay and Lesbian Couples

- 2004–Massachusetts ruled gay couples had a right to marry
- Trend is toward greater acceptance of homosexual relationships
- Most gay couples with children are raising offspring of previous heterosexual unions; others adopt
- Gay parenting challenges traditional ideas
  - Shows that many gay couples value family life as highly as heterosexuals

---

Singlehood

- Nine out of ten people in U.S. marry
  - Singlehood seen as a temporary stage of life
- Rising number of single young women
  - Women have greater participation in the labor force
  - Women who are economically secure view a husband as a matter of choice rather than a financial necessity, marry later or not at all
- By midlife, many unmarried women sense a lack of available men
  - Older, more educated, better job; the more difficulty finding a husband

---

New Reproductive Technologies and Family

- New reproductive technologies are changing families
- In vitro fertilization
  - Doctors unite a woman's egg and man's sperm "in glass"
- Allow some couples who cannot conceive normally to have children
- Raises difficult and troubling questions
  - In divorce, who is entitled to frozen embryos?
  - Genetic screening?

Families: Looking Ahead

- Divorce rate is likely to remain high even though children are at higher risk for poverty
- Family life in the future will be more diverse
- Men will play a limited role in child rearing
- Families will continue to feel the effects of economic change
- The importance of new reproductive technologies will increase

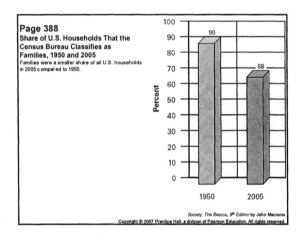

Page 388
Share of U.S. Households That the Census Bureau Classifies as Families, 1950 and 2005
Families were a smaller share of all U.S. households in 2005 compared to 1950.

RELIGION: BASIC CONCEPTS

- **Profane**
  - *Occurring as an ordinary element of everyday life*
- **Sacred**
  - *Set apart as extraordinary, inspiring awe and reverence*
- **Religion**
  - *A social institution involving beliefs and practices based on recognizing the sacred*
- **Faith**
  - *Belief based on conviction rather than on scientific evidence*

THEORETICAL ANALYSIS OF RELIGION

- Structural- Functional Analysis
- Symbolic Interaction Analysis
- Social-Conflict Analysis

Functions of Religion: Structural-Functional Analysis

- Totem
  - An object in the natural world collectively defined as sacred
- Three major functions of religion
  - Social Cohesion
  - Social Control
  - Providing meaning and purpose

- **Critical Review**
  - Downplays religion's dysfunctions
    - Strongly held beliefs can generate social conflict
  - In light of recent world events
  - Few people would deny that religious beliefs have provoked more violence in the world than differences in social class

Constructing the Sacred: Symbolic-Interaction Analysis

- Religion, like all of society, is socially constructed
- Through rituals, people sharpen the distinction between the sacred and profane
- Placing our small brief lives within some "cosmic frame of reference" gives us the appearance of "ultimate security and permanence"

- **Critical Review**
  - The sacred's ability to give meaning and stability to society depends on ignoring the fact that it is socially constructed
  - How much strength could be gained from sacred beliefs if they were seen as merely a means of coping with tragedy
  - Ignores religion's link to social inequality

Inequality and Religion: Social-Conflict Analysis

- Approach highlights religion's support of social inequality
  - Religion serves elites by legitimizing the status quo and diverting people's attention from social inequities
- Religion and social inequality also linked through gender
  - Virtually all the world's major religions are patriarchal
  - Most religions now have women in leadership roles

- **Critical Review**
  - Religion also promotes change toward equality
    - Religion played an important role in the abolition of slavery
    - Religion was at the core of the Civil Rights Movement
    - Clergy actively opposed the Vietnam War and support progressive causes such as feminism and gay rights

---

APPLYING THEORY
Religion

	Structural-Functional Approach	Symbolic-Interaction Approach	Social-Conflict Approach
What is the level of analysis?	Macro-level	Micro-level	Macro-level
What is the importance of religion for society?	Religion performs vital tasks, including uniting people and controlling behavior. Religion gives life meaning and purpose.	Religion strengthens marriage by giving it (and family life) sacred meaning. People often turn to sacred symbols for comfort when facing danger or uncertainty.	Religion supports social inequality by claiming that the social order is just. Religion turns attention from problems in this world to a "better world to come."

Applying Theory (p. 394)

RELIGION AND SOCIAL CHANGE

- Religion has promoted dramatic social change
  - Protestantism and Capitalism
  - Liberation Theology

Max Weber: Protestantism and Capitalism

- Believed that particular religious ideas set into motion a wave of change that brought about industrialization
- Rise of industrial capitalism encouraged by Calvinism
  - *Predestination*
  - The plight of the poor was a mark of God's rejection
  - Embraced technological advances
  - Resulted in a profane "Protestant Work Ethic"

Liberation Theology

- *The combining of Christian principles with political activism, often Marxist in character*
- Started late in the 1960s
  - Social oppression runs counter to Christian morality, so as a matter of faith and justice, Christians must promote greater social equality
- Condemned by Pope John Paul II
  - Distorting church doctrine with left-wing politics
- Grown in Latin America
  - People's Christian faith drive them to improve conditions for the world's poor

TYPES OF RELIGIOUS ORGANIZATIONS

- Sociologists categorize hundreds of different religious organizations in the U.S. along a continuum
- Church at one end and sects at the other
- And then there are Cults

Church

- **Church**
  - *A type of religious organizations that is well integrated into the larger society*
    - Persisted for centuries
- **State Church**
  - *A church formally allied with the state*
    - Considers everyone in the society a member
- **Denomination**
  - *A church, independent of the state, that recognizes religious pluralism*
    - Hold to their own beliefs but recognize rights of others

Sect

- **Sect**
  - *A type of religious organization that stands apart from the larger society*
    - Rigid religious convictions and deny beliefs of others
- **Charisma**
  - *Extraordinary personal qualities that can infuse people with emotion and turn them into followers*
- Generally form as break away groups
- Actively recruit (proselytize) new members
- Churches and sects differ in composition
  - Churches (high social standing); Sects (social outsiders

Cults

- **Cult**
  - *A type of religious organization that is largely outside a society's cultural traditions*
- Most spin off from conventional religion
- Typically forms around a charismatic leader
- Because some principles and practices are unconventional, viewed as deviant or evil
- Nothing wrong with this religious organization
  - Christianity, Islam, and Judaism began as cults
- Many demand adoption of radical lifestyle
  - Sometimes accused of brainwashing

Religion in History

- **Animism**
  - *The belief that elements of the natural world are conscious life forms that affect humanity*
  - Embraced by early hunter/gatherers
- Belief in a single divine power arose with pastoral and horticultural societies
- Religion becomes more important in agrarian societies
- Industrial Revolution introduced science
  - People looked to physicians and scientists for the knowledge and comfort they got from priests

RELIGION IN THE UNITED STATES

- Analysts disagree about the strength of religion in U.S. society
- Research shows that changes are underway and confirms that religion remains important in social life

Religious Commitment

- Eight in ten people claim "comfort and strength" from religion
  - Half of U.S. adults are Protestants
  - 1/4th are Catholics
  - 2% are Jews
- Religious diversity stems from constitutional ban on government sponsored religion and high immigrant population
- Identification with religion varies by region
- **Religiosity**
  - *The importance of religion in a person's life*

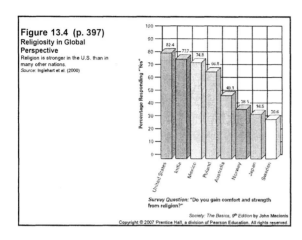

Figure 13.4 (p. 397)
Religiosity in Global Perspective

Religion is stronger in the U.S. than in many other nations.

Source: Inglehart et al. (2000)

Survey Question: "Do you gain comfort and strength from religion?"

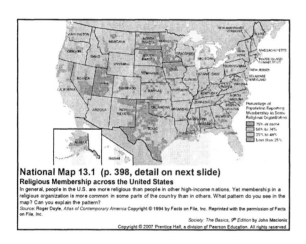

National Map 13.1 (p. 398, detail on next slide)
Religious Membership across the United States

In general, people in the U.S. are more religious than people in other high-income nations. Yet membership in a religious organization is more common in some parts of the country than in others. What pattern do you see in the map? Can you explain the pattern?

Source: Roger Doyle, Atlas of Contemporary America Copyright © 1994 by Facts on File, Inc. Reprinted with the permission of Facts on File, Inc.

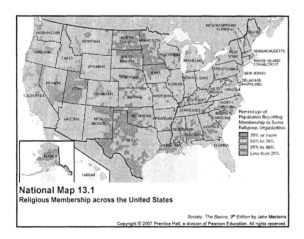

National Map 13.1
Religious Membership across the United States

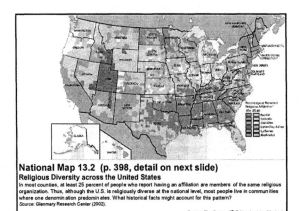

National Map 13.2 (p. 398, detail on next slide)
Religious Diversity across the United States
In most counties, at least 25 percent of people who report having an affiliation are members of the same religious organization. Thus, although the U.S. is religiously diverse at the national level, most people live in communities where one denomination predominates. What historical facts might account for this pattern?
Source: Glenmary Research Center (2002).

Society: The Basics, 9th Edition by John Macionis

National Map 13.2
Religious Diversity across the United States

Society: The Basics, 9th Edition by John Macionis

- Though many people claim to be religious, probably no more than 1/3rd actually are
- Religiosity varies among denominations
  - Members of sects are most religious
- Number of social patterns linked to strong religious beliefs
  - Low rates of delinquency
  - Low rates of divorce
  - Helps unite children, parents, and local communities
  - Enhances educational achievement of young people

Religion: Class, Ethnicity, and Race

- **Social Class**
  - Among high achievers
    - 33% are Episcopalians, Presbyterians, and United Church of Christ members
    - Account for less than 10% of the population
  - Jews also enjoy high social position
  - Methodists and Catholics have moderate social standing
  - Baptists, Lutherans, and members of sects have typically low social standing
  - Considerable variation within all denominations

- **Ethnicity**
  - Religion tied to ethnicity throughout the world
    - Because one religion stands out in a single nation or geographic region
  - Religion and national identity are joined to a certain extent in the U.S.
  - Result from the arrival of immigrants from nations with a distinctive major religion
  - Nearly every ethnic category displays some religious diversity

- **Race**
  - Church is the oldest and most important institution in the African American community
  - Blended Christian beliefs with elements of African religions brought with them
  - Resulting in rituals that seem by European standards more spontaneous and emotional
  - Migration from the South, church played a role in addressing problems
    - dislocation, poverty, and prejudice
  - Provided avenue of achievement for talented men and women
  - Increase in non-Christian African Americans
    - Largest group is Islam

RELIGION IN A CHANGING SOCIETY

- Religion is changing in the U.S.
- Sociologists focus on the process of:
  - **Secularization**
- Includes
  - Civil Religion
  - "New Age" Seekers
  - Religious Revival

Secularization

- *The historical decline in the importance of the supernatural and the sacred*
- Commonly associated with modern, technologically advanced societies
  - Science is the major way of understanding
- More likely to experience birth, illness, and death in the presence of physicians rather than church leaders
- Will religion disappear some day?
  - Sociologists say NO!

- Majority of people in U.S. profess belief in God
- Conservatives view secularization as a mark of moral decline
- Progressives view secularization as liberation from dictatorial beliefs
- Secularization sparked by U.S. Supreme Court ban on prayer in schools (1963)
- 1990, Court permitted meeting of voluntary religious groups outside of school hours if students ran the meeting

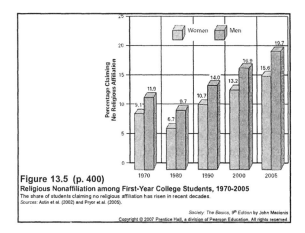

Figure 13.5 (p. 400)
Religious Nonaffiliation among First-Year College Students, 1970-2005
The share of students claiming no religious affiliation has risen in recent decades.
Sources: Astin et al. (2002) and Pryor et al. (2005).

Society: The Basics, 9th Edition by John Macionis

Civil Religion

- *A quasi-religious loyalty binding individuals in a basically secular society*
- Religious qualities of citizenship
- People find religious qualities in political movements
- Involves a range of rituals
  - Standing to sing the National Anthem
  - Waving the flag at parades
- U.S. flag serves as a sacred symbol of our national identity and expect people to treat it with respect

---

"New Age" Seekers: Spirituality Without Formal Religion

- Approach has five core values:
  - *Seekers believe in a higher power*
  - *Seekers believe we're all connected*
  - *Seekers believe in a spirit world*
  - *Seekers want to experience the spirit world*
  - *Seekers pursue transcendence*
- Important new form of religious interest in the modern world

347

Religious Revival: "Good Old-Time Religion"

- **Fundamentalism**
  - *A conservative religious doctrine that opposes intellectualism and worldly accommodation in favor of restoring traditional, otherworldly religion*
- Distinctive in five ways:
  - Fundamentalists take the words of sacred texts literally
  - Fundamentalists reject religious pluralism
  - Fundamentalists pursue the personal experience of God's presence
  - Fundamentalists oppose "secular humanism"
  - Many fundamentalists endorse conservative political goals

Religion: Looking Ahead

- Religion will remain a major part of modern society for decades to come
  - Popularity of media ministries
  - Growth of religious fundamentalism
  - New forms of spirituality
  - Connection of millions to mainstream churches
- New technology raises difficult moral questions
- People look to their faith for guidance and hope

Chapter 14

Education and Medicine

LEARNING OBJECTIVES

- To understand the relationship between schooling and economic development.
- To describe the different role of education in low-income and high-income countries.
- To consider how education supports social inequality.
- To discuss the major issues and problems facing contemporary education in the United States today.
- To recognize how race, social class, and age affect the health of individuals in our society.
- To describe the role of health care in low-income and in high-income nations.
- To discuss cigarette smoking, eating disorders, and sexually transmitted diseases as serious health problems in our society.
- To be familiar with the medical establishment on a global level.
- To begin to understand the viewpoints being provided by the three major sociological perspectives.

CHAPTER OUTLINE

I.   Education: A Global Survey
      A.   Schooling and Economic Development
      B.   Schooling in India
      C.   Schooling in Japan
      D.   Schooling in the United States

II.   The Functions of Schooling

III. Schooling and Social Interaction
      A.   The Self-Fulfilling Prophecy

IV.   Schooling and Social Inequality
      A.   Public and Private Education
      B.   Access to Higher Education
      C.   Greater Opportunity: Expanding Higher Education
      D.   Community Colleges
      E.   Privilege and Personal Merit

V.   Problems in the Schools
      A.   Discipline and Violence
      B.   Student Passivity

EDUCATION, HEALTH, AND MEDICINE

CHAPTER 14

- **How** are schooling and health linked to social inequality in the United States?

- **What** changes in schooling and health have taken place in the United States in recent generations?

- **Why** do people in poor nations have little access to schooling and medical care?

EDUCATION: A GLOBAL SURVEY

- *EDUCATION*
  - *The social institution through which society provides its members with important knowledge, including basic facts, job skills, and cultural norms and values*
- *SCHOOLING*
  - *Formal instruction under the direction of specially trained teachers*

Schooling and Economic Development

- The extent of schooling in any society is tied to its level of economic development
- Low-income countries have little schooling
- 1/3rd of the world's people cannot read or write
- Global comparisons made between
  - India
  - Japan
  - United States

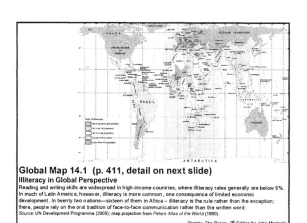

Global Map 14.1 (p. 411, detail on next slide)
Illiteracy in Global Perspective
Reading and writing skills are widespread in high-income countries, where illiteracy rates generally are below 5%. In much of Latin America, however, illiteracy is more common, one consequence of limited economic development. In twenty two nations—sixteen of them in Africa – illiteracy is the rule rather than the exception; there, people rely on the oral tradition of face-to-face communication rather than the written word.
Source: UN Development Programme (2005): map projection from *Peters Atlas of the World* (1990).

Society: The Basics, 9th Edition by John Macionis

Global Map 14.1
Illiteracy in Global Perspective
Society: The Basics, 9th Edition by John Macionis

Table 14.1 (p. 412)
Educational Achievement in
the United States,
1910-2004

TABLE 14-1

Educational Achievement in the United States,
1910–2004[*]

Year	High School Graduates	College Graduates	Median Years of Schooling
1910	13.5%	2.7%	8.1
1920	16.4	3.3	8.2
1930	19.1	3.9	8.4
1940	24.1	4.6	8.6
1950	33.4	6.0	9.3
1960	41.1	7.7	10.5
1970	55.2	11.0	12.2
1980	68.7	17.0	12.5
1990	77.6	21.3	12.4
2000	84.1	25.6	12.7
2004	85.2	27.7	n/a

[*]For people twenty-five years of age and over. Percentage of high school graduates includes those who go on to college. Percentage of high school dropouts can be calculated by subtracting percentage of high school graduates from 100 percent.

Source: U.S. Census Bureau (2005).

The Functions of Schooling

- Structural-functional analysis:
  - Socialization
  - Cultural innovation
  - Social integration
  - Social placement
  - Latent functions

- CRITICAL REVIEW
  - Overlooks how the classroom behavior of teachers and students can vary from one setting to another
  - Says little about many problems of the educational system and how schooling helps reproduce the class structure in each generation

SCHOOLING AND SOCIAL INTERACTION

- *THE SELF FUL-FILLING PROPHECY*
  - *People who expect others to act in certain ways often encourage that very behavior*
- Jane Elliott
  - "Blue Eyes"
- **CRITICAL REVIEW**
  - People do not just make up beliefs about superiority and inferiority
  - These beliefs are built into a society's system of social inequality

SCHOOLING AND SOCIAL INEQUALITY

- Social-conflict challenges structural-functional idea that schooling develops everyone's talents and abilities
- Three ways schooling causes and perpetuates social inequality
  - **Social control**
  - **Standardized testing**
  - **Tracking**
    - *Assigning students to different types of educational programs*

Public and Private Schools

- Parochial "Of the Parish"
  - Catholic schools
- Protestant private schools
  - Christian Academies
- Students in private schools outperform those in public schools
  - Smaller classes, demanding coursework, greater discipline
- Public Schools
  - Difference in funding between rich and poor communities result in unequal resources

355

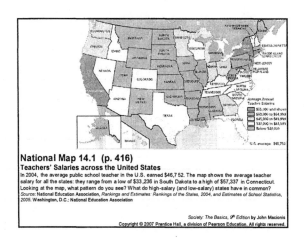

National Map 14.1 (p. 416)
Teachers' Salaries across the United States
In 2004, the average public school teacher in the U.S. earned $46,752. The map shows the average teacher salary for all the states; they range from a low of $33,236 in South Dakota to a high of $57,337 in Connecticut. Looking at the map, what pattern do you see? What do high-salary (and low-salary) states have in common?
Source: National Education Association, Rankings and Estimates: Rankings of the States, 2004, and Estimates of School Statistics, 2005. Washington, D.C.: National Education Association

Society: The Basics, 9th Edition by John Macionis

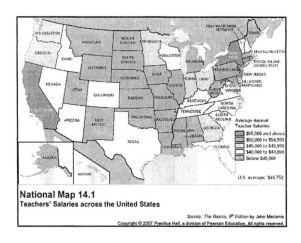

National Map 14.1
Teachers' Salaries across the United States

Society: The Basics, 9th Edition by John Macionis

- Schools in more affluent areas offer better schooling than in poor communities
- Social Capital
  - Students whose families value schooling
  - Read to their children
  - Encourage the development of imagination
- Home environment is an important influence on school performance
- Differences in home and local neighborhood matter most in children's learning

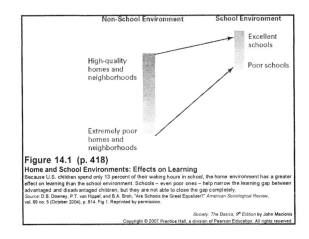

Figure 14.1 (p. 418)
Home and School Environments: Effects on Learning
Because U.S. children spend only 13 percent of their waking hours in school, the home environment has a greater effect on learning than the school environment. Schools – even poor ones – help narrow the learning gap between advantaged and disadvantaged children, but they are not able to close the gap completely.
Source: D.B. Downey, P.T. von Hippel, and B.A. Broh, "Are Schools the Great Equalizer?" American Sociological Review, vol. 69 no. 5 (October 2004), p. 614, Fig 1. Reprinted by permission.

Access to Higher Education

- 67% of U.S. high school graduates enroll in college immediately after graduation
- Crucial factor affecting access is income
- Economic differences is reason for education gap between minorities and whites
- Completing college brings rewards
  - Higher earnings

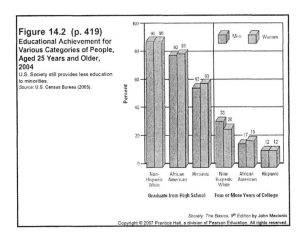

Figure 14.2 (p. 419)
Educational Achievement for Various Categories of People, Aged 25 Years and Older, 2004
U.S. Society still provides less education to minorities.
Source: U.S. Census Bureau (2005).

Greater Opportunity: Expanding Higher Education

- U.S. world leader in providing college education to its people
- Education is the key path to better jobs
  - Government makes money available to help certain categories of people pay for college
- ***Community Colleges***
  - Low cost provides access to millions
  - Special importance to minorities
  - Attracts students from all over the world
  - Priority of faculty is teaching, not research

Privilege and Personal Merit

- Schooling transforms social privilege into personal merit
- ***Credentialed Society***
  - *Society that evaluates people based on schooling*
- Process helps those who are already advantaged and hurts those who are already disadvantaged
- CRITICAL REVIEW
  - Social-conflict overlooks the extent to which schooling provides upward mobility to the talented from all backgrounds and changes social inequality on many fronts

Education

	Structural-Functional Approach	Symbolic-Interaction Approach	Social-Conflict Approach
What is the level of analysis?	Macro-level	Micro-level	Macro-level
What is the importance of education for society?	Schooling performs many vital tasks for the operation of society, including socializing the young and encouraging discovery and invention to improve our lives. Schooling helps unite a diverse society by teaching shared norms and values.	How teachers and others define students can become real to everyone and affect students' educational performance.	Schooling maintains social inequality through unequal schooling for rich and poor. Within individual schools, tracking provides privileged children with a better education than poor children.

Applying Theory (p. 420)

PROBLEMS IN THE SCHOOLS

- Discipline and Violence
  - Schools do not create violence
  - Spills in from surrounding society
- Student Passivity
  - TV and iPods claim more of young people's time than schooling
- Five ways bureaucracy undermine education
  - Rigid uniformity
  - Numerical ratings
  - Rigid expectations
  - Specialization
  - Little individual responsibility

- Passivity common among college and university students
- Four teaching strategies that can bring students to life in classrooms
  - Calling on students by name when they volunteer
  - Positively reinforcing student participation
  - Asking analytical rather than factual questions and giving students time to answer
  - Asking for students' opinions even when no one volunteers an answer

- Dropping Out
  - Quitting before earning even a high school diploma
  - Leaves young people unprepared for work and high-risk of poverty
- Least common among whites
- More likely among African Americans and Hispanics
- Causes
  - Trouble with the English language
  - Work to support family

- Academic Standards
  - Functional Illiteracy
    - A lack of the reading and writing skills needed for everyday living
- Nation at Risk
- U.S. spend more on schooling than almost any other country
  - U.S. placed 16th in science and 19th in math
- Cultural values play a part in how hard students work at their schooling

---

RECENT ISSUES IN U.S. EDUCATION

- *School Choice*
  - Create a market for education so parents and students can shop for best value
- Magnet Schools
  - Offer special facilities and programs to promote educational excellence
- Charter Schools
  - Public schools that are given more freedom to try new policies and programs
- Schooling for Profit
  - School systems operated by private profit-making companies rather than government

- *Home Schooling*
  - Parents do not believe public education is doing a good job
  - Students who learn at home outperform those who learn in school
- *Schooling People With Disabilities*
  - Resulted from persistent efforts by parents and other concerned citizens
  - *Mainstreaming*
    - *Including students with disabilities in the education program*
    - Inclusive Education

- *Adult Education*
  - Many return to advance a career or train for a new job
- *The Teacher Shortage*
  - Final challenge for U.S. schools
  - Factors
    - Low salaries
    - Frustration
    - Retirement
    - Rising enrollment and reductions in class size

HEALTH AND MEDICINE

- *MEDICINE*
  - *The social institution that focuses on fighting disease and improving health*
- *HEALTH*
  - *A state of complete physical, mental, and social well-being*

Health and society

- Society affects health in four major ways:
  - Cultural patterns define health
  - Cultural standards of health change over time
  - A society's technology affects people's health
  - Social inequality affects people's health

HEALTH: A GLOBAL SURVEY

- **Health in Low-Income Countries**
  - Poverty cuts decades off of life expectancy
  - Poor sanitation and malnutrition
- **Health in High-Income Countries**
  - Industrialization raised living standards
  - Better nutrition
  - Safer housing
  - Medical advances in science to control infectious disease

Health in the United States

- *Social Epidemiology*
  - *The study of how health and disease are distributed throughout a society's population*
- **Age and Gender**
  - Death now rare among young people
  - AIDS changing this trend
  - Male aggression
- **Social Class and Race**
  - Poverty
  - Infant mortality twice as high for the disadvantaged

TABLE 14-3

Leading Causes of Death in the United States,
1900 and 2004

1900	2004
1. Influenza and pneumonia	1. Heart disease
2. Tuberculosis	2. Cancer
3. Stomach and intestinal disease	3. Stroke
4. Heart disease	4. Lung disease (noncancerous)
5. Cerebral hemorrhage	5. Accidents
6. Kidney disease	6. Diabetes
7. Accidents	7. Alzheimer's disease
8. Cancer	8. Influenza and pneumonia
9. Disease in early infancy	9. Kidney disease
10. Diphtheria	10. Blood disease

Sources: Information for 1900 is from William C. Cockerham, *Medical Sociology*, 2d ed. (Englewood Cliffs, N.J.: Prentice Hall, 1986), p. 24; information for 2004 is from Arialdi M. Miniño, Melonie P. Heron, & Betty L. Smith, *National Vital Statistics Reports*, vol. 54, no. 19 (Hyattsville, Md.: National Center for Health Statistics, 2006).

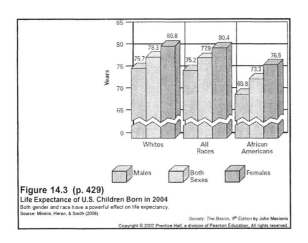

Figure 14.3 (p. 429)
Life Expectancy of U.S. Children Born in 2004
Both gender and race have a powerful effect on life expectancy.
Source: Miniño, Heron, & Smith (2006).

- **Cigarette Smoking**
  - Tops list of preventable health hazards in U.S.
  - Many smoke to cope with stress
  - 440,000 die prematurely yearly
    - Exceeds alcohol, cocaine, heroin, homicide, suicide, auto accidents, and AIDS
  - $83 billion dollar industry
    - Increased marketing abroad where there is less regulation of tobacco
  - Ten years after quitting, ex-smoker's health is as good as someone who never smoked

- *Eating Disorders*
  - *An intense type of dieting or other unhealthy method of weight control driven by the desire to be very thin*
  - **Anorexia Nervosa**
    - Dieting to the point of starvation
  - **Bulimia**
    - Binge eating followed by induced vomiting to avoid weight gain
  - **Obesity**
    - 2/3rd of U.S. adults are obese
    - Limit physical activity and raise risk of serious diseases
    - Live in a society in which most people have sedentary jobs

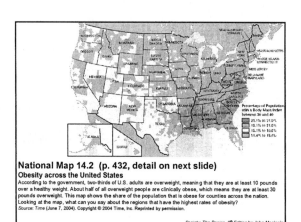

National Map 14.2 (p. 432, detail on next slide)
Obesity across the United States
According to the government, two-thirds of U.S. adults are overweight, meaning that they are at least 10 pounds over a healthy weight. About half of all overweight people are clinically obese, which means they are at least 30 pounds overweight. This map shows the share of the population that is obese for counties across the nation. Looking at the map, what can you say about the regions that have the highest rates of obesity?
Source: *Time* (June 7, 2004). Copyright © 2004 Time, Inc. Reprinted by permission.

Society: The Basics, 9th Edition by John Macionis

National Map 14.2
Obesity across the United States

Society: The Basics, 9th Edition by John Macionis

Sexually Transmitted Diseases

- *Venereal Disease*
  - **Gonorrhea and Syphilis**
    - Cured easily with antibiotics
  - **Genital Herpes**
    - 45 million adults in U.S. and is incurable
  - **AIDS**
    - Most serious of all sexually transmitted diseases
    - Incurable and almost always fatal
    - Risk behaviors are anal sex, sharing needles, use of any drug including alcohol
    - Education most effective weapon

Global Map 14.2 (p. 434, detail on next slide)
HIV/AIDS Infection of Adults in Global Perspective
64% of all global HIV infections are in sub-Saharan Africa. In Swaziland, one-third of people between the ages of 15 and 49 are infected with HIV/AIDS. This very high infection rate reflects the prevalence of other sexually transmitted diseases and infrequent use of condoms, two factors that promote transmission of HIV. All of Southeast Asia accounts for about 17% of global HIV infections. In Cambodia, nearly 2% of people aged 15 to 49 are now infected. All of North and South America taken together account for 8 percent of global HIV infections. In the U.S., 0.6% of people aged 15 to 49 are infected. The incidence of infection in Muslim nations is extremely low by world standards.
Sources: Population Reference Bureau (2003, 2006) and United Nations (2006); map projection from Peters *Atlas of the World* (1990).

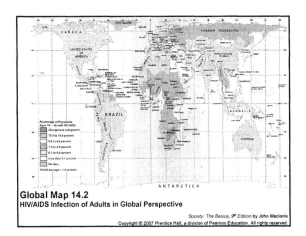

Global Map 14.2
HIV/AIDS Infection of Adults in Global Perspective

Ethical Issues Surrounding Death

- *Defined as an irreversible state involving no response to stimulation, no movement or breathing, no reflexes, and no indication of brain activity*
- *Euthanasia*
  - *Assisting in the death of a person suffering from an incurable disease*
  - "Right to die" one of today's most difficult issues
  - Supporters view circumstances when death preferable to life
  - Critics cite abuse

THE MEDICAL ESTABLISHMENT

- Emerged as a social institution as societies became more productive and people took on specialized work

Holistic Medicine

- *An approach to health care that emphasizes prevention of illness and takes into account a person's entire physical and social environment*
- Three foundations of holistic health care
  - Treat patients as people
  - Encourage responsibility, not dependency
  - Provide personal treatment

Paying for Medical Care: A Global Survey

- **People's Republic of China**
  - Government controls most health care
- **Russian Federation**
  - Transforming from state-dominated to more of a market system
- **Sweden**
  - *Socialized Medicine*
    - *A medical care system in which the government owns and operates most medical facilities and employs most physicians*

- **Great Britain**
  - Also established socialized medicine
- **Canada**
  - "single-payer" model of care that provides care to all Canadians
  - Less state of the art technology
  - Responds more slowly, people may wait months to receive major surgery
- **Japan**
  - Approach medical care like Europe
  - Most medical expenses paid through the government

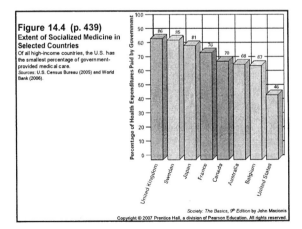

Figure 14.4 (p. 439)
Extent of Socialized Medicine in Selected Countries
Of all high-income countries, the U.S. has the smallest percentage of government-provided medical care.
Sources: U.S. Census Bureau (2005) and World Bank (2006).

Paying for Medical Care: U.S.

- *Direct-fee system*
  - *A medical care system in which patients pay directly for the services of physicians and hospitals*
- Rich can buy best medical care in the world
- Poor are worse than European counterparts
- No national medical care program
  - Culture stresses self-reliance
  - Political support for national medical program not strong
  - AMA and insurance industry strongly and consistently oppose national medical care

---

- **Private Insurance Programs**
  - 68% of U.S. population has private insurance
- **Public Insurance Programs**
  - *Medicare* pays costs for people over age 65
  - *Medicaid* pays for the poor
- **Health Maintenance Organizations**
  - An organization that provides comprehensive medical care to subscribers for a fixed fee
  - Criticized for refusing to pay for medical procedures they consider unnecessary
  - Congress currently debating the extent to which patients can sue HMO's to obtain better care

---

The Nursing Shortage

- Fewer people are entering the nursing profession
  - Today's young women have a wide range of job choices
  - Nurses are unhappy with their working conditions
- Hopeful sign
  - Increase in salaries
  - Recruitment of more minorities

Theoretical Analysis of Health and Medicine

- Structural-Functional Analysis: Role Theory
  - *The Sick Role*
    - *Patterns of behavior defined as appropriate for people who are ill*
  - *Physician's Role*
    - *Use specialized knowledge and expect patient's to follow "doctor's orders" to complete treatment*
- **CRITICAL REVIEW**
  - Sick-role concept applies to acute conditions
  - Sick person's ability to assume the sick role depends on person's resources
  - Illness is not completely dysfunctional

- *Symbolic-Interaction Analysis: The Meaning of Health*
  - **The Social Construction of Illness**
    - *Our response to illness is based on social definitions*
    - *Psychosomatic disorders*
      - *When state of mind guides physical sensations*
  - **The Social Construction of Treatment**
    - *Doctor's tailor their physical surroundings and their behavior so that others see them as competent and in charge*
- CRITICAL REVIEW
  - Implies that there are no objective standards of well-being

---

- **Social-Conflict and Feminist Analysis**
  - Points out the connection between health care and social inequity
- Access to care
  - Capitalism provides excellent health care for the rich at the expense of the rest of the population
- The Profit Motive
  - Real problem is not access to medical care but capitalist medicine itself
  - Profit motive turns doctors, hospitals, and the pharmaceutical industry into multibillion-dollar corporations
  - Society tolerant of doctor's financial interest in tests and procedures they order

Health

	Structural-Functional Approach	Symbolic-Interaction Approach	Social-Conflict and Feminist Approaches
What is the level of analysis?	Macro-level	Micro-level	Macro-level
How is health related to society?	Illness is dysfunctional for society because it prevents people from carrying out their daily roles. The sick role releases people who are ill from responsibilities while they try to get well.	Societies define "health" and "illness" differently according to their living standards. How people define their own health affects how they actually feel (psychosomatic conditions).	Health is linked to social inequality, with rich people having more access to care than poor people. Capitalist medical care places the drive for profits over the needs of people, treating symptoms rather than addressing poverty and sexism as causes of illness.

Applying Theory (p. 442)

- Medicine as Politics
  - Scientific medicine takes sides on significant social issues
    - Medical establishment opposes government medical programs
    - Recently allowed women to join ranks of physicians
    - Racial and sexual discrimination kept women and people of color out of medicine
    - Scientific medicine explains illness in terms of bacteria and viruses ignoring poverty, racism, and sexism
- CRITICAL REVIEW
  - Minimizes the advances in U.S. health brought about by scientific medicine and higher living standards

Population, Urbanization, and Environment

LEARNING OBJECTIVES

- To learn the basic concepts used by demographers to study populations.
- To compare Malthusian theory and demographic transition theory.
- To gain an understanding of the worldwide urbanization process, and to be able to put it into historical perspective.
- To describe demographic changes in the U.S. throughout its history.
- To consider urbanism as a way of life as viewed by several historical figures in sociology.
- To consider the idea of urban ecology.
- To develop an understanding of how sociology can help us confront environmental issues.
- To be able to discuss the dimensions of the "logic of growth" and the "limits to growth" as issues and realities confronting our world.
- To identify and discuss major environmental issues confronting our world today.

CHAPTER OUTLINE

I.   Demography: The Study of Population
    A.   Fertility
    B.   Mortality
    C.   Migration
    D.   Population Growth
    E.   Population Composition

II. History and Theory of Population Growth
    A.   Malthusian Theory
    B.   Demographic Transition Theory
    C.   Global Population Today: A Brief Survey
          1.   The Low-Growth North
          2.   The High-Growth South

III. Urbanization: The Growth of Cities
    A.   The Evolution of Cities
          1.   The First Cities
          2.   Preindustrial European Cities

POPULATION, URBANIZATION, AND ENVIRONMENT

CHAPTER 15

- **Why** should we worry about the rapid rate of global population increase?

- **What** makes city and rural living different?

- **How** is the state of the natural environment a social issue?

Demography: The Study of Population

- *Demography*
  - *The study of human population*
- *Fertility*
  - *The incidence of childbearing in a country's population*
- *Crude Birth Rate*
  - *The number of live births in a given year for every 1,000 people in a population*

- *Mortality*
  - *The incidence of death in a country's population*
- *Crude Death Rate*
  - *The number of death's in a given year for every 1,000 people in a population*
- *Infant Mortality Rate*
  - *The number of deaths among infants under one year of age for each 1,000 live births in a given year*
- *Life Expectancy*
  - *The average life span of a country's population*

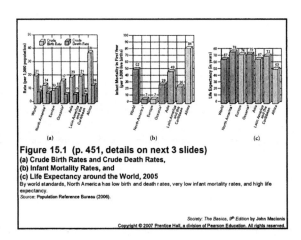

Figure 15.1 (p. 451, details on next 3 slides)
(a) Crude Birth Rates and Crude Death Rates,
(b) Infant Mortality Rates, and
(c) Life Expectancy around the World, 2005
By world standards, North America has low birth and death rates, very low infant mortality rates, and high life expectancy.
Source: Population Reference Bureau (2006).

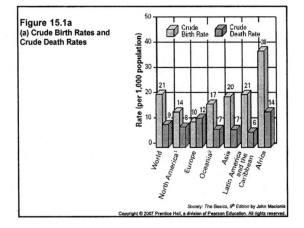

Figure 15.1a
(a) Crude Birth Rates and Crude Death Rates

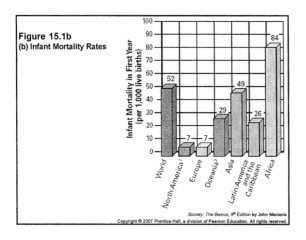

Figure 15.1b
(b) Infant Mortality Rates

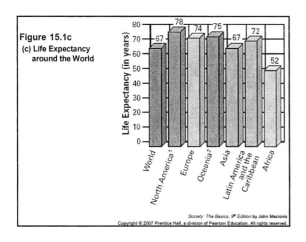

Figure 15.1c
(c) Life Expectancy around the World

- *Migration*
  - *The movement of people into and out of a specified territory*
  - *Immigration*
    - In-migration rate
      - Number of people entering an area for every 1,000 people in the population
  - *Emigration*
    - Out-migration rate
      - The number of people leaving for every 1,000 people
  - Both types usually happen at once
    - *Push-Pull factors*

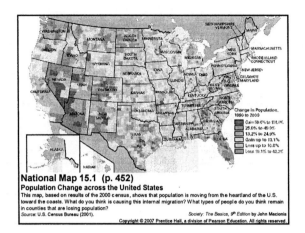

National Map 15.1 (p. 452)
Population Change across the United States
This map, based on results of the 2000 census, shows that population is moving from the heartland of the U.S. toward the coasts. What do you think is causing this internal migration? What types of people do you think remain in counties that are losing population?
Source: U.S. Census Bureau (2001).
Society: The Basics, 9ᵗʰ Edition by John Macionis

Population Growth

- Affected by fertility, mortality, and migration
- Population growth of U.S. and other high-income nations is well-below world average
- Highest growth region is Africa
  - Troubling because these countries can barely support existing populations

---

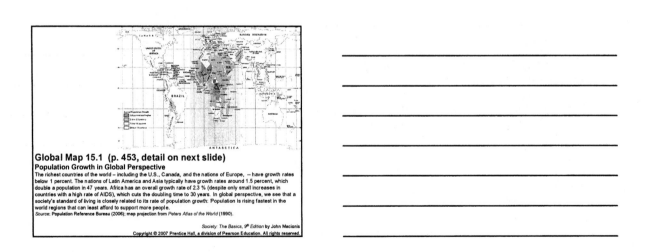

Global Map 15.1 (p. 453, detail on next slide)
Population Growth in Global Perspective
The richest countries of the world -- including the U.S., Canada, and the nations of Europe, -- have growth rates below 1 percent. The nations of Latin America and Asia typically have growth rates around 1.5 percent, which double a population in 47 years. Africa has an overall growth rate of 2.3 % (despite only small increases in countries with a high rate of AIDS), which cuts the doubling time to 30 years. In global perspective, we see that a society's standard of living is closely related to its rate of population growth: Population is rising fastest in the world regions that can least afford to support more people.
Source: Population Reference Bureau (2006); map projection from *Peters Atlas of the World* (1990).

Society: The Basics, 9ᵗʰ Edition by John Macionis

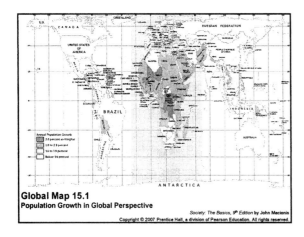

Global Map 15.1
Population Growth in Global Perspective

Society: The Basics, 9th Edition by John Macionis

Population Composition

- *Sex Ratio*
  - *The number of males for every 100 females in a nation's population*
- *Age-sex Pyramid*
  - *A graphic representation of the age and sex of a population*
    - Lower-income nations are wide at the bottom

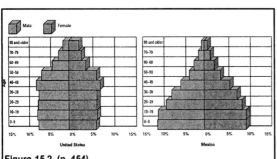

Figure 15.2 (p. 454)
Age-Sex Population Pyramids for the United States and Mexico, 2005
By looking at the shape of a country's population pyramid, you can tell its level of economic development and predict future levels of population increase.
Source: U.S. Census Bureau (2005).

Society: The Basics, 9th Edition by John Macionis

History and Theory of Population Growth

- *Malthusian Theory*
  - Rapid population increase would lead to social chaos
  - *Geometric Progression of population*
    - Doubling of population (2, 4, 8, 16, 32, etc.)
  - *Arithmetic Progression of food production*
    - Limited farmland (2, 3, 4, 5, 6, etc.)
  - Reproduction beyond what the planet could feed
  - Birth control and sex abstention may change prediction

- CRITICAL REVIEW
- Prediction flawed
  - Birth rate began to drop with industrialization
  - Underestimated human ingenuity
- Ignored the role of social inequality in world abundance and famine
- Lesson:
  - Habitable land, clean water, fresh air are limited resources

---

- *Demographic Transition Theory*
  - *A thesis that links population patterns to a society's level of technological development*
  - Stage 1 – Pre-industrial Agrarian societies
    - High birth rate; High death rate
  - Stage 2 – Industrialization
    - Death rate falls; Birth rates remain high
  - Stage 3 – Mature Industrial Economy
    - Birth rate drops; Death rate drops
  - Stage 4 – Postindustrial Economy
    - Demographic transition complete
    - Low-birth rate; steady death rate
    - Japan, Europe, and U.S.

	Stage 1	Stage 2	Stage 3	Stage 4
Birth Rate Death Rate		Natural Increase		
Level of Technology	Preindustrial	Early Industrial	Mature Industrial	Postindustrial
Population Growth	Very Slow	Rapid	Slowing	Very Slow

Figure 15.3 (p. 456)
Demographic Transition Theory
Demographic transition theory links population change to a society's level of technological development.

- CRITICAL REVIEW
  - Linked to Modernization Theory
    - Optimism that poor countries will solve their population problems as they industrialize
  - Dependency Theorists
    - Unless there is redistribution of global resources
    - Division into affluent enjoying low population growth
    - Poor struggling in vain to feed more and more people

Global Population Today: A Brief Survey

- *The Low-Growth North*
  - *Zero Population Growth*
    - *The level of reproduction that maintains population at a steady level*
  - Factors that hold down population
    - High proportion of men and women in labor force
    - Rising costs of raising children
    - Trends toward later marriage
    - Singlehood
    - Wide use of contraceptives
  - Concern for *under-population*

- *High-Growth South*
  - Population is critical problem in poor nations of Southern Hemisphere
  - Advanced medical technology provided by rich nations has lowered death rate
    - Poor societies account for 2/3 of world's population
    - To limit population increase
      - M ust control births as successful as fending off death

Urbanization: The Growth of Cities

- **Urbanization**
  - The concentration of population into cities
  - The First Cities
    - First urban revolution
  - Preindustrial European Cities
  - Industrial European Cities
    - Second urban revolution

The Growth of U.S. Cities

- Colonial Settlements, 1565-1800
- Urban Expansion, 1800-1860
- The Metropolitan Era, 1860-1950
  - *Metropolis*
    - *A large city that socially and economically dominates an urban area*
- Urban Decentralization, 1950-Present
  - Occurred as people left downtown areas for outlying *Suburbs*
    - *Urban areas beyond the political boundaries of a city*

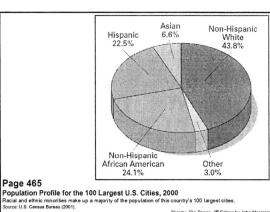

Suburbs and Urban Decline

- Loss of higher-income taxpayers to suburbs
  - Left cities struggling to pay for expensive social programs for the poor
- Cities fell into crisis leading to inner-city decay
- Decline in the importance of public space
- Spread of TV, Internet, and other media people can use without leaving home

Postindustrial Sun Belt Cities and Sprawl

- 60% of U.S. population live in sunbelt cities
  - LA, Houston
- Argument
  - Growth follows no plan
  - Traffic congestion
  - Poorly planned housing developments
  - Overcrowded schools

Megalopolis: The Regional City

- *Megalopolis*
  - *A vast urban region containing a number of cities and their surrounding suburbs*
  - Metropolitan Statistical Areas (MSA's)
    - One city with 50,000 or more people
  - Micropolitan Statistical Areas
    - Urban areas with at least one city with 10,000 to 50,000 people
  - Core-based Statistical Areas (CBSA's)
    - Include metropolitan and micropolitan areas
    - New York and adjacent urban areas

- **Edge Cities**
  - *Business centers some distance from the old downtowns*
  - No clear physical boundaries
- **The Rural Rebound**
  - *3/4 of rural communities across the U.S. gained population*
  - Scenic and recreational attractions
  - Companies relocating to rural communities
    - Increased economic opportunities for rural populations

Urbanism as a Way of Life

- *Gemeinschaft*
  - *A type of social organization in which people are closely tied by kinship and tradition*
- *Gesellschaft*
  - *A type of social organization in which people come together only on the basis of individual self-interest*
  - Motivated by own needs rather than desire to help improve the well-being of everyone

Mechanical and Organic Solidarity

- *Emile Durkheim*
- *Mechanical Solidarity*
  - *Social bonds based on common sentiments and shared moral values*
  - Similar to Gemeinschaft
- *Organic Solidarity*
  - *Social bonds based on specialization and interdependence*
  - Similar to Gesellschaft

The Blasé Urbanite

- *Georg Simmel*
- *Tuning out much of what goes on around one*
- City dwellers keep distance as a survival strategy

The Chicago School: Robert Park and Louis Wirth

- City is a living organism – a human kaleidoscope
- Define the city as a setting with a large, dense, and socially diverse population
  - City dwellers know others not in terms of
    - *Who they are **but** what they do*
- Impersonal nature of urban relationships with greater diversity makes city dwellers more tolerant than rural villagers

---

- CRITICAL REVIEW
  - Overlook the effects of class, race, and gender
  - Many kinds of urbanites

Urban Ecology

- *The study of the link between they physical and social dimensions of cities*
- *Concentric Zones*
- *Wedge-shaped Sectors*
- *Multicentered Model*
- *Social Area Analysis*
  - Households with fewer children cluster towards city's center
  - Social class differences are responsible for sector-shaped districts
  - Racial and ethnic neighborhoods consistent with muticentered model

Urban Political Economy

- *Urban political-economy model*
  - Applies Marx's analysis of conflict in the workplace to conflict in the city
- Political economists reject ecological approach of city as a natural organism
  - See city life as defined by people with power
- CRITICAL REVIEW
  - Focus on U.S. cities during a limited period of history
  - Unlikely any single model can account for full range of urban diversity

_____

_____

_____

_____

_____

_____

_____

Urbanization in Poor Nations

- Two revolutionary expansion of cities in world history
  - 1st began about 8000 B.C.E.
  - 2nd began in 1750 and lasted two centuries
- 3rd urban revolution is under way
  - Result of many poor nations entering high-growth stage 2 of demographic transitions theory
  - Cities offer more opportunities than rural areas
    - Provide no quick fix for problems of escalating population and grinding poverty

_____

_____

_____

_____

_____

_____

ENVIRONMENT AND SOCIETY

- *ECOLOGY*
  - *The study of the interaction of living organisms and the natural environment*
- *NATURAL ENVIRONMENT*
  - *Earth's surface and atmosphere, including living organisms, air, water, soil, and other resources necessary to sustain life*

_____

_____

_____

_____

_____

_____

_____

The Global Dimension

- *Ecosystem*
  - *A system composed of the interaction of all living organisms and their natural environment*
- Change in any part of the natural environments sends ripples through the entire global ecosystem
  - The Ecological Viewpoint of the Hamburger

Technology and the Environmental Deficit

- *I=PAT*
  - *Environmental impact (I) reflects a society's population (P), its level of affluence (A), and its level of technology (T).*
- Societies at intermediate stages of sociocultural evolution have somewhat greater capacity to affect the environment
- Environmental impact of industrial technology goes beyond energy consumption

---

- *Environmental Deficit*
  - *Profound long-term harm to the natural environment caused by humanity's focus on short-term material affluence*
- Environmental concerns are sociological
- Environmental damage to air, land, or water is unintended
- Environmental deficit is reversible
  - Societies create environmental problems
  - Societies can undo many of them

Culture: Growth and Limits

- ***The logic of growth***
  - Material comfort, Progress, Science
- *Holds that more powerful technology has improved lives and new discoveries will continue to do so in the future*
- Progress can lead to unexpected problems
  - Strain on the environment
- Environmentalists
  - Logic of growth flawed
  - Assumes natural resources will always be plentiful

- ***The limits of Growth***
  - Cannot invent our way out of the problems created by the logic of growth
  - Growth must have limits
- *Humanity must put into place policies to control population increase, pollution, and use of resources to avoid environmental collapse*
- Shares Malthus's pessimism about the future

Solid Waste: The Disposable Society

- U.S. is a disposable society
  - Consume more products than virtually any other nation on earth
  - Countless items are designed to be disposable
  - Rich society consumes hundreds of times more energy, plastics, lumber, and other resources
  - 80% never goes away
    - Ends up in landfills
    - Can pollute groundwater under Earth's surface
  - *Recycling – reuse of resources*

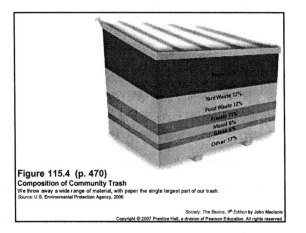

Figure 115.4 (p. 470)
Composition of Community Trash
We throw away a wide range of material, with paper the single largest part of our trash.
Source: U.S. Environmental Protection Agency, 2006

- **Water and Air**
  - *Hydrologic Cycle*
    - *Planet naturally recycles water and refreshes the land*
  - Two major concerns
    - Supply and pollution
- **Water Supply**
  - 1% of Earth's water is suitable for drinking
  - Water rights prominent in laws around the world
  - Rising population and development greatly increased world's needs for water
  - Face the reality that water is a valuable and finite resource

---

- **Water Pollution**
  - In large cities, people have no choice but to drink contaminated water
  - Quality in U.S. good by global standards
  - Special problem is Acid Rain
    - Rain made acidic by air pollution which destroys plant and animal life
  - Global phenomenon
    - Regions that suffer may be thousands of miles from source of the pollution

- **Air Pollution**
  - People in U.S. more aware of air pollution than contaminated water
  - Air quality improved in the final decades of the 20th century
  - Rich nations passed laws banning high-pollution heating
  - Problem serious in poor nations
    - Reliance on coal, wood, peat, or other "dirty" fuels for heating

Rain Forests

- *Regions of dense forestation, most of which circle the globe close to the equator*
  - Largest in South America, West-Central Africa, and Southeast Asia
  - 7% of Earth's total land surface
- Losing rainforests to hardwood trade
  - People in rich nations
    - *Love parquet floors, fine furniture, fancy paneling, weekend yachts, and high-grade coffins*
  - No rainforests – no protection of Earth's biodiversity and climate

Global Warming

- *A rise in Earth's average temperature due to an increasing concentration of carbon dioxide in the atmosphere*
  - Carbon dioxide increasing while amount of plant life on Earth is shrinking
  - Rainforests being destroyed by burning
- Global warming is a problem that threatens the future for all

Declining Biodiversity

- Clearing rainforests reduces Earth's biodiversity
- Rainforests home to almost half of planet's living species
- **Four reasons for concern:**
  - *Earth's biodiversity provides a varied source of human food*
  - *Earth's biodiversity is a vital genetic resource used by medical and pharmaceutical researchers*
  - *Beauty and complexity of natural environment are diminished*
  - *Extinction of any species is irreversible and final*

Environmental Racism

- ***Patterns that make environmental hazards greatest for poor people, especially minorities***
- Factories that spew pollution stood near neighborhoods housing poor and people of color
  - Poor drawn to factories for work
  - Low incomes led to affordable housing in undesirable neighborhoods

Toward a Sustainable Society and World

- ***Ecologically Sustainable Culture***
  - *A way of life that meets the needs of the present generation without threatening the environmental legacy of future generations*
- Three strategies
  - *Bring population growth under control*
  - *Conserve finite resources*
  - *Reduce waste*

Global Population Increase

	Births	Deaths	Net Increase
Per year	130,860,569	56,579,396	74,281,173
Per month	10,905,047	4,714,950	6,190,098
Per day	358,522	155,012	203,510
Per hour	14,938	6,459	8,480
Per minute	249	108	141
Per second	4.1	1.8	2.4

Page 475
Global Population Increase

- Dinosaurs dominated for 160 million years
- Humanity is far younger
  - 250,000 years
- Compared to dimwitted dinosaurs, humans have the great gift of intelligence
- *What are the chances that humans will continue to flourish 160 million years or even 1,000 years from now?*
- Answer depends on the choices made by one of the 30 million species living on Earth
  - *HUMAN BEINGS*

<table>
</table>

Chapter 16

Social Change: Modern and Postmodern Societies

LEARNING OBJECTIVES

- To identify and describe the four general characteristics of social change.
- To identify and illustrate the different sources of social change.
- To be able to discuss the perspectives on social change as offered by Ferdinand Tönnies, Emile Durkheim, Max Weber, and Karl Marx.
- To identify and describe the general characteristics of modernization.
- To identify the key ideas of two major interpretations of modern society: mass society and class society.
- To be able to discuss the ideas of postmodernist thinkers and critically consider their relevance for our society.

CHAPTER OUTLINE

I. What Is Social Change?

II. Causes of Social Change
   A. Culture and Change
   B. Conflict and Change
   C. Ideas and Change
   D. Demographic Change
   E. Social Movements and Change
      1. Types of Social Movements
      2. Claims Making
      3. Explaining Social Movements
      4. Stages in Social Movements
   F. Disasters: Unexpected Change

III. Modernity
   A. Ferdinand Tönnies: The Loss of Community
   B. Emile Durkheim: The Division of Labor
   C. Max Weber: Rationalization
   D. Karl Marx: Capitalism

IV. Structural-Functional Theory: Modernity as Mass Society
   A. The Mass Scale of Modern Life
   B. The Ever-Expanding State

SOCIAL CHANGE: MODERN AND POSTMODERN SOCIETIES

CHAPTER 16

- **Why** do societies change?

- **How** do social movements both encourage and resist social change?

- **What** do sociologists say is good and bad about today's society?

What is Social Change?

- *SOCIAL CHANGE*
  - *The transformation of culture and social institutions over time*
- Four major characteristics
  - Social change happens all the time
    - *Cultural lag*
      - *Material culture (things) changes faster than nonmaterial culture (ideas and attitudes)*
  - Social change is sometimes intentional but often unplanned
  - Social change is controversial
  - Some changes matter more than others

Causes of Social Change

- *Culture and Change*
  - Three important sources of cultural change
    - Invention produces new objects, ideas, and social patterns
    - Discovery occurs when people take notice of existing elements of the world
    - Diffusion creates change as products, people, and information spread from one society to another
  - Material things change more quickly than cultural ideas

- *Conflict and Change*
  - Inequality and conflict within a society also produce change
  - Marx correctly foresaw that social conflict arising from inequality would force changes in every society
- *Ideas and Change*
  - Weber acknowledged that conflict could bring about change
  - Traced roots of most social changes to ideas
  - Revealed how religious beliefs of Protestants set the stage for spread of industrial capitalism

- *Demographic Change*
  - Population patterns also play a part in social change
  - Migration within and between societies promotes change
- *Social Movements and Change*
  - *Social Movement*
    - *An organized activity that encourages or discourages social change*

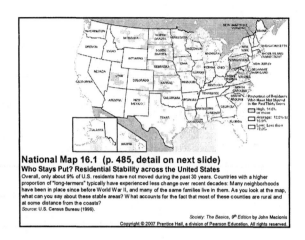

National Map 16.1 (p. 485, detail on next slide)
Who Stays Put? Residential Stability across the United States
Overall, only about 9% of U.S. residents have not moved during the past 30 years. Countries with a higher proportion of "long-termers" typically have experienced less change over recent decades: Many neighborhoods have been in place since before World War II, and many of the same families live in them. As you look at the map, what can you say about these stable areas? What accounts for the fact that most of these counties are rural and at some distance from the coasts?
Source: U.S. Census Bureau (1996).

_____
_____
_____
_____
_____
_____

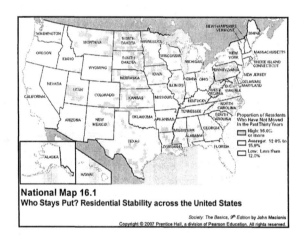

National Map 16.1
Who Stays Put? Residential Stability across the United States

_____
_____
_____
_____
_____
_____
_____

- *Types of Social Movements*
  - *Alternative Social Movements*
    - *The least threatening to the status quo because they seek limited change*
  - *Redemptive Social Movements*
    - *Target specific individuals and seek more radical change*
  - *Reformative Social Movements*
    - *Aim for limited change but target everyone*
  - *Revolutionary Social Movements*
    - Most extreme
    - *Working for major transformation of an entire society*

_____
_____
_____
_____
_____
_____
_____

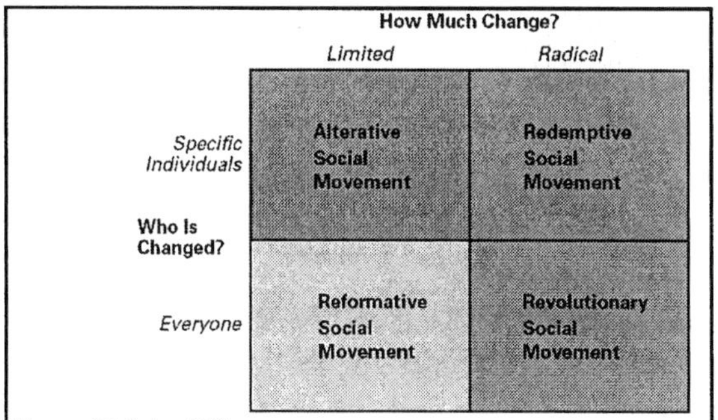

Figure 16.1 (p. 486)

	How Much Change?	
	Limited	Radical
Specific Individuals	Alterative Social Movement	Redemptive Social Movement
Who Is Changed?		
Everyone	Reformative Social Movement	Revolutionary Social Movement

Figure 16.1 (p. 486)
Four Types of Social Movements
There are four types of social movements, reflecting who is changed and how great the change is.
Source: Based on Aberle (1966).

Claims Making

- *The process of trying to convince the public and public officials of the importance of joining a social movement to address a particular issue*

- For a social movement to form, some issue has to be defined as a problem that demands public attention

Explaining Social Movements

- *Deprivation Theory*
  - Social movements arise among people who feel deprived of something
  - *Relative Deprivation*
    - *A perceived disadvantage arising from some specific comparison*
- *Mass-Society Theory*
  - Social movements attract socially isolated people who join a movement in order to gain a sense of identity and purpose

- **Resource Mobilization Theory**
  - Links the success of any social movement to available resources
    - Money, human labor, mass media
- **Culture Theory**
  - Social movements depend not only on money and other material resources but also on cultural symbols
- **New Social Movements Theory**
  - Points out distinctive character of recent social movements in postindustrial societies
  - Movements are typically national or international in scope and focus on quality of life issues

Stages in Social Movements

- Four stages:
  - **Emergence**
    - Occurs as people think all is not well
  - **Coalescence**
    - Social movement defines itself and develops strategy for attracting new members
  - **Bureaucratization**
    - Movement becomes established
  - **Decline**
    - Resources dry up, group faces overwhelming opposition, members achieve goals and lose interest

Disasters: Unexpected Change

- **Disaster**
  - *An event that is generally unexpected and that causes extensive harm to people and damage to property*
- **Three types:**
  - **Natural disasters**
    - Floods, earthquakes, hurricanes
  - **Technological disasters**
    - Widely regarded as an accident
    - More accurately the result of our inability to control technology
  - **Intentional disaster**
    - One or more organized groups intentionally harm others

- *Kai Erikson*
  - **Three conclusions about social consequences of disasters**
    - *Disasters harm people and destroy property but also damages human communities*
    - *Social damage is more serious when an event involves some toxic substance*
      - Com mon with technological disasters
    - *Social damage is most serious when the disaster is caused by the actions of other people*
      - T echnological disasters
      - I ntentional disasters

Modernity

- *Social patterns resulting from industrialization*
- Four major characteristics of modernization
  - *The decline of small, traditional communities*
  - *The expansion of personal choice*
  - *Increasing social diversity*
  - *Orientation toward the future and a growing awareness of time*

TABLE 16-1
The United States: A Century of Change

	1900	2000
National population	76 million	281 million
Percentage urban	40%	80%
Life expectancy	46 years (men), 48 years (woman)	74 years (men), 79 years (women)
Median age	22.9 years	35.3 years
Average household income	$8,000 (in 2000 dollars)	$40,000 (in 2000 dollars)
Share of income spent on food	43%	15%
Share of homes with flush toilets	10%	98%
Average number of cars	1 car for every 2,000 households	1.3 cars for every household
Divorce rate	about 1 in 20 marriages	about 8 in 20 marriages
Average gallons of petroleum products consumed per person per year	34	1,100

Table 16.1 (p. 490)
The United States: A Century of Change

The Loss of Community

- *Ferdinand Tonnies*
  - Viewed modernization as the progressive loss of Gemeinschaft
  - Emphasis on Gesellschaft
  - Inevitable tensions and conflicts divided these communities
  - Modernity turns society inside out so that people are essentially separated in spite of uniting factors
- *CRITICAL REVIEW*
  - Modern life, though impersonal, still has some degree of Gemeinschaft

The Division of Labor

- *Emile Durkheim*
- *Division of Labor*
  - Specialized economic activity
  - Becomes more pronounced with modernization
  - Less mechanical solidarity and more organic solidarity
- **CRITICAL REVIEW**
  - Anomie
    - A condition in which society provides little moral guidance to individuals
  - Yet shared norms and values seem strong enough to give most people a sense of purpose

Rationalization

- *Max Weber*
- Modernity meant replacing a traditional worldview with a rational way of thinking
- Modern society is disenchanted
- **CRITICAL REVIEW**
  - Science is carrying us away from more basic questions about the meaning and purpose of human existence
  - Rationalization, especially in bureaucracies, would erode human spirit with endless rules and regulations

Capitalism

- *Karl Marx*
- *Capitalist Revolution*
  - Marx's view of Industrial Revolution
  - Modernity weakened small communities, increased division of labor, and encouraged a rational worldview
    - Conditions necessary for capitalism to flourish
  - Though critic of capitalism
  - Marx's view of modernity incorporates optimism
- **CRITICAL REVIEW**
  - In socialist societies, bureaucracy turned out to be as bad or worse than dehumanization of capitalism

Structural-Functional Analysis: Modernity as Mass Society

- *Mass Society*
  - *A society in which prosperity and bureaucracy have weakened traditional social ties*
  - Productive, on average, people have more income
  - Marked by weak kinship and impersonal neighborhoods

Mass Scale of Modern Life

- *Mass Society Theory*
  - The scale of modern life has greatly increased
  - Increasing population, growth of cities, and specialized economic activity altered social patterns
  - Face-to-face communication replaced by impersonal mass media
  - Geographic mobility, mass communication, exposure to diverse ways weakened traditional values
  - Mass media gave rise to a national culture

The Ever-Expanding State

- Technological innovation allowed government to expand
- Government assumed more responsibility
  - Schooling, wage regulation, working conditions, establishing standards, providing financial assistance
- Power resides in large bureaucracies
  - Left people with little control over their lives

- **CRITICAL REVIEW**
  - Mass society theory romanticizes the past
  - Ignores problems of social inequality
  - Attracts social and economic conservatives who defend conventional morality and are indifferent to the historical inequality of women and other minorities

---

Traditional and Modern Societies: The Big Picture

Elements of Society	Traditional Societies	Modern Societies
Cultural Patterns		
Values	Homogeneous; sacred character; few subcultures and countercultures	Heterogeneous; secular character; many subcultures and countercultures
Norms	Great moral significance; little tolerance of diversity	Variable moral significance; high tolerance of diversity
Time orientation	Present linked to past	Present linked to future
Technology	Preindustrial; human and animal energy	Industrial; advanced energy sources
Social Structure		
Status and role	Few statuses, most ascribed; few specialized roles	Many statuses, some ascribed and some achieved; many specialized roles
Relationships	Typically primary; little anonymity or privacy	Typically secondary; much anonymity and privacy
Communication	Face to face	Face-to-face communication supplemented by mass media
Social control	Informal gossip	Formal police and legal system
Social stratification	Rigid patterns of social inequality; little mobility	Fluid patterns of social inequality; high mobility
Gender patterns	Pronounced patriarchy; women's lives centered on the home	Declining patriarchy; increasing number of women in the paid labor force
Settlement patterns	Small-scale; population typically small and widely dispersed in rural villages and small towns	Large-scale; population typically large and concentrated in cities

Summing Up (p. 495, continued on next slide)

Traditional and Modern Societies: The Big Picture

Elements of Society	Traditional Societies	Modern Societies
Cultural Patterns		
Values	Homogeneous; sacred character; few subcultures and countercultures	Heterogeneous; secular character; many subcultures and countercultures
Norms	Great moral significance; little tolerance of diversity	Variable moral significance; high tolerance of diversity
Time orientation	Present linked to past	Present linked to future
Technology	Preindustrial; human and animal energy	Industrial; advanced energy sources
Social Structure		
Status and role	Few statuses, most ascribed; few specialized roles	Many statuses, some ascribed and some achieved; many specialized roles
Relationships	Typically primary; little anonymity or privacy	Typically secondary; much anonymity and privacy
Communication	Face to face	Face-to-face communication supplemented by mass media
Social control	Informal gossip	Formal police and legal system
Social stratification	Rigid patterns of social inequality; little mobility	Fluid patterns of social inequality; high mobility
Gender patterns	Pronounced patriarchy; women's lives centered on the home	Declining patriarchy; increasing number of women in the paid labor force
Settlement patterns	Small-scale; population typically small and widely dispersed in rural villages and small towns	Large-scale; population typically large and concentrated in cities

Summing Up (p. 495, continued on next slide)

Society: The Basics, 9th Edition by John Macionis
Copyright © 2007 Prentice Hall, a division of Pearson Education. All rights reserved.

Traditional and Modern Societies: The Big Picture

Elements of Society	Traditional Societies	Modern Societies
Social Institutions		
Economy	Based on agriculture; much manufacturing in the home; little white-collar work	Based on industrial mass production; factories become centers of production; increasing white-collar work
State	Small-scale government; little state intervention in society	Large-scale government; much state intervention in society
Family	Extended family as the primary means of socialization and economic production	Nuclear family retains some socialization functions but is more a unit of consumption than of production
Religion	Religion guides worldview; little religious pluralism	Religion weakens with the rise of science; extensive religious pluralism
Education	Formal schooling limited to elites	Basic schooling becomes universal, with growing proportion receiving advanced education
Health	High birth and death rates; short life expectancy because of low standard of living and simple medical technology	Low birth and death rates; longer life expectancy because of higher standard of living and sophisticated medical technology
Social Change	Slow; change evident over many generations	Rapid; change evident within a single generation

Summing Up (p. 495 continued)

Society: The Basics, 9th Edition by John Macionis
Copyright © 2007 Prentice Hall, a division of Pearson Education. All rights reserved.

Two Interpretations of Modernity

	Mass Society	Class Society
Process of modernization	Industrialization; growth of bureaucracy	Rise of capitalism
Effects of modernization	Increasing scale of life; rise of the state and other formal organizations	Expansion of the capitalist economy; persistence of social inequality

Summing Up (p. 498)

Society: The Basics, 9th Edition by John Macionis
Copyright © 2007 Prentice Hall, a division of Pearson Education. All rights reserved.

Social Conflict Analysis: Modernity as Class Society

- *Class Society Theory*
- **Capitalism**
  - A capitalist society with pronounced social stratification
  - Increasing scale of social life in modern times has resulted from the growth and greed of capitalism
  - Capitalism supports science as an ideology that justifies the status quo
  - Businesses raise the banner of scientific logic to increase profits through greater efficiency

- *Persistent Inequality*
  - Elites persist as capitalist millionaires
  - In U.S., richest 5% own 60% of all privately held property
  - Mass Society Theorists argue:
    - State works to increase equality and fight social problems
  - Marx disagreed
    - Doubted that state could accomplish more than minor reforms
  - Other class-society theorists
    - Grater political rights and higher living standards result of political struggle not government good-will

- *CRITICAL REVIEW*
  - Overlooks the increasing prosperity of modern societies
    - Discrimination based on race, ethnicity, religion, and gender is now illegal and widely regarded as a social problem
  - Most people in the U.S. do not want an egalitarian society
    - Prefer a system of unequal rewards that reflects personal differences in talent and effort

404

Modernity and The Individual

- *Mass Society: The Problems of Identity*
  - Mass society is socially diverse and rapidly changing
  - People unable to build a personal identity
  - *Social Character*
    - *Personality patterns common to members of a particular society*
  - **Tradition-Directedness**
    - *Rigid conformity to time-honored ways of living*
  - **Other-Directedness**
    - *Openness to the latest trends and fashions often expressed by imitating others*

Class Society: Problems of Powerlessness

- Persistent inequality undermines modern society's promise of individual freedom
- Modernity
  - Great privilege for some
  - For others everyday life means coping with uncertainty and powerlessness
  - Greater for racial and ethnic minorities
  - Society still denies a majority of people full participation in social life

---

- Although modern capitalist societies produce unparalleled wealth
- Poverty remains the plight of more than 1 billion people
- Technological advances further reduce people's control over their own lives
  - Conferred a great deal of power on a core of specialists
  - Not the people
- Counters view that technology solves the world's problems

Modernity and Progress

- Progress
  - A state of continual improvement
  - By contrast, stability seen as stagnation
- Cultural bias in favor of change
  - Regard traditional cultures as backward
- Rising standard of living
  - Live longer and materially more comfortable
  - Many people wonder whether routines are too stressful
- New technology a mixed blessing

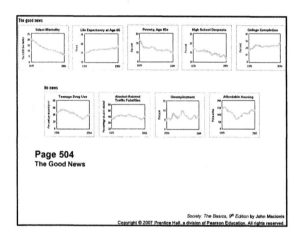

Page 504
The Good News

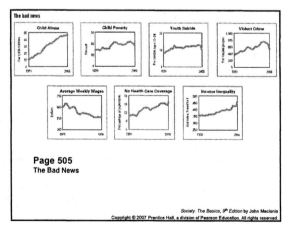

Page 505
The Bad News

Postmodernity

- *Social patterns characteristic of post-industrial societies*
- Postmodern thinking shares five themes:
    - In important respects, modernity has failed
    - The bright light of "progress" is fading
    - Science no longer holds the answers
    - Cultural debates are intensifying
    - Social institutions are changing
- CRITICAL REVIEW
    - Modernity fails to meet human needs
    - Science is bankrupt and progress is a sham but no alternatives

_____

_____

_____

_____

_____

_____

_____